MW00344073

"Renewed attention to the doctrine of the church is a notable feature of recent Protestant works of systematic theology. This collection offers an array of informed and insightful essays that not only address but also develop the current dialogue in creative ways. This volume thus marks a warmly welcome addition to the ongoing conversation."

—PAUL T. NIMMO, University of Aberdeen

"With so many controversies, scandals, and stories of deconstruction, it is hard to think of an area in theology that has as much cynicism swirling around it these days as ecclesiology; that means it is exactly the time for us to revisit the topic. Thankfully, this volume brings trusted voices together to remind us of the indispensability of the church for Christian faith and life."

—KELLY M. KAPIC, Covenant College

"Not only is the Christian church in the West in freefall, but the face of the church is rapidly changing because of compromises with the world's agenda and the reaction of people who vote with their feet. The authors of these valuable studies take these current problems on board. With insightful analysis, they draw on the riches of Scripture and the historic Christian tradition to suggest new paths. A challenging read for all those concerned by the question—Wither the church?"

—PAUL WELLS, Faculté Jean Calvin, emeritus

"*Engaging Ecclesiology* alerts us to questions, texts, conversations, and challenges that are important for ecclesiology in the twenty-first century. It will be a help to Reformed Christians of various stripes and even to many from other traditions as it models a multi-aspectival analysis of the doctrine of church."

—MICHAEL ALLEN, Reformed Theological Seminary, Orlando

"As the first edition of the newly conceived Rutherford Centre for Reformed Theology, *Engaging Ecclesiology* brings together eight essays from significant British scholars, each reflecting on the nature, identity, formation, and challenges of the Reformed church and churches more generally. In a world of miserable deconstruction, this volume is a work of constructive dogmatics. The abiding theme of the essays is hope and a confident, but realistic, view of the church."

—MYK HABETS, Laidlaw College

Engaging Ecclesiology

THE RUTHERFORD CENTRE FOR REFORMED THEOLOGY ECCLESIOLOGY SERIES

SERIES EDITORS

A. T. B. McGowan and John McClean

The Rutherford Centre for Reformed Theology (RCRT), based in Scotland, has established "The Ecclesiology Project" to enable some serious reconsideration of the Reformed doctrine of the church. The project will be carried out in partnership with the Theological Commission of the World Reformed Fellowship (WRF) which is also currently engaged in a study on ecclesiology.

On many of the doctrines of the Christian faith, there is broad agreement within the community of Reformed Christians. If we were considering the Trinity, the Person and Work of Christ, the doctrines which make up our understanding of salvation (effectual calling, regeneration, justification, adoption, repentance etc.) then the disagreements among us would be minor. When it comes to the doctrine of the church, however, there is no such agreement. We believe that there is a great need today for clarity in our understanding of the church, not least its nature and purpose.

In the seventeenth century, the ministers and theologians who wrote the *Westminster Confession of Faith* had a very "high" view of the church. They affirmed that the church is, "the kingdom of the LORD Jesus Christ, the house and family of God, out of which there is no ordinary possibility of salvation." In the twentieth century, many people have a very "low" view of the church, seeming to regard the church almost as an optional extra. Within the community of churches which trace their origins back to the sixteenth century Reformation, both of these views are represented and also everything in between. How then should we formulate a doctrine of the church that is true to our roots, and which is also fit for purpose in the twenty first century?

In this series there will be several monographs on the subject, two of them being on aspects of the unity of the church, which we believe to be a vital topic in our divided church situation. Given our Reformed beliefs that the church should be confessional and that its worship should conform to the "Regulative Principle" (the idea that we may only do in worship what God commands) we are including in the series the WRF Statement of Faith (a new Reformed confessional statement) and a new edition of the *Reformed Book of Common Order*. Also included will be the papers from the Edinburgh Dogmatics Conference which took place at the beginning of June 2021 and was focused on the subject of ecclesiology. We hope in due course to add other volumes to the series.

We hope that you will both enjoy and benefit from this series.

A.T.B. McGowan (editor)
Director of the Rutherford Centre for Reformed Theology (www.rcrt.scot)

John McClean (deputy editor)
Vice Principal of Christ College, Sydney (https://christcollege.edu.au)

Engaging Ecclesiology

Papers from the
Edinburgh Dogmatics Conference 2021

EDITED BY
A.T.B. McGowan

PICKWICK *Publications* · Eugene, Oregon

ENGAGING ECCLESIOLOGY
Papers from the Edinburgh Dogmatics Conference 2021

The Rutherford Centre for Reformed Theology Ecclesiology Series

Copyright © 2023 Wipf and Stock Publishers. All rights reserved. Except for brief quotations in critical publications or reviews, no part of this book may be reproduced in any manner without prior written permission from the publisher. Write: Permissions, Wipf and Stock Publishers, 199 W. 8th Ave., Suite 3, Eugene, OR 97401.

Pickwick Publications
An Imprint of Wipf and Stock Publishers
199 W. 8th Ave., Suite 3
Eugene, OR 97401

www.wipfandstock.com

PAPERBACK ISBN: 978-1-6667-2869-9
HARDCOVER ISBN: 978-1-6667-2071-6
EBOOK ISBN: 978-1-6667-2072-3

Cataloguing-in-Publication data:

Names: McGowan, A. T. B., editor.

Title: Engaging ecclesiology : papers from the Edinburgh dogmatics conference 2021 / edited by A. T. B. McGowan.

Description: Eugene, OR: Cascade Books, 2023. | The Rutherford Centre for Reformed Theology Ecclesiology Series. | Includes bibliographical references and index.

Identifiers: ISBN 978-1-6667-2869-9 (paperback). | ISBN 978-1-6667-2071-6 (hardcover). | ISBN 978-1-6667-2072-3 (ebook).

Subjects: LSCH: Church. | Reformed Church—Doctrines—Congresses. | Conference papers and proceedings. | Evangelicalism—Congresses.

Classification: BX9422.3 E56 2023 (print) | BX9422.3 (ebook)

Contents

Introduction

As CHAIRMAN OF THE eighteenth Edinburgh Dogmatics Conference, I am delighted to write this introduction to the published version of the papers delivered at that conference. For those who do not know of this conference, let me begin by providing some background details.

Rutherford House was established in 1982 in Edinburgh by the Rev William Still and others, as an evangelical and Reformed research and study center. In its early phase of life, it was a residential library and a publisher, and, in addition, organized or sponsored numerous reading groups, study groups, and conferences. It also sought to promote biblical and evangelical thinking in the churches, by organizing training for ministers and elders, producing journals and by engaging with the major issues of the day from an evangelical perspective. Its major academic contribution is the Edinburgh Dogmatics Conference, which has taken place every two years since 1985. Since the Tyndale Fellowship, of which some of us were members, focused on biblical studies, it was thought that we could make a parallel contribution by devoting ourselves to systematic and historical theology, through hosting a conference on Christian Dogmatics. The vision behind the conferences was to create a forum where academic Reformed theology could be presented in a positive way, in engagement with others who perhaps did not share all of our theological views but were broadly sympathetic and were themselves writing and teaching constructive Protestant theology. In this way, we created an opportunity for academics and ministers from various traditions to come together and encounter one another. It was agreed that the conference would be biennial, alternating with the Fellowship of European Evangelical Theologians' conference, which is also biennial and which some of us attend.

The titles of the first few conferences indicate the range of topics under consideration: "The Challenge of Evangelical Theology: Approach

& Method" (1985); "Issues in Faith and History" (1987); "The Power & Weakness of God: Impassibility & Orthodoxy" (1989); "Universalism and the Doctrine of Hell" (1991); and "The Trinity in a Pluralistic Age" (1993). The normal practice was to produce a book after each conference and some notable volumes were published. Prominent speakers were invited to all of these conferences, and this resulted in serious and sustained debate. It would take up too much space to list all of the contributors over the years, but they have included T. F. Torrance, Paul Helm, Colin Gunton, Henri Blocher, Cynthia Brown, Bruce McCormack, David Wright, Julie Canlis, Kelly Kapic, Oliver O'Donovan, Elizabeth Shively, Michael Horton, N. T. Wright, Karla Wubbenhorst, Lewis Ayres, Francis Watson, Katherine Sonderegger, Don Carson, John Webster, David Fergusson, Donald Macleod, Kees van der Kooi, Kevin Vanhoozer, and many more. The conferences have attracted many speakers and attendees from overseas. For example, in 2017, papers were given by scholars from the UK, France, the Netherlands, the USA, Australia and Hong Kong.

In 2019, Rutherford House was renamed the "Rutherford Centre for Reformed Theology" and moved from Edinburgh to an office in the Highland Theological College in Dingwall. The vision for the work has been clarified and sharpened (see www.rcrt.scot) but the core commitments remain in place. There was no Dogmatics Conference in 2019, as these transitions were taking place, but we were determined to resume in 2021.

It had been intended that the eighteenth Edinburgh Dogmatics Conference would be held in Palmerston Place Church, Edinburgh, from the first to the third of June 2021. Unfortunately, due to the pandemic, the decision was reluctantly taken to hold the conference by Zoom. Although this was disappointing, there were also significant benefits. People from all over the world, who would have been unable to travel to Edinburgh, were able to take part. Over seventy people signed up to attend the conference, from eleven countries: the Netherlands, Germany, the USA, Canada, Australia, Malaysia, Singapore, Indonesia, Japan, Colombia, and the UK. This was the highest number attending an Edinburgh Dogmatics Conference for some years and was certainly the conference with the highest number of countries represented. Indeed, we had many subsequent contacts from participants in Asia who said that normally they would not be able to attend such a conference in Scotland because of the travel and accommodation costs involved and thanked us for making their participation possible. This is to say nothing of those who faced a travel ban due to the pandemic.

We were planning the conference just as the pandemic was breaking and we did not know if anyone would be allowed to travel to Edinburgh, so we did something we had never done before: we chose all of our speakers from the UK. Our reasoning was that, even if borders were closed, they should be able to attend. This did not in any way lower the standard of excellence of the speakers. The papers were presented by a veritable pantheon of fine scholars: Professor Oliver Crisp; Professor Tom Noble; Professor Tom Greggs; Professor Gerald Bray; Professor Stephen Williams; Dr Andrew Clarke; Professor Tony Lane; and Professor David Fergusson. In the event, they were not required to travel, and the event became a Zoom conference. We are very grateful to the Rev Stuart Love who organized the technical aspects of the conference and to Mr. Mark Stirling of RCRT for his support.

The subject of the conference was ecclesiology, the doctrine of the church. Within RCRT there is a current focus on ecclesiology and this book is one of an initial six volumes to be published in this area by in the Pickwick Publications imprint of Wipf and Stock Publishers, under the general title of the "RCRT Ecclesiology Series."

The church, especially in Europe, is in steep decline. Many mainstream denominations are losing tens of thousands of members each year, seem unable to attract and hold the attention of young people and have seen hundreds of church buildings closing their doors. In contrast, many churches in Latin America, Africa and Asia are growing. How are we to account for this? The other major problem is the disunity of the church with schisms and secessions and disruptions meaning that many towns and cities have dozens of churches, each maintaining an independent existence. This is to say nothing of the proliferation of new churches, independent fellowships, house churches and more. Given Jesus' prayer that the church might be "one," how can we justify our divisions? Another problem concerns the worship, liturgy, and doctrine of the church with its many "options." This is to say nothing of the outreach of the church, its mission and evangelism. Are we fulfilling the Great Commission?

Perhaps even more significant questions revolve around the nature and purpose of the church. For many professing Christians today, the church seems almost to be an optional extra. This is in marked contrast to the Westminster Divines who, in the Westminster Confession of Faith 20:2, said: "The visible Church, which is also catholic or universal under the gospel (not confined to one nation as before under the law), consists of all those throughout the world that profess the true religion; and of their children: and is the kingdom of the Lord Jesus Christ, the house and family of God, out of which there is no ordinary possibility of salvation." This statement stands in the tradition of Cyprian and other early Fathers. How are we to negotiate the differences between these "low" and "high" views of the church?

As evangelical Christians in the Reformed tradition, RCRT believes that these problems and questions can only be answered and dealt with through a careful biblical and theological examination. Hence our current preoccupation with ecclesiology. Having said that we stand in the Reformed tradition, it should be noted that we espouse a particular type of Reformed theology. There is an increasing tendency among some to narrow the scope of what may be called "Reformed" in a somewhat partisan manner, convinced that only their particular version of Reformed theology is worthy of the name. This is deeply unhealthy and is entirely contrary to the true nature and spirit of Reformed theology, to say nothing of authentic Christian discipleship. From the beginning, Reformed theology has been a "school" of thought with many "strands." In the earliest days of the Reformation, scholars throughout Europe were developing Reformed ideas. These various "strands" in the "school" of Reformed theology did not always agree and often came to contradictory conclusions. They also produced confessional statements, which were different from one another in structure and content, yet all were recognized as "Reformed." There was a healthy debate between the "strands" and no one strand was regarded as having all the truth. Those who hold to the Reformed faith today must resist recent attempts to insist that only one "strand" of Reformed theology is acceptable. Like the early Reformers, we must learn to show respect for Reformed brothers and sisters who choose to express their theology in different language and with different emphases. The RCRT seeks to espouse a humble, gracious, faithful, and respectful Reformed theology.

With those convictions and that attitude to fellow Christian scholars, the 2021 Edinburgh Dogmatics Conference presented the opportunity to think theologically about the church. The papers presented covered a number of significant topics, ranging from patristic commitments (Gerald Bray) to Reformation studies (Stephen Williams) to doctrinal issues (Oliver Crisp) to the sacramental (Tony Lane) and to issues both practical and critical (Andrew Clarke and David Fergusson). Finally, we had two essays exploring Tom Greggs book *The Priestly Catholicity of the Church,* the first in a projected three volumes on Dogmatic Ecclesiology.

I hope that you enjoy reading these essays and that, in doing so, you are drawn deeper into thinking about the life of the church and its significance in the purposes of God for the salvation of the world, as it declares the Gospel of the Lord Jesus Christ.

Professor A.T.B. McGowan

Abbreviations

ANF	Ante-Nicene Fathers
CCC	*Catechism of the Catholic Church*, with Modifications from the Editio Typica. New York, Doubleday, 1997
JSNTSup	Journal for the Study of the New Testament Supplement Series
LNTS	Library of New Testament Studies
NPNF1	Nicene and Post-Nicene Fathers, First Series
NPNF2	Nicene and Post-Nicene Fathers, Second Series
SNTSMS	Society for New Testament Studies Monograph Series
WUNT	Wissenschaftliche Untersuchungen zum Neuen Testament

Contributors

Gerald Bray was librarian of Tyndale House, Cambridge from 1975 to 1978, when he was ordained in the Church of England and served in the parish of St Cedd, Canning Town (Diocese of Chelmsford) until 1980. From 1980 to 1992 he taught ecclesiastical history and doctrine at Oak Hill Theological College in London. From 1993 to 2006 he taught at Beeson Divinity School, where he is now a research professor. He is now also Distinguished Professor of Historical Theology at Knox Theological Seminary. He is the director of research at the Latimer Trust at Oak Hill Theological College in London.

Andrew Clarke is Honorary Professor in biblical studies at the University of Aberdeen. He served as research librarian at Tyndale House from 1990–1995 and then as senior lecturer in New Testament at the University of Aberdeen (1995–2015). He currently serves as Leadership Development Lead with the Scottish Baptist Union. His role is to work with ministers and church leaders as they look to develop their gifts and skills in leadership and ministry.

Oliver Crisp is the Professor of Analytic Theology and Director of the Logos Institute for Analytic and Exegetical Theology. He joined the Divinity School in the autumn of 2019, having previously taught at Fuller Theological Seminary in California (2011–2019), the University of Bristol (2006–2011), and the University of St Andrews (2002–2004). He has also held postdoctoral research fellowships at the Center for Philosophy of Religion, University of Notre Dame (2004–5; 2019), and the Center of Theological Inquiry, Princeton (2008–2009).

David Fergusson is Regius Professor of Divinity in the University of Cambridge, having formerly been professor of systematic theology in the University of Edinburgh. He serves as dean of the Chapel Royal in Scotland

and dean of the Order of the Thistle. He is also a Fellow of the Royal Society of Edinburgh (2004) and a Fellow of the British Academy (2013).

Tom Greggs holds the Marischal Chair of Divinity (the oldest separated Divinity chair established in 1616) at the University of Aberdeen and is a founding co-director of the Aberdeen Centre for Protestant Theology. He also currently serves as head of Divinity at Aberdeen. He previously held a chair in historical and doctrinal theology and, until 2011, when he joined the University of Aberdeen, was professor of systematic theology at the University of Chester. He has also taught at the University of Cambridge. In 2019, he was elected a Fellow of the Royal Society of Edinburgh.

Tony Lane is professor of historical doctrine at the London School of Theology. He studied mathematics and theology at Oxford and Cambridge before joining the school's faculty in 1973. He was course leader for the school's BA program for twelve years before becoming director of research from 1996–2008. In 2000 he was recognized by Brunel University as professor of historical theology and in 2004 he was awarded the degree of Doctor of Divinity by Oxford University.

Tom Noble is professor of theology at the Nazarene Theological Seminary, Kansas City. He taught theology at Nazarene Theological College, Manchester (UK), for twenty years, serving also for twelve years as academic dean, before joining the NTS faculty. He was secretary of the Tyndale Fellowship for Biblical and Theological Research for five years, and now serves as chairman of the Christian Doctrine study group. He is on the board of the Manchester Wesley Research Centre and has served as President of the Wesleyan Theological Society.

Stephen Williams holds MA degrees in modern history from the University of Oxford and theology from the University of Cambridge. After a period there as Henry Fellow, he received his PhD from Yale University (Department of Religious Studies) in 1981. He served for a brief period in Oxford at the Whitefield Institute for theological research before his appointment as professor of theology in the United Theologal College, Aberystwyth (1980–1991) and then as professor of systematic theology in Union Theological College, Belfast (1994–2017). He was appointed honorary professor of theology at Queen's University, Belfast, in 2017 and elected Fellow of the Learned Society of Wales in 2018.

Mapping the Church

Current Challenges of History and Mission

David Fergusson

In what follows I seek to articulate three key claims. First, we should avoid simple definitions of the church by favoring instead a models-based approach that suggests a plurality of ways of being and acting. Second, we should contest the relentless deconstruction of church history by seeking a more nuanced account that balances repentance with appreciation. And third, we should inspect some of the inflated claims around mission for the sake of a more sober reading of our current condition and our likely short-term future.

The Church as a Necessary Condition of Christian Faith

From my time as an undergraduate in the 1970s, I recall a talk by Professor Murdo Ewan McDonald in Glasgow. He tackled the claim by Malcolm Muggeridge that we should dispense with the church and concentrate on Jesus only. Provoked by this suggestion, Murdo Ewan wanted to engage Muggeridge in public debate. He indicated that he would put two points to him. Did not Jesus gather around himself a group of disciples who were the harbingers of the church? The formation of a body of followers was surely integral to Jesus' ministry—any attempt to separate these is anachronistic. His second claim was that the only way in which the story of Jesus could be transmitted is through the medium of the church. The gospels themselves are the product of the early church and without the sustained witness of the institution through the centuries neither he nor Muggeridge would have received the faith. These two points remain fundamentally correct in my opinion and provide an argument for the necessity of the church. But there is a third claim that also needs to be articulated which is part of the case against separation of Jesus and the church. As the body of Christ, the church is the community in which Christian faith is experienced, nurtured, and celebrated. The Christian life may not be confined to the church, but it cannot be lived except in this communal setting with other Christians. Its significance is not merely instrumental. There are of course examples of people who have managed to keep the faith while separated from the church. Confined to his prison cell, Bonhoeffer is one heroic case. Yet his separation from fellow Christians was a constant source of lament, especially on Sundays when he was acutely conscious of his absence from the worshipping community. In a seminal essay, Andrew Walls has written,

> [T]he first effect of Christian expansion is not the production of saved or enlightened individuals, but of congregations . . . The influence of Jesus not only produces group response; it works by means of groups, and is expressed in groups. The influence of Jesus, that is, operates in terms of social relations.[1]

The sacrament of baptism makes good sense in this respect. As a mark, recognized by the ecumenical church, it signals not only a commitment to Christ but membership of his body, the church. These remain inseparable. Calvin is insistent on this point, repeating Cyprian's claim that you cannot have God as your Father if you do not have the church as your Mother.[2]

The Need to Inflect Traditional Ecclesial Dictums

In one sense, there has always been a doctrine of the church, if we intend by this a substantial body of theological literature that reflects upon the church as both a divine creation and a human institution. And there have been

---

1. Walls, *The Cross-Cultural Process in Christian History*, 10–11.
2. Calvin. *Institutes*, 1012.

some notable contributions to this in recent years, not least by Tom Greggs.[3] At the same time, we should note Pannenberg's observation that the church was not a subject of sustained theological investigation until relatively late. He points out that the doctrine of the church did not become a separate locus of theological study until the late middle ages and the Reformation.[4] While theologians wrote about the church, especially Cyprian and Augustine, they did so in occasional ways, often in other contexts and drawing upon a multiplicity of images. Despite some schisms, notably that of the Donatists in Augustine's time, the doctrine of the church was not developed in the manner of other loci since it was not the site of major ecclesiastical division. The claim that the church was one, holy, catholic, and apostolic was made in Cyril of Jerusalem's *Catecheses* (c350), these four adjectives later appearing in the Nicene Creed (381). Notwithstanding this body of work, Pannenberg maintains that the Reformers were the first to introduce the church as a discrete dogmatic theme, for example in the final edition of the *Institutes* (1559) with Calvin's extended treatment of the true church, its marks, offices, and sacraments. The task here was not to defend innovation as to indicate continuity with and recovery of apostolic themes.

Despite the historical consensus, some of the better-known slogans in ecclesiology have recently been problematized and are in need of some restatement, if not discarding. The aforementioned Nicene Creed speaks of the church as one, holy, catholic, and apostolic. This has been widely accepted throughout the ecumenical church, though questions were raised in the sixteenth century about where it was to be located and how it was to be recognized. The marks or notes of the church in the Reformed confessions were an attempt to address this problem. The church was visible through Word and sacrament—the preaching of the Word of God and the correct administration of the two sacraments. The ecumenical advantage of this claim lay in part in its minimalism. The *satis est* of the Augsburg Confession enabled recognition of any church where Word and sacrament could be discerned.[5] This enables us to view different churches, despite still lacking full visible unity, as making a vital contribution to the wider body of the universal church. In our own time, the project of receptive ecumenism seems to be governed by this assumption.[6] Notwithstanding the failure of

---

3. Greggs, *Dogmatic Ecclesiology*, vol. 1.

4. Pannenberg, *Systematic Theology*, 21–27.

5. Augsburg Confession VII.

6. Murray, *Receptive Ecumenism and the Call to Catholic Learning*.

ecumenical aspirations in the late twentieth century, the need for greater visible unity remains a Scriptural and missional imperative.

The Augustinian distinction between the visible and invisible church was frequently employed at the Reformation. By separating these, one could distinguish the invisible company of the elect through the ages from the visible church into which entire populations were baptized. The visible church could thus remain an authentic church of Word and sacrament, even though not all its adherents belonged to the elect. One could also hold that the elect might include some not adhering to the visible church through the mark of baptism, though this remained a point of division amongst the Reformers.[7]

With the tendency in modern theology to reconfigure the relationship between the church and the world, the distinction between the visible and the invisible church has had to be recast, both in Catholic (Vatican II) and Protestant theology.[8] If the church is witness, foretaste, and sign of the coming kingdom of God, then its fundamental identity is visible.[9] A purer invisible church requires a doctrine of election that stresses a decreed and final separationism. This has generally not commended itself to modern ecumenical theologians. Yet the visible-invisible distinction does not need to be abandoned entirely. If notion of an invisible church can provide us with a keen sense of our links in the *communio sanctorum* to the church across space and time, then it continues to serve a useful function. This need not be tied to earlier assumptions about the nature of Christendom and the doctrine of election.

A further difficulty with characterizing the visible church in terms of its two marks is the lack of sufficiency in the definition. Word and sacrament are necessary but what about church order, offices, oversight, government, and forms of historical continuity? Such concerns moved Bucer and the authors of the Scots Confession to add a third mark, namely that of pastoral discipline. Today we are nervous around this supplementary note, partly owing to its subsequent preoccupation with sexual morality. Yet its

---

7. These ecclesial distinctions were not without their practical tensions after the Reformation. Was the church a national institution into which everyone was to be baptized or a gathered company of those adhering to the true faith? See Spurlock, "Boundaries of Scottish Reformed Orthodoxy 1560–1700," 359–76.

8. For example, Barth, *Church Dogmatics* IV/3, 722–55.

9. George Lindbeck points out that there was never a doctrine of the invisible Israel. "The Church," 179–208.

intention was to underscore the importance of order, justice, and the common good of both church and society.

Problems around the sufficiency of any one definition of the church have led to contrasting approaches that are shaped by a series of models; these have roots in the multiplicity of Scriptural images of the church. This has obvious advantages. A plethora of images in the New Testament is evident, e.g., the body of Christ, the household of God, the creation of the Holy Spirit, the people of faith, the called, and the elect. Other notions such as the vine, the bride and the flock illustrate both the relationship of church to Christ and of the members to one another. Paul Minear discerns a startling ninety-six images.[10] The unity of the church, the diversity of gifts and ministries distributed by the Spirit, the equality of the members, the emergence of disparate offices and the need for order: these are all important and reflect various crises during the apostolic age. Given its complexity, we need images rather than an Aristotelian definition to capture the richness and multi-dimensionality of the church. There is a danger of essentializing it with one single image or account of order, thus missing its diverse expressions by excluding all but one form. This recognition is an ecumenical breakthrough.

Avery Dulles's treatment of the models of the church has become something akin to a modern classic. He distinguishes six models, while exploring the value and limitations of each. His argument is that all are needed to generate a balanced and rounded ecclesiology that avoids an over-determination of one perspective or set of actions. His six models comprise the church as an institution (a traditional Catholic notion), the church as a mystical body (including the body of Christ and people of God), the church as a sacramental sign (reflecting the Vatican 2 notion of "sign"), the church as herald (a more Protestant notion of witness), the church as servant (a greater stress on the diaconal role of the church to the world is provided here), and as community of disciples (the links to Jesus' calling of the twelve are explicit here). Dulles registers some telling criticisms of each but acknowledges that there should be room for all in tackling an agenda of contemporary problems. His last model was added to the 2002 edition of the work in an attempt to find a setting in which the other five can be anchored.[11]

---

10. Minnear, *Images of the Church in the New Testament*.

11. Dulles, *Models of the Church*.

Two additional problems can be detected in the classical Reformation statement of the dual marks of the church, and these will form the bulk of what remains in this essay. One concerns history and the other mission. The historical problem is already evident in what became known as the Protestant time warp. With the perceived need to secede from the Roman Catholic Church, the Reformers faced the dual challenge of establishing their links with the apostolic church of the New Testament and the early centuries, while simultaneously so stressing the corruption of the institution that was being abandoned that its continuity with the apostolic church could be contested. This generated a vague sense that a thousand years of church history were a dark age that had now been corrected by a sudden return to a purified church. Although this is something of a caricature when we consider the liturgical, theological, and legal continuities with the late middle ages, nevertheless elements have persisted in the Protestant mindset. No doubt that has often been encouraged by a theological curriculum which too quickly jumped from Augustine to the Reformers in its attention to doctrinal matters.

But the problem of church history runs deeper today. To make sense of the church, we have to tell a story about ourselves. (This applies *mutatis mutandis* to other institutions too). The story requires to be positive and to have a measure of plausibility under the scrutiny of the historian. In the case of the church, there are strong theological reasons for assuming that the emergence of the Christian faith made a difference both to its adherents and to the wider world. The transformative potential of the gospel in the lives of the followers of Jesus confirms its claims. A constitutive feature of Christian faith is that the appearance of a new and unique society of believers in the first century, together with its many subsequent expressions, made a positive difference. These claims are already ventured in the New Testament, particularly in the first attempt to write a history of the church in the Acts of the Apostles. From this inheritance, our own practice of the faith is enriched and connected with that of the ecumenical church. Yet the problem today is that such claims are the target of a relentless hermeneutics of suspicion with the exposure of dubious practices, mixed motives, and shameful episodes; these then fuel secular narratives about shaking off the yoke of traditional faith claims. Nietzsche got there before the new atheists with his oft-quoted remark. "Better songs they will have to sing for me before I learn to believe in their redeemer; more redeemed his disciples would have to look."[12]

A further lacuna is that the two marks make no reference to mission, a subject that has become central to many recent theological descriptions of the church, not to mention policy shifts regarding the deployment of resources. Why the Reformers did not regard mission as significant and when this shifted in the Protestant mindset are interesting historical questions on which more work is needed.[13] No doubt, the priority of reforming the church rather than extending its reach is part of the story. But the apparent absence of mission from the *notae* counts as a serious omission by many today. Is the church now to be defined in terms of mission, perhaps proceeding from the *missio Dei* as its ground? Or does this suffer too from the narrowing of purpose, form and activity that afflicted earlier approaches?[14]

Dismal Stories?

An underlying meta-narrative of the secular age is that we have now broken free from the irrational and damaging hold of religion upon our society. We have entered, so the narrative continues, a new age of liberation, peace, sexual freedom, and individual rights. I take this to be a historical story (as opposed to a philosophical or scientific claim) which underlies skepticism, new atheism, and a more diffused secular antipathy towards the church. The narrative features some shameful examples (the Crusades, the Inquisition, sectarianism, violence, burning of witches, and recent exposure of chronic child abuse—admittedly, these are not difficult to find) and tends to view these as indicative of the practical effects of Christian faith across the ages. Hence the triple claim that religion is irrational, damaging and inhibiting is supported by a historical story that we have now internalized as a culture. This has particular appeal in the secular west—the examples indeed are largely drawn from western history. Since the 1960s, the rapid process of secularization has confirmed the plausibility of this new meta-narrative for many of our fellow citizens. It enables critics to castigate Christian attitudes

---

12. Nietzsche, *Thus Spoke Zarathustra*, 71.

13. David J. Bosch points out that Anabaptist missions provided an exception. See *Transforming Mission*, 246.

14. For discussion of Reformed attitudes to mission, see Guder, "Reformed Theology, Mission and Ecumenism," 319–34.

as "medieval" and to view its rejection as accompanied by greater freedoms, the end of a cramping institutional authority, and life-enhancing practices.

I offer three types of response to this story of liberation from the dark ages of Christianity.

i) Repentance is required of the churches for previous abuses of faith and power. This is needed for the purification of memory and for the constant task of reformation in our own age. Humility is the first flower that grows at the foot of the cross. We should also acknowledge that the secular world may have much to teach us. In the past, the churches have often been too slow to appreciate the importance of democracy, the equality of the sexes, tolerance, the provision of legislation for divorce and remarriage, and human rights, even though resources within the tradition can be deployed to support these. Some forms of secularism offer a blanket condemnation of Christianity. But we should not repeat the same mistake by making a blanket judgement about secularism, as if its benefits must be entirely deleterious.

The representatives of any contemporary institution have a responsibility to reckon with its history. In belonging to the church, we position ourselves *a fortiori* in continuity with those who preceded us and invested in its practices and beliefs. Implicit in the belonging is a claim about institutional origins and standards, and our alignment with these. Edmund Burke famously stated that if an institution is worth preserving, we should be prepared to reform it. The converse also holds. If an institution is worth reforming, we must be ready to defend its preservation. This will involve a reckoning with the past and a readiness to admit its defects and lapses. The act of reforming should be accompanied by an appropriate acknowledgement of where we and our predecessors went wrong. That may involve apology and reparations to other groups or individuals who have been harmed, sometimes grievously, and honest historical excavation of the past, both remote and recent, and what was undertaken in the name of the institution. Repentance may take different forms, depending on time and circumstance, but it is a pre-requisite for the work of preservation and reform. Though its roots are medieval and catholic, the ancient slogan of *semper reformanda* is often associated with the Reformed churches. If we always need to be reformed, then we must stand in a dialectical relationship to the past in both interrogating its failings and lauding its achievements.[15]

---

15. For discussion of the slogan see Koffeman, "'Ecclesia reformata semper reformanda,'" 1–5.

The Christian mediocrity of which Augustine spoke constantly afflicts the life of the church. Diarmaid MacCulloch's verdict is therefore unsurprising. Christian faith "has brought human beings to acts of criminal folly as well as to the highest achievements of goodness, creativity, and generosity."[16]

ii) Nevertheless, a close scrutiny of the historical evidence reveals that much of the contemporary secular narrative is unbalanced—the entries are mostly in the debit column. Yet the early Christians were critical of the violence and corruption of the Graeco-Roman empire. They espoused high standards, as many of their opponents conceded. Despite popular caricatures, the middle ages were a time in which monasteries and cathedrals were built, schools and universities founded, patterns of commerce developed, and care for the sick and poor practiced. The just war theory and popular concepts of political authority were articulated by medieval scholars. And, after the Reformation, the case for freedom of conscience and religious tolerance was argued forcefully by dissident Protestant groups, particularly in England, before secular arguments for autonomy emerged. Newton, Kelvin, and Clerk Maxwell saw no conflict between their faith and their science. The oft-quoted cases of Galileo and Darwin were never a simple clash of a recondite religion with an enlightened science.[17] In modern times, Christians have also been involved in reform movements, in political radicalism, in making the case for social welfare, and in supporting education and health care provision wherever the church spread in the world. We need to tell these stories. And despite developments surrounding marriage, it remains a surprisingly persistent institution that has been adapted rather than abandoned by our contemporaries. Meanwhile, the record of atheist regimes in the twentieth century and since has often been deplorable.

Except in a piecemeal way, the challenge of offering a more positive narrative of the church has not generally been met by theologians and church historians. This remains an important apologetic task, though it has not been pursued with the same vigor as have responses to scientific and philosophical challenges. One notable exception is Rowan Williams measured analysis in *Why Study the Past?*[18] Here Williams identifies the need to move towards a post-critical reading of church history to find a way of understanding the institution to which we belong without evading necessary critical questions. We must shun both a progressivist account in which

16. MacCulloch, *A History of Christianity*, 13.
17. See Numbers, *Galileo Goes to Jail.*
18. Rowan Williams, *Why Study the Past?*.

we see ourselves as improving steadily upon the past and also the claim that there was once a pristine age of the church which has been lost but now recaptured in some fresh way. Yet monotonous deconstruction will cause fatal damage to our sense of belonging to the body of Christ.[19] Proper criticism must be combined with an appreciation of the past. Further support has arrived from less likely quarters, for example in the recent work of Tom Holland which sees the treasures of the Enlightenment not as a release from the inheritance of Christianity but as reposing upon it.[20]

iii) Much Christian service takes places in local and concealed ways that are not immediately evident in the textbooks of historians. In his 1949 study of *Christianity and History*, Herbert Butterfield wrote of how the standing work of the churches through the ages amongst local communities has made an incalculable practical change to the quality of life and yet how difficult it can be for historians to factor into their work the inner spiritual life of the church and its parochial activities. This may be the most important way in which the meta-narrative of secularism can be contested. Today we speak of the social capital generated by faith communities with their resilience and positive significance. Throughout our country, Christians quietly visit the sick, run food banks, establish credit unions, maintain youth organizations, raise money for work overseas, and support refugees. This requires to be taken into account as a pointer to a very different story that undergirds faith. If we cannot overturn the mind-set of our age with immediate effect, we can at least find ways of contesting it both intellectually and practically.

In their study *American Grace*, Robert Putnam and David Campbell suggest that those frequenting a church or synagogue are more likely to do voluntary work for a charity and offer multiple forms of support to those in need. Frequent, rather than occasional, worshippers are significantly more active citizens. This is practice, not belief. Taking part is what counts, rather than giving intellectual assent to a creedal position. Putnam and Campbell "speculate that an atheist who went regularly to church (perhaps because of a spouse) would be more likely to volunteer in a soup kitchen than a believer who prays alone."[21] These actions of the church tend to be local, individual, and seemingly modest in their impacts. Yet their cumulative effect, when assessed in such studies, is striking. Much of this activity does

---

19. Williams, *Why Study the Past?*, 27.

20. Holland, *Dominion: The Making of the Western Mind*.

21. Putnam and Campbell, *American Grace*, 427–28.

not make for a headline story or a single episode available for historical scrutiny, yet its persistence is remarkable in its own way.[22]

Mission in Perspective

A stress on the local provides a salutary reminder of the multiple forms of social engagement that take place in most Christian congregations. This is not the privileged domain of so-called national churches but is apparent in many other traditions and increasingly in other faith communities. To defend a national church on the grounds that it cares for everyone in its parish and not only its own members is a misrepresentation of other groups that are equally impressive in their outreach, witness, and generation of social capital.

Nevertheless, one of the frequent complaints of those who advocate mission as the central component of ecclesial strategy is that this has been neglected throughout much of our history. In transitioning from a maintenance model of church life to a missional one, the church is urged to adopt a strategy that has mission at the heart of everything it does. While it is certainly the case that the discourse of mission does not feature much in early Reformed texts, much of what might count as mission today has been exhibited for many centuries. Although the term "mission" was not in common currency, the aim of social transformation runs deep in the Reformed churches. These were concerned with the shaping of society and not merely the church. The ideal of a "godly commonwealth" became a powerful expression of the importance of Christian transformation, as did its predecessor concept of the "common good" in medieval thought. To this extent, the church maintained an outward focus beyond its walls. Its members were sent into the secular world to suffuse it with their Christian standards, while the church itself sought to enter into a partnership with the political state.[23]

To cite my own Scottish context, our nineteenth-century predecessors were also heavily engaged in forms of mission—church planting, education

22. Jeffrey Stout's study *Blessed are the Organized: Grassroots Democracy in America*, similarly demonstrates the ways in which local activism is necessary for the preservation of a democratic culture. This again may illustrate ways in which western democracies remain more indebted than is often recognized to the faith communities that they host.

23. Luther's secularization of vocations is an important element of this outward focus and provides a stronger social theology than is sometimes recognized. See Laffin, *The Promise of Martin Luther's Political Theology*.

of the people, foreign missions and forms of social service and health care. Having suffered the trauma of the Disruption in 1843 in which it lost one third of its ministers and one half of its members, the Church of Scotland recovered largely through this concerted missional effort. By the end of the century, it had become the largest Presbytery grouping. This renewal took place partly through the work of evangelicals who remained within the ranks of the Kirk, but also by a broader church party that was persuaded of the value of an established parish church. By the time of the 1929 re-union, the auld Kirk was almost twice the size of the United Free Church. Its commitment to education, liturgical reform, new church development, overseas work, social outreach, and uniformed organizations was central in this process of recovery. The base from which these activities emerged was the local parish church which transmitted the faith to new generations and generated the human and financial resources for the accomplishment of its work.

Also worth pondering are the innovations of the twentieth century, many of them undertaken by some of the most gifted people that the Scottish churches have produced. When we consider the array of new ideas and initiatives that produced the Iona Community, counselling services, Christian education, Tell Scotland, and Scottish Churches House, we realize that fresh expressions were already developed by earlier generations.[24] We continue to learn from these creative initiatives and movements. The history of the Scottish churches in the twentieth century has yet to be written, but these initiatives will surely feature.

Why then has the language of mission suddenly attained such prominence? Much of this has its roots in the *missio Dei* theologies of the twentieth century.[25] With the spreading of the Christian faith to the global south, mission assumed a new salience that had not characterized western church life at earlier periods. The stress on God's mission, moreover, enabled a keener sense of the distinction between the kingdom of God and the work of the church. God intended not only a church. Rooted in the teaching of Jesus, the kingdom or commonwealth of God provided a more capacious concept with universalist and eschatological aspects. The sending of the church, therefore, was for the wider purpose of witnessing to and working for the kingdom. This enabled the language of mission to assume a more critical socio-political edge. As theologians developed the *missio Dei*, an

24. Forsyth, *Mission by the People*.
25. See Bosch, *Transforming Mission*, 389–92.

important trinitarian inflection was discerned. The mission of Christ upon which the church reposed, was generated by the missions of the triune God in the *opera Trinitatis ad extra*. The sending of the Son and the Spirit into the world reflected the eternal begetting and the eternal proceeding of their persons in the life of the Trinity.[26] For this reason, the entire economy of creation and salvation could be characterized in terms of mission, a going forth of God to make and save the cosmos. With the renaissance of trinitarian theology, this wider hermeneutical context has resulted in an inflation of missiological discourse.

Yet a more proximate cause for the predominance of the language of mission in contemporary ecclesiastical strategies is surely the sudden loss of Christendom status in the west. As parish churches have declined and large swathes of the population have become disconnected from the Christian faith, a rapid move from maintenance to mission seems required of the contemporary church. At times, it is difficult not to feel a sense of anxiety creeping into the rhetoric of mission. Unless we mend our ways, extinction threatens. Church strategy needs to be driven by missional priorities.

First developed within the Church of England, the "five marks of mission" are worth considering.

1. To proclaim the Good News of the Kingdom

2. To teach, baptize and nurture new believers

3. To respond to human need by loving service

4. To seek to transform unjust structures of society, to challenge violence of every kind and to pursue peace and reconciliation

5. To strive to safeguard the integrity of creation and sustain and renew the life of the earth.

These have evolved since 1984, the fourth one being most recently expanded. The breadth of missional work is apparent here from proclamation and conversion through to socio-political activism and ecological preservation. Undoubtedly, there is Scriptural support for grouping these actions of the church under the banner of mission. Jesus sends out the twelve and the seventy to proclaim. At the close of Matthew's gospel, the church is commissioned to teach and baptize the nations. In John, the disciples are to follow the example of Jesus in loving service. "As the Father has sent me, so I send

26. For discussion of how the *missio Dei* became the *missio Trinitatis*, see Flett, *The Witness of God*.

you" (John 20:21). The commitment to justice and cosmic wholeness is also deeply embedded in the Psalms, the law, the prophets, and the teaching of Jesus. The apocalyptic vision that concludes the New Testament is one that encompasses the nations and transforms social life.

Yet the five marks are not comprehensive. Perhaps most surprisingly, the name of Jesus is never mentioned though doubtless it is implicit in marks one and two. Other actions of the church seem to be missing. Worship, pastoral care, Christian education, and the eucharist do not feature explicitly in the five marks. What this suggests is that though the five marks may be useful for benchmarking the work of congregations, they are not intended to provide a comprehensive list of essential activities, an ordered set of priorities, or a menu from which only some may be selected.[27] The raison d'être of the church is not exhausted by their citation. The focus on "sending" in missional theology becomes Procrustean when the entire range of ecclesial action is grouped under this one heading.

Once again, the necessary multiplicity of ecclesiological models may prove relevant here. In the 2002 edition of his work, Dulles introduced the model of the community of disciples which he argued could ground the other five models.[28] This had the advantage of being close to the experience of Christians and readily assimilated in their understanding. Within this foundational model, he sees both assembling and sending as activities that should be inter-related.

> The church is never more church than when it gathers for instruction and worship. On such occasions it becomes most palpably the "the sacrament of Christ" as proposed in the third model. But it would not be completely church unless it went forth from its assemblies to carry on Christ's work in the world. The church's existence is a continual alternation between two phases. Like systole and diastole in the movement of the heart, like inhalation and exhalation in the process of breathing assembly and mission succeed each other in the life of the church. Discipleship would be stunted unless it included both the centripetal phase of worship and the centrifugal phase of mission.[29]

27. Zink, "Five Marks of Mission," 144–66. Zink suggests that such lists have a useful function in uniting the ecumenical church and in balancing local with global concerns. But their shelf-life is likely to be not much more than ten to twenty years, after which they will be supplanted.

28. Dulles, *Models of the Church*, 195–217.

29. Dulles, *Models of the Church*, 211.

This insight has some practical outcomes for the contemporary church. The over-determining of mission may be just as bad as neglecting it. The church has many functions—the glorifying of God in its worship, the education and nurture of its people, the care of the sick and the dying, and the bearing witness to the gospel in the life of the world. The activities of the church are necessarily plural, even as we affirm that there is one faith and one LORD.

Yet none of this is to imply that the church does not find itself today in a very different historical position. If we begin with a sad lament for its former status, then we will tend to present the solution as merely reversing that decline with mission becoming a project of restoration. This neglects the way in which we have shifted from a culture of obligation to one of consumption, the ways in which people increasingly choose their religion or spirituality, and function as seekers rather than dwellers.[30] Much sociological evidence and analysis supports these conclusions. Secularization is not the fault of the church—this is simply where we find ourselves. Our post-Christian setting is a new one in the history of the church. We have to opt-in rather than opt-out. For most, the default setting is one of market choice rather than cultural obligation. This entails that churchgoing and religious observance must compete with a range of other leisure-time pursuits—hence the difficulty in attracting and retaining young people. Vicarious religion, sympathetic indifference, forms of Christian affiliation outside the institutional churches—these are novel features of our condition that we have not hitherto experienced as a society. Other western European societies are experiencing similar shifts, and the USA may not be so far behind, despite earlier claims for its exceptionalism.

The future of the church in our society seems set to be one in which it is smaller. Predictions of transformational events are notoriously imprecise and uncertain. Who predicted the collapse of communism and the Berlin Wall, 9/11, the credit crunch in 2008, and Covid-19? Our pollsters couldn't even foresee Brexit and the election of Trump. So, prediction is a hazardous business. Maybe we'll be surprised by the sudden revival of the churches when it happens, as well as by its causes. But for the moment, the church needs to recognize that it will be much smaller in the coming generation and to figure out how to function effectively with a reduced capacity. A missional strategy that is based upon taking us back to a position of cultural pre-eminence is profoundly mistaken. We need to become a humbler

30. Davie, *Religion in Britain*, 133–74.

church, recognizing that we have lost our cultural standing to a significant degree. This will mean fewer buildings and congregations. People may need to travel a bit further to attend church. But some consolidation is inevitable and hard decisions about finance and fabric are necessary. In particular, we need to concentrate focus on buildings and worship to provide a transformative experience on a Sunday morning and at other times in the week, from which a range of activities can then follow. Liturgical reinvigoration, not least through church music, may be vital to our missionary strategy. People should leave church feeling much better than when they entered, not merely relieved that an act of observance is over for another week.

We should also be realistic in what we can expect and ready to accommodate those who want to attend only occasionally without generating too many obligations. Perhaps this explains why Saturday night mass is popular in many Roman Catholic churches and why cathedral worship has grown significantly in England. In this context, to impose too many missional obligations on the church may actually be to its detriment.

Within our towns and cities we should offer greater variety to people in terms of styles of worship, theology, and outreach. The Church of England may be rather better at this than the Church of Scotland. Spirituality and religion will not be provided wholesale to an entire population. Different products and retail outlets will be required for people who are increasingly educated, selective, and mobile in relation to institutions. Large evangelical churches should be allowed to flourish with a greater degree of autonomy, as should cathedrals and other historic buildings that offer more traditional patterns of worship. We need to encourage local initiatives and diversity at grass roots level. Declining congregations should be given a menu of options with encouragement to reflect upon what might work best for them. Many of the churches that continue to flourish are those with strong connections to their surrounding communities; these are able to offer lively worship and a range of activities for people of all ages. This embeddedness of churches in their localities is what earns them respect, especially where this is evident in forms of service and support to hard-pressed people. The parish model continues to have traction in different places.[31]

The saddest element in recent research about leaving the church are the stories of those who failed to find friendship and love or were not

---

31. For a missiological defense of the parish model, see Newbigin, *A Word in Season*, 48–65.

allowed to express their doubts and lack of convictions.[32] Feeling pressurized to conform, they became impatient with the persistent refusal to embrace change and grew weary of ever-increasing demands. Any missionary strategy for the future needs to be alert to the causes of alienation within the body of Christ itself.

In permitting diversity and enabling local initiatives, by adopting a more humble posture and a realistic recognition of what can be expected of people, we may arrive at a place where the Spirit surprises us. This is by no means to forsake mission, especially the obligation to transmit the faith to those who come after us. But we should release ourselves from unrealistic burdens and expectations to serve God as best we can in our own day. Freed from strategic postures induced by either panic or denial, we can better appreciate and be grateful for the multiplicity of ways in which the church continues to live and act in the name of Christ.

32. Aisthorpe, *The Invisible Church*; Stockitt and Dawson, *Leaving Church*.

2

The Mystical Body of Christ

Oliver D. Crisp

In CHRISTIAN THEOLOGY SALVATION is not just about the reconciliation of the *individual* with God through Christ by means of the agency of the Spirit. It is also concerned with the whole of Redeemed Humanity, that is, those who are united with Christ in his act of reconciliation. For the members of Redeemed Humanity form the new society created by Christ's reconciling work, which is the church.[1] The New Testament writings speak variously of the church in the language of organic metaphors as (among other things) the vine, the body, the bride of Christ, and the household of faith (e.g., John 15; Rom 12:4–5; 1 Cor 10:17, 12; 2 Cor 11:12; Gal 6:10; Eph 5; Col 1:24; 1 Pet 2:5; Rev 21:9).[2] It is not incidental that the reconciling work of Christ brings about not just the salvation of individuals, but of the church as a whole. For the goal of Christ's soteriological work is not

1. I presume that the church is co-terminus with Redeemed Humanity. It may be that some members of Redeemed Humanity are not outwardly members of the church or do not have access to the sacramental life of the church. (For instance, a member of Redeemed Humanity may live in a country where there is no expression of the Christian church, or may be the adherent of another faith, or may have lived before the message of the Gospel was proclaimed. Nevertheless, such persons, being members of Redeemed Humanity, are also members of the invisible church scattered down through the centuries because they are united to Christ by the Holy Spirit and regenerate even if they are not members of the visible church at a particular moment in history.

2. Joshua Cockayne notes that "In Scripture, there are at least 96 metaphors used to explain the nature of the Church." In "Analytic Ecclesiology," 103.

just the reconciliation of fallen human persons as a kind of collection or bundle of particulars. It is the formation of the church as a new society intimately united with Christ. The relation between Christ and the members of this group that is the church scattered through space and time is a kind of union formed by the Holy Spirit. Though we may go some way toward understanding this relation between God and his redeemed people, it is not something that we can fully fathom this side of the grave. For this reason, theologians have characterized the entity that is generated by the soteriological work of the divine persons as a *mystical* work, and the society formed by this work, *the mystical body of Christ*. In this connection a mystical work is one that has a certain symbolic or metaphysical significance that transcends human understanding. It is mysterious.

In this paper I want to focus on the relationship between Christ's act of atonement and the church formed as a consequence of that reconciling act—what we might call the question of the formation and ontology of the church in relation to Christ as its head. My thesis is this: *How does the reconciling work of Christ unite the believer with Christ and with other members of Redeemed Humanity in the mystical body of Christ that is the Church?* We will set about addressing this thesis by dividing our discussion of the matter into three parts. In the first, I shall discuss the way in which the saving benefits of Christ's reconciling work are applied to the believer, with particular reference to eternal justification as the ground of the work of the Holy Spirit in regeneration. Then, in the second part, I will turn to the manner in which the Spirit unites the believer to Christ so that she may begin to enjoy the benefits of Christ's saving work, and so participate in the divine life. In the third part, I will fold these two things, the application of Christ's benefits to the believer, and the union of the believer with Christ, into the larger soteriological work of forming the mystical body of Christ, which is the church, drawing in particular on recent work in this area by the analytic theologian and Anglican clergyman, Joshua Cockayne. Some of the elements of the first two sections of this chapter draw on my previous work in this area, applied to the present concern.[3] The third section takes forward the discussion in a constructive way, and in conversation with the recent philosophical literature on social ontology and group theory.

---

3. Particularly, *Deviant Calvinism*, chaps. 5–6, 10.

Applying Christ's Reconciling Work

Suppose we think of the application of the benefits of Christ's atonement as a twofold action of the Holy Spirit. The first aspect of this action entails the moral and spiritual transformation made possible by Christ's reconciling work via the Holy Spirit in regeneration. The second aspect of this action involves the Spirit uniting the believer with Christ. We begin by considering the first, regenerative aspect of this divine act. It is predicated upon God's eternal decision to save a particular number of fallen humanity and to justify them by means of the reconciling work of Christ. In order to see this more clearly, let us turn first to the doctrine of justification from eternity. Then we will be in a position to consider the particular way in which this eternal act is applied to the believer in regeneration.

Justification from Eternity

The doctrine of justification has been the source of significant division in the Christian church, especially since the Protestant Reformation.[4] For many in the Roman Catholic tradition, justification is a process that begins with baptism, and that continues throughout the life of the individual. But for Protestants standing in the tradition of the Magisterial Reformation, justification is typically regarded as a kind of declarative act by means of which a person's status before God is transformed by the imputation of the alien righteousness of Christ brought about by atonement. What happens in life after the moment of justification is the ongoing sanctification of the justified person—not that person's continued gradual justification over time. This process of the justification and transformation of the individual believer are two parts of what is usually known as the *ordo salutis*, that is, the order of salvation. This is usually thought to comprise the following elements in Protestant thought: calling, regeneration, faith, justification, sanctification, perseverance, and glorification.[5] As divines reflected further on these matters in post-Reformation Protestantism, the shape of the *ordo salutis* was more carefully parsed with some theologians providing

---

4. The standard scholarly history of the doctrine in English is McGrath, *Iustitia Dei: A History of the Christian Doctrine of Justification*. For a useful snapshot of recent debate on this topic, see Beilby and Eddy, *Justification: Five Views*.

5. The origin and development of the term is discussed in Muller, *Calvin and the Reformed Tradition*, chap. 6.

sophisticated accounts of how the Holy Spirit works in the lives of believers.[6] The discussion was not just about distinguishing the different facets of the *ordo salutis* as it normally unfolded in the life of the Christian. It was also pushed back into eternity as it was brought into contact with the doctrine of divine election and the divine decrees more generally. What started as an attempt to describe the manner in which the sinner is transformed into a believer became a framework by means of which the whole sweep of human salvation could be viewed from the effectual calling of the believer by the Holy Spirit all the way through to glorification postmortem.

Our focus is constructive rather than historical. That is, I am interested in setting forth a view and defending it, rather than reporting on the development of a particular doctrinal trajectory in the history of doctrine. But of course, the two tasks are not unrelated. In high Reformed theology, as justification was viewed in its eternal aspect as one of the divine decrees of God in creation, the doctrine of God's eternal justification emerged. This is the idea that the justification of some number of fallen humanity is an eternal divine decision consistent with God's plans in providing effectual atonement in the reconciling work of Christ.[7] What begins in eternity as God's decision to save that particular number, the elect, can be distinguished into the act by means of which this group is eternally justified in the purposes of God, and the manner of securing the soteriological grounds for such justification in Christ's atonement.[8]

In earlier work in this area, I distinguished between two ways in which the doctrine of eternal justification could be construed. The first was *justification in eternity*, the second was *justification from eternity*.[9] According

6. Consider, for example, the famous "golden chain" of salvation, which was a table of how God's plans in election are worked out based on Rom 8: 28–30, and made popular in Reformed piety by William Perkins *A Golden Chain or Description of Theology*.

7. Notable Reformed theologians who have held versions of this view include William Twisse, prolocutor of the Westminster Assembly, John Gill, Tobias Crisp, and Abraham Kuyper. It is often, mistakenly, thought to imply antinomianism—the idea that we may "carry on sinning that grace may abound" (cf. Rom 6:1).

8. The assumption here is that God either cannot or does not simply declare righteous some group of humanity independent of some means by which that declaration is grounded in atonement. In other words, those justified are justified on the basis of Christ's atoning work, which is the means by which reconciliation with God is made possible. God does not simply declare some group of humanity righteous irrespective of a work of atonement. The two things are intertwined, the atonement being the ground and means by which justification is made possible.

9. See the discussion in Crisp, *Deviant Calvinism*.

to the doctrine of justification in eternity, God's declarative act of justification obtains at the eternal "moment" when God ordains it. What happens in history is that those who are eternally justified are made aware of their status when they are given the gift of faith by the susurrus working of the Holy Spirit. But importantly, on this view, the Spirit's secret work in the life of the believer does not transform the individual from a state of alienation to a state of justification. For the individual is already eternally justified. Rather, what happens is that an epistemic change takes place. It is like the case of King Arthur drawing the sword from the stone. In drawing the sword Arthur comes to understand that he is the heir to the throne and of royal blood, being a Pendragon. He does not *become* heir to the throne or a member of the royal line in the act of drawing the sword from the stone. The change is an epistemic one, not an ontological one. The same is true of the believer in the doctrine of justification in eternity.

By contrast, in the doctrine of justification from eternity, the transformation that takes places in the believer in time is completed, as it were, in history at the moment the individual comes to understand that they are justified by means of Christ's atoning work in the act of faith. This transformation is epistemic, but it is also legal and moral: the individual in question is changed from a state of alienation to a state of reconciliation. Although this is an act that is ordained in eternity in the purposes of God, it is completed at that moment in which the gift of faith is communicated to the believer by the secret work of the Holy Spirit. It seems to me that of these two versions of eternal justification, the doctrine of justification from eternity is preferable. For it tracks better with the sort of view one finds in the New Testament documents, as well as in subsequent tradition. We can express the justification from eternity view like this:

JUSTIFICATION FROM ETERNITY

1. God eternally decrees the number of the elect. (That is, *Redeemed Humanity*.)

2. God eternally decrees that Christ is the mediator of salvation.

3. Christ is the ground of election (given that God the Son, the divine person who voluntarily assumes human nature, is a member of the divine Trinity) and the means by which election is brought about as the Elect One and mediator of our election.

4. God knows all those who are elect. (That is, all the members of Redeemed Humanity.)

5. God knows that all the elect (i.e., members of Redeemed Humanity other than Christ) will be saved through the work of Christ as mediator.

6. God knows that all the elect will be justified through the work of Christ by God's divine grace alone, according to God's will and purpose (Eph. 1:5).

7. It is eternally true that the members of Redeemed Humanity (other than Christ) are justified by Christ's meritorious work alone (not by their own merit).

8. The secret work of the Holy Spirit applies the benefits of Christ's work to each individual member of the elect.

9. This application normally obtains by means of the gift of faith, bestowed on the elect individual by the Holy Spirit, uniting that individual to Christ in regeneration.[10]

10. The application of faith to the elect individual completes the eternal act of justification; justification is an eternal act of divine grace that obtains in time at the very moment in which the Holy Spirit applies the benefits of Christ to the individual.

11. The application of faith to the elect individual enables that person to understand that she is included within the ambit of divine election and that she is justified.

12. The application of faith to the elect individual brings about an epistemic change to the person concerned.

13. The application of faith also brings about a moral and (perhaps) a legal change in the elect individual.[11]

Given that justification obtains on the basis of Christ's reconciling work, it is logically consequent to the atonement in the divine decrees. God desires that human beings participate in his divine life; He ordains Christ as the prototypical human, and as the means by which humans may

10. The caveat "normally" provides some wiggle room for those that may be elect, and members of Redeemed Humanity, but who are incapable of exercising faith, e.g., the severely mentally impaired, and infants that die before the age of maturity.

11. Adapted from *Deviant Calvinism*, 51–53.

participate in the divine life as a kind of divine-human hub; and he sees that in creating this world, human beings will need to be redeemed by means of an atonement, provided by the God-man.[12] Those he ordains to salvation on the basis of this reconciling work are justified from eternity. And the way in which this divine act of justification is made effectual in the life of the believer is through the gift of faith, and transformation brought about by the secret work of the Holy Spirit in regeneration.[13]

Regeneration as Infusion

There are different ways in which the doctrine of regeneration might be characterized. One promising avenue of exploration is the *infusion model* that can be found in the work of Jonathan Edwards.[14] On this view, it is the Spirit himself that is communicated to the believer in regeneration, and who is said to indwell the believer infusing into her a new disposition that rectifies the moral disorder brought about through the removing of the Spirit's presence and the introduction of original sin that occurred in the primeval fall. Edwards describes this divine act as infusing in the believer a new *spiritual sense*. He writes,

> this new spiritual sense is not a new faculty of understanding, but it is a new foundation laid in the nature of the soul, for a new kind of exercises of the same faculty of understanding. So that new holy disposition of heart that attends this new sense, is not a new

12. I have discussed the topic of Christ as the prototypical human in *The Word Enfleshed,* and supralapsarian Christology in *Analyzing Doctrine.* Readers are directed to those works for further elaboration of these matters.

13. Calvin thought that the efficient cause of salvation is the good pleasure of God. The material cause is Christ. The instrumental cause is faith, and the final cause is the praise of God's grace. See the discussion of this in Muller, *Calvin and the Reformed Tradition,* 172. Though I am not casting the order of salvation in the language of the four-fold Aristotelian causes, and though my view differs in detail from that of Calvin, there is clearly a family resemblance.

14. I have discussed this more detail in "Regeneration Reconsidered," *Freedom, Redemption and Communion,* chap. 7. The infusion account is one version of what Adonis Vidu calls the uncreated grace model of divine indwelling, which can be traced back at least to Peter Lombard. See Vidu, "The Indwelling of the Holy Spirit," 259–260. For a digest of historic Reformed thinking on this matter that reflects the uncreated grace model, see Heppe, *Reformed Dogmatics,* chap. XX.

> faculty of will, but a foundation laid in the nature of the soul, for a
> new kind of exercises of the same faculty of will.[15]

This strikes me as a plausible way of thinking about the manner in which the transformative experience of regeneration applies the benefits of Christ's atonement and God's eternal justification, to the individual. We might summarize it thus:

> REGENERATION: the divine action by means of which the Holy
> Spirit is communicated to the believer, indwelling the believer, and
> *infusing* a new supernatural disposition or habit into a fallen hu-
> man person that provides a spiritual sense by means of which the
> regenerate person may begin to live a life pleasing to God.

In keeping with a broadly Edwardsian sensibility about the manner of salvation, we may add to this infusion account of regeneration a proviso about the nature of this divine act. Like atonement and justification, in historic Reformed thought regeneration is regarded as entirely a work of divine grace from beginning to end—including the very gift of faith itself (Eph 2:8–9). Fallen human beings are incapable of saving themselves absent divine grace so that even the exercise of faith itself is a product of God's enabling of fallen human beings to act in a particular manner. In this process, according to traditional Reformed teaching, the fallen human being, bound by sin, is incapable of placing herself in a soteriologically advantageous position. It is not even the case that fallen human beings may come to a point at which they cease to resist God and open themselves up to divine grace.[16] For, so the Reformed have thought, this too is a work of grace.[17] As the influential seventeenth century Reformed divine, William Ames, puts it in his discussion of conversion as an aspect of God's calling of an individual in the *ordo salutis*, "The will is the proper and prime subject of this grace; the conversion of the will is the effectual principle in the conversion

---

15. Edwards, *Religious Affections, The Works of Jonathan Edwards,* 206. Elsewhere in his writings, Edwards says "there is no other principle of grace in the soul than the very Holy Ghost dwelling in the soul and acting there as a vital principle." Edwards, *Writings on the Trinity, Grace and Faith,* 196.

16. In recent theology this sort of view has been touted by Eleonore Stump. See Stump, *Aquinas,* 389–404. See also the discussion of this in Kittle, "Grace and Free Will: Quiescence and Control," 89–108. I discuss Stump's view in "Regeneration Reconsidered."

17. Useful discussion of this can be found in Muller, *Calvin and the Reformed Tradition,* chap. 6.

of the whole man."[18] What is more, it is not merely the enlightening of the mind that brings about this change. Rather, says Ames, "the will in this first receiving plays the role neither of a free agent nor a natural bearer, but only of an obedient subject."[19] The reception of this divine grace is, he maintains, "an elicited act of faith."[20] Although it is the act of the individual human agent, it is only by means of divine grace in the provision of faith that this action is feasible.[21] Such a view might be characterized as *monergism*, that is, the singular work of God in the heart of the believer. It is typical of the sort of approach to this question favored by those in the Reformed tradition. We could put it like this:

> MONERGISM: the doctrine according to which the application of the benefits of Christ's reconciling work by the agency of the Holy Spirit in REGENERATION is wholly a work of divine grace; in this process the human agent is entirely passive, but not quiescent.

Union with Christ

By means of the infusion of uncreated grace. the Holy Spirit indwells the believer, regenerating her and providing a new disposition to live in a way pleasing to God. Yet this action also unites the believer with the meritorious cause of this reconciling work, namely, Christ. But how? How is union with Christ brought about? It is one thing to say that by means of the agency of the Holy Spirit the believer is transformed in the act of regeneration. For we can conceive, however dimly, the idea of God indwelling and changing us from the inside out, so to speak. Nevertheless, this leaves unexplained how this also brings about the union of the believer with Christ. This is the next thing we must consider, as the second aspect of the consequence of Christ's atonement. In order to do so we will need to take a step back from the particular issues raised by the calling of the believer and the act of regeneration, to think about how God sets up the *conditions* by means of which union with Christ might obtain. For as we looked first at justification from eternity as the ground of regeneration in the believer, so here we will need to consider the way in which God ordains the incarnation as the conduit by means of which redeemed human beings may be "hooked up" to

18. See Ames, *The Marrow of Theology*, 159.

19. Ames, *The Marrow of Theology*, 159.

20. Ames, *The Marrow of Theology*, 159.

21. Ames, *The Marrow of Theology*, 159.

the divine so as to be united to Christ, and thereby participate in the divine life. We may then connect this to the notion of union with Christ in order to provide a more complete account of this relation.

Thus, to begin with, we will need to say something about Christ as the hub between divinity and humanity, or the interface between God and humans that makes union with God possible. We can put it like this. Christ interfaces between God and humans as the prototypical human being, the one in whose image all subsequent humans are formed (2 Cor 4:4; Col 1:15; Heb 1:3).[22] He is literally the *firstborn over all creation*—not as one who is merely a creature or angelic figure, as the Arians supposed, but as one who assumes creatureliness into his own divine life in order that he may interface with creaturely existence and unite it with Godself. Although the human nature assumed by the Son begins to exist at a particular moment in time in the womb of the Virgin, it was (so it seems to me) eternally ordained as the prototypical human nature on the basis of which all other human natures were created. An analog may help illuminate the point here. In contemporary transhumanism literature there is the aspiration to unite the organic and the digital by means of "wet" interfaces—that is, implants—that might enable suitably enhanced human beings to directly access data via digital superhighways. Analogously, the incarnation is a means by which God may interface with his creatures. In fact, the human nature of Christ is ordained by God as the prototypical human creature that the Word may "interface" with, "uploading" himself into the human nature that is miraculously generated for him in the womb of the Virgin.[23]

But this interface between divinity and humanity is ordained irrespective of human sin. It is, we might think, a function of God's desire to be united with his human creatures that he forms the human nature of Christ. For by means of this hub between divinity and humanity, God enables other human beings to be united to Godself. Elsewhere I have likened this to the way in which an internet hub may provide a connection to the

---

22. I have argued for this claim at greater length in Crisp, *The Word Enfleshed*, chap. 4.

23. This account of the incarnation I elaborate upon in more detail in Crisp, *Divinity and Humanity*, chap. 2. Lest I be misunderstood, I want to keep distinct two things here. These are, first, a claim about the human nature of Christ being the prototypical image of God on the basis of which we all are made to image the divine, and second, the claim that the incarnation brings about an interface between divinity and humanity in the theanthropic person of Christ. These two things are distinguished in more expansive terms in *The Word Enfleshed*, and I direct interested readers to the discussion there.

World Wide Web by means of an interface one end of which is hardwired to a telephone connection, enabling the hub to directly access the internet, with the other end calibrated to send and receive radio signals from particular laptop computers that may be wirelessly connected to the hub via Bluetooth technology.[24] The laptops send and receive the radio signals that connect the user to the internet by means of the hub. This is a common enough feature of contemporary life. In a similar fashion Christ as the hub between divinity and humanity is "hardwired" to the divine nature, and is able, via the secret working of the Holy Spirit, to connect individual believers to the divine nature by means of his human nature. We are, as it were, united to Christ by the Spirit, who acts like the radio signals connecting the laptop computer to the hub, which is Christ. What is more, Christ unites us directly to the divine nature as we interface with his humanity by means of the Spirit's agency.

Of course, an internet hub is only of use if the laptop *is able* to connect to it wirelessly. The laptop computer must itself be switched on and capable of such connection, and it must have the technology necessary to connect to the hub activated—usually Bluetooth capability. If the computer is closed, or switched off, or if its Bluetooth capability is inactive, it will not be able to access the internet via the hub. This is true even if the hub is active and ready to receive radio signals from the laptop in question. This points us to a further dimension of the notion of union with Christ. It is this. To be united to Christ the believer must be "activated," that is, regenerate, by mean of the secret work of the Holy Spirit. Once the believer is regenerate and in a position to send and receive the "signals" carried by the Holy Spirit necessary to be united with Christ, she may be joined with Christ in a spiritual manner, as the beginnings of the work of sanctification that leads to ever greater union with God in Christ and to participation in the divine life through Christ.

Lest it be thought that this image of union with Christ is rather too strong, and even something that does not reflect the sort of views one finds in historic Reformed theology, consider the following passage from William Ames's *Marrow of Theology*. It is anything but quotidian:

> The relationship is so intimate that not only is Christ the church's and the church Christ's. Song of Solomon 2:16, but Christ is *in* the church and the church *in him*, John 15:4; 1 John 3:24. Therefore, the church is *mystically called Christ*, 1 Corinthians 12:12, and the

24. See discussion in Crisp, *The Word Enfleshed*; and Crisp, *Analyzing Doctrine*.

Fullness of Christ, Ephesians 1:23. The church is metaphorically called the bride and Christ the bridegroom; the church a city and Christ the king; the church a house and Christ the householder; the church the branches and Christ the vine; and finally the church a body and Christ the head. But these comparisons signify not only the union and communion between Christ and the church but also the relation showing Christ to be the beginning of all honor, life, power, and perfection in the church. *This church is mystically one, not in a generic sense, but as a unique species or individual*—for it has no species in the true sense.[25]

Other Reformed divines have been even more emphatic in this respect. Consider. for example, Jonathan Edwards:

God's respect to the creature's good, and his respect to himself, is not a divided respect; but both are united in one, as the happiness of the creature aimed at is happiness in union with himself. The creature is no further happy with this happiness which God makes his ultimate end than he becomes one with God. The more happiness the greater union: when the happiness is perfect, the union is perfect. And as the happiness will be increasing to eternity, the union will become more and more strict and perfect; nearer and more like to that between God the Father and the Son; who are so united, that their interest is perfectly one. If the happiness of the creature be considered as it will be, in the whole of the creature's eternal duration, with all the infinity of its progress, and infinite increase of nearness and union to God; in this view, the creature must be looked upon as united to God in an infinite strictness.[26]

Just as the relation between Christ and those he comes to reconcile to Godself is a kind of *sui generis* representative atonement ordained by divine fiat, so also the mystical union brought about by Christ's work in the formation of the church is itself both mystical and unique. Because of this, our groping after language and images that that may express something of these matters is always going to be piecemeal and partial at best. That said, the image of the wireless hub (Christ), the radio signals (the Holy Spirit), and the laptop computer (the believer) connected to the internet gives us some conceptual grip on these matters, even if it is at best analogous.

---

25. Ames, *The Marrow of Theology*, 176–77. Emphasis added. Ames's views are representative of much Reformed thought on this matter, rather than eccentric, and were influential on a number of subsequent Reformed thinkers, rather than marginal.

26. Edwards, *Concerning the End for which God Created the World*, 533–34.

Nevertheless, it would be helpful to have some more formal way of thinking about the relation of union with Christ. So, let us say this. The relation of union is *binary* (having two relata: the believer and God in Christ communicated by the Holy Spirit who is the medium or bond connecting the two relata[27]) and *symmetrical* (connecting the believer to Christ, and Christ to the believer by means of the Holy Spirit). But it is also *monergistic.* That is, it is generated and sustained entirely by divine agency, in this case, the agency of the Holy Spirit in uniting the believer to Christ, and Christ to the believer. It is also true in much Reformed theology that this relation is sustained and strengthened through the use of the sacraments. Thus, as Calvin points out, in the celebration of the eucharist the believer is mystically united to Christ by feeding upon the sacramental elements. The bread and wine also (somehow) facilitate the spiritual feeding of the believer on the benefits of Christ's saving work via the Spirit. He writes: "Now Christ is the only food of our souls, and therefore our Heavenly Father invites us to Christ, that, refreshed by partaking of him, we may repeatedly gather strength until we shall have reached heavenly immortality."[28] This "mystery of Christ's secret union with the devout is by nature incomprehensible,"[29] avers Calvin. And yet, not only does the sacrament remind us of the "wonderful exchange"[30] by way of the Son of God taking on human flesh for our salvation, it also nourishes the soul of the believer through the real presence of Christ. As he goes on to say,

> Even though it seems unbelievable that Christ's flesh, separated from us by such great distance, penetrates to us, so that it becomes our food, let us remember how far the secret power of the Holy Spirit towers above all our senses, and how foolish it is to wish to measure his immeasurableness by our measure. What, then, our mind does not comprehend, let faith conceive: that the Spirit truly unites things separated in space.[31]

The feeding of the believer upon Christ by the power of the Spirit is, for Calvin, a real union, and an outward means of strengthening the union with Christ by the means of grace—one that offers a real, though mystical

---

27. In Calvin's memorable phrase, "the Holy Spirit is the bond by which Christ effectually unites us to himself." *Institutes of the Christian Religion*, 3.1.1.

28. Calvin, *Institutes*, 4.17.1.

29. *Calvin, Institutes,* 4.17.1.

30. *Calvin, Institutes,* 4.17.2.

31. *Calvin, Institutes,* 4.17.10.

rather than merely corporeal communion with the body and blood of Christ. Plausibly, the sacrament of baptism performs a similar function. For it unites the one baptized to the visible church in faith, and in the expectation of a fuller union that will be actualized as the child baptized comes of age, and owns that faith for herself.[32] In this way, the union with Christ is fortified by the sacramental life of the church, though it is, in origin, a work of grace consequent upon the calling of the believer and the secret work of regeneration.

The Mystical Body of Christ

Thus far we have examined how God ordains the justification of Redeemed Humanity in eternity, though this obtains in time at the particular moment at which a given individual is regenerated by the infusion of the Holy Spirit. This monergistic work is transformative, and sets the believer on the path toward ever greater union with God in Christ that goes on into the world to come in theosis. Union with Christ is the means by which the believer is united to God via the saving benefits of Christ's atoning work. Thus, there is a movement from God through the agency and reconciling work of Christ via the Holy Spirit to the believer in regeneration. At the same time, there is another movement from the believer via the Spirit in union with Christ, aided by the sacramental life of the church. This brings us to the question of the church as the mystical body of Christ.

Not only are there organic analogies for the church embedded in the New Testament witness. There is a long tradition of theological reflection on these images, as well as attempts to express them in various models and doctrines of the church. Thus, for instance, in Reformed theology we can find substantive use made of these images in Calvin's humanist-imbued thought, in Edwards's empiricist-idealist understanding of the church, or in nineteenth century ways of thinking about the church as the body of Christ that are indebted to German idealism such as views expressed by the Mercersberg theologian, John Williamson Nevin.[33]

Recently, the British Anglican analytic theologian, Joshua Cockayne, has weighed into the discussion of these matters in an account of the ontology of the church that takes seriously the biblical and historical ways in

32. See, e.g., *Calvin, Institutes*, 4.16.20.

33. See Nevin, *The Mystical Presence*. I have discussed Nevin's views in "John Williamson Nevin on the Church," *Retrieving Doctrine*, chap. 8.

which the church has been understood as the mystical body of Christ, and that explores the social ontology literature as providing material for modelling this. In this section I want to consider Cockayne's work as a resource for thinking about the ontology of the church as the mystical body of Christ.

In the social ontology literature, there is a distinction between group theories that include the notion that groups have agency, and those that do not. Group theories that include the notion of group-level agency are, it seems to me, problematic. There are legal and political ways in which such language is co-opted, and sometimes this is for very good reason. This is the case in situations where corporations are treated as entities that may be the subject of legal action, including the corporation's assets as parts of one complex whole.[34] Political theorists have also thought of societies in an analogous way too, with Thomas Hobbes being a particular notorious historic example.[35] Such accounts may be said to be realist about certain kinds of entities, whether legal, social, or political. But, as Cockayne following the broader social ontology literature points out, in such cases we do not think of the entities in question as bearing agency as a collective, or as a whole. The entities posited are thought to be real, but agency is not at the group level. Rather, it is a function of the collective will of the individuals that make up the group. For instance, in the case of Hobbesian monarchies, the society authorizes the monarch whereupon the monarch is able to act on behalf of the group as a kind of political body or "person" that he represents. These Cockayne describes as *redundant realist* groups because "while this model is realist about the ontology of groups, the explanation of how groups think, act, and deliberate is entirely explicable by giving an account of how the authorized individual thinks, acts, and deliberates."[36]

Those who opt for thoroughgoing realist approaches to groups that include some idea of group agency Cockayne categorizes into two genera. The first, more historical approach, involves positing some sort of unifying

34. As an interesting historical footnote, according to Christian List and Philip Pettit this sort of notion goes back to an edict issued by Pope Innocent IV: "The classical connection between corporate responsibility and personhood was made in a debate about the exposure of a group agent or *universitas* to excommunication. In 1246 Pope Innocent IV argued against the excommunication of any such corporate entity on the grounds that although it might be a person—this important concession was made in passing—it was a *persona ficta*, a fictional or artificial person, and did not have a soul". List and Pettit, *Group Agency*, 153.

35. See, e.g., Hobbes, *Leviathan*, I. 16, 107. This is also picked up by Cockayne, "Analytic Ecclesiology," 109.

36. Cockayne, "Analytic Ecclesiology," 109.

principle or spirit on the basis of which we may speak of some kind of group agency. These Cockayne characterizes as *animation* theories. Examples might include the sort of views expressed by the nineteenth and early twentieth century British Hegelianism of philosophers like F. H. Bradley.[37] But one might just as easily look to theological forebears of this view like Nevin for whom the mysterious uniting principle is none other than the Holy Spirit himself.[38]

However, more recently, philosophers like Peter French, and subsequently Mitchell Haney, Christian List, and Phillip Pettit, have ventured other thoroughgoing realist accounts of group agency that are *functionalist* in nature.[39] The distinguishing feature of functionalist accounts of mind is that "what makes something a mental state of a particular type does not depend on its internal constitution, but rather on the way it functions, or the role it plays, in the system of which it is a part."[40] According to List and Pettit, an agent can be a system that has representational states, motivational states, and a capacity to act on such states. A representational state is one that "plays the role of depicting the world" and a motivational state is one that motivates action.[41] It is the functional role that these states play that is the focus of their attention in thinking about group agency. Thus, a corporation may be a group agent in the relevant functionalist sense if it has ways of representing the world, e.g., in the scope of business conducted by the corporation, has motivational states that enable the corporation to act in a particular way with respect to its clients and products, and is able to act as a group to these ends. Naturally, in such groups the interaction of particular individuals in units and in the whole is vital, and certain individuals may be authorized to act in particular ways on behalf of the group, e.g., a CEO or a board or a manager.

Cockayne does an admirable job of attempting to motivate the application of a functionalist account of group agency to the church drawing on the work of List and Pettit in particular. He advocates a *Modified Functionalist Model* of ecclesial group agency. On this way of thinking, "the church

37. See Cockayne, "Analytic Ecclesiology," 110.

38. For useful discussion of this, see Evans, *Imputation and Impartation*, chap. 5.

39. See, e.g., French, "The Corporation as a Moral Person," 207–15; and French, *Corporate Ethics*; Haney, "Corporate Loss of Innocence for the Sake of Accountability," 391–412; List and Pettit *Group Agency*.

40. See Levin, "Functionalism."

41. See List and Pettit, *Group Agency*, 20–21, and Cockayne "Analytic Ecclesiology," 111.

is a unified group which functions as an agent with representation and motivational states and is capable of acting on these states. It is constituted by individual Christian disciples and is united by the internal promptings of the Holy Spirit . . . and the external commands of the Holy Spirit."[42] The Holy Spirit unites us to Christ, on his view, and communicates Christ's will to the church.[43] The Spirit shapes and guides the church in its relation to Christ. But the church can disregard or rebel against the secret work of the Spirit in this regard, and sin. This is important for Cockayne, who worries that some accounts of the church are too idealistic, or imply that God is sinful by tying God's agency too closely to that of the church and its members. But he also thinks that other existing accounts of group agency are either too strong in their realism (so that the collective—the church—becomes more "real" or more fundamental that the individual agents making up the church), or too weak (so that insufficient attention is paid to the corporate role of the church, rather than on the church as a collection of individual agents). He summarizes his view like this:

> According to MFM [the Modified Functionalist Model], the Church is constituted by individual Christian disciples, who in turn, coalesce into gathered collectives . . . The unity of the Church is brought about by the work of the Spirit, who through instruction and guidance made possible by the liturgies of the Church, and his indwelling the mind of each individual believer, shapes the actions of the individual constituent parts to form motivational and representational states, which meet the necessary conditions for agency . . . The Spirit enacts this work in line with the will of Christ, the head of the Church . . . Finally, since each constituent member of the Church can reject or act in defiance of the will of Christ made manifest by the Holy Spirit, the actions of gathered collectives and individual disciples can diverge from the purposes of God, thereby bringing about apparent disunity within a united whole.[44]

42. Cockayne, "Analytic Ecclesiology," 118.

43. Cockayne, "Analytic Ecclesiology," 118.

44. Cockayne, "Analytic Ecclesiology," 120. This summary is set against a series of desiderata with which he begins his account of the nature of the church. These are: (1) The church is constituted by individual Christians; (2) these individuals at times coalesce into gathered collectives; (3) these collectives and individuals that partially constitute the church are not united in practice, theology, or belief; (4) such disunity arises in part due to human sin; (5) the Spirit unites the constituent parts of the church to respond to God in worship through Christ; and (6) Christ has authority and headship over the church. (Adapted from "Analytic Ecclesiology," 103).

However, I worry that functionalist models of group agency involve rather forced and peculiar ways of thinking about how groups actually work. For one thing, it seems to me that all attempts to analyze group agency that imply that the group *qua* group has propositional attitudes (i.e., attitudes toward particular propositions such as "it is raining outside") seem mired in real conceptual difficulties. Not the least of these is that it is very difficult to see what can be meant by the notion that groups *qua* groups may have propositional attitudes that does not ultimately reduce to the claim that it is, in fact, a collection of individuals that share a propositional attitude in common, such as when a group of schoolboys stay inside their classroom at lunchtime because they share the belief that it is raining outside.

But, perhaps more importantly, Cockayne's analysis of the ontology of the church in terms of group action does raise some important differences between the church as the body of Christ on the one hand with Christ as its head, and Christ as the one whose work atones for the sins of the members of Redeemed Humanity, on the other hand. Christ is authorized (by God) to act on behalf of Redeemed Humanity. He represents them in atonement. This is a *sui generis* relation that is divinely constituted. By contrast, the church, which comprises the members of Redeemed Humanity, is joined together by the agency of the Holy Spirit in calling and regeneration, and in union with Christ. The Spirit is the agent that, as it were, binds the members of the church together. This much animation models of group theory applied to the church have gotten right. For the church is animated and bound together by the agency of the Spirit, which is a necessary condition for the existence of the church. But the church as such does not act by means of an authorized *merely human* agent or representative in communing with Christ. Rather, the different members of the church act together by means of a *divine agent*, that is, the Holy Spirit who calls and regenerates them individually, and unites them to Christ and to one another as members of the mystical Body of Christ. So, it seems to me that animation models of group action articulate something fundamental concerning the nature of the church that should not be set aside. Although I think that Cockayne is right about much of his analysis of the nature of the church, it seems to me to err too much on the side of the individual in providing a functionalist account of the church. He writes, "we do not need to appeal to any mysterious force to explain the unity of the whole [church]. Indeed, unlike the animation model, this unity is provided by means of the will of a person, or group of persons." His view "does not appeal to some metaphysically strange force which emerges each time groups are formed."[45] Instead, it is the will of the Trinity that is the "driving force of the church's unity."[46] But how is this mediated to the church if not by the "mysterious force" of the Holy Spirit? And how is the church to act together if not by means of the same Spirit who calls and regenerates the individual believers and unites them to Christ? The church is significantly unlike a corporation or even a collective like a hive. The reason for this is precisely that there *is* a mysterious "force" at work uniting the different members of the church together in a whole, that is, the Holy Spirit, without whose agency the church would not exist as a group at all.

Of course, the church fails in important respects. The very fact that the historic fabric of the One, Holy, Catholic, and Apostolic church is torn and patched, and misaligned in all sorts of ways reflects the fact that the church does not act in accordance with the will of God expressed in the reconciling work of Christ, and the salvific agency of the Holy Spirit. Nevertheless, it is in attending to this agency, and in the infusion of uncreated grace that comes in being a member of Redeemed Humanity, that the individual believer is united with other believers as members of the mystical body of Christ. If anything, it seems to me that the church should be thought of in what Cockayne calls redundant realist terms, as a special case of a group that acts by means of an authorized agent, the Holy Spirit, who unites the members of the church one another and to Christ as the head of the church.[47] The Spirit animates the church; without his agency there would be no church, though there may be a collective or a corporation. Although the church *qua* church does not have agency as such, it is able to act together by means of the agency of Holy Spirit, and as the members of the church seek to be conformed to the image of God in Christ, to whom they are mystically united.

---

45. Cockayne, "Analytic Ecclesiology," 119.

46. Cockayne, "Analytic Ecclesiology," 120.

47. The Holy Spirit is "authorized" for this work by God, not by members of the group. In this way, and in a manner similar to the account given of the atonement in the previous chapter, the Holy Spirit's agency in the church is both mysterious and *sui generis*.

Conclusion

In this paper I have provided an account of how it is that the benefits of Christ's reconciling work are applied to the believer, and form the church as the new society of Redeemed Humanity, which is the mystical body of Christ. The argument was divided into three sections. In the first, I reasoned that those who are members of Redeemed Humanity are justified by an act of sheer divine grace from eternity. This is "actualized" in the work of regeneration that brings about what Jonathan Edwards called "a new sense of things" in the heart of the believer through the infusion of uncreated grace, and the reordering and reorientation of the fallen individual through the secret work of the Spirit. Then we considered the second aspect of the way in which the Spirit applies the benefits of Christ to the believer. This has to do with uniting the believer to Christ, and through Christ to the divine nature. In this way the believer is reconciled to God and enabled to begin the process of participation in the divine life that begins with justification, calling, and regeneration, and continues through the process of sanctification. But this only deals with the relation of the individual to Christ. It does not address the corporate aspect of this union, in the mystical body of Christ. This we tackled in the third section of the chapter. Using some ideas culled from recent work in social ontology, and filtered through the helpful recent work of Joshua Cockayne, I argued for a special case of a realist and pneumatic account of the church as the mystical body of Christ.

3

The Four Marks of the Church

Today and Tomorrow

GERALD BRAY

Introduction

A FEW YEARS AGO, I wrote a book about the church which I subdivided into historical periods.[1] For each period I considered the meaning of the four traditional marks of the church as we recite them in the Nicene Creed—unity, holiness, catholicity, and apostolicity. I pointed out that these basic principles, which have survived the test of time, and which are agreed by virtually all Christians, have been understood in quite different ways at different times by different groups of people. Today the legacy of this history is apparent in the many denominations that make up the world of Christendom. Each of them looks back to some past time when their particular ecclesiology was either dominant or else emerging in the face of opposition from what was then the establishment. To varying degrees everybody tries to ground their doctrine of the church on the Bible, but this can be frustrating, because the Scriptures often give us enough to justify our own positions but not enough to exclude others. For example, in 1 Cor 11 there is quite detailed information about the celebration of the LORD's Supper, but there are some surprising gaps. The Apostle Paul never

1. Bray, *The Church.*

mentions who should preside at it, and that has been a major bone of contention for centuries. The man who went on to say "Let all things be done decently and in order" would hardly have assumed that it would all just happen, but we have no idea who was in charge at Corinth![2]

I mention this because so much of what is written about ecclesiology is theoretical and idealistic, rather than a guide to what works in practice. People tend to expound what they think the church ought to be rather than describe what it actually is. Arguments for episcopacy, Presbyterianism or independency concentrate on their positive aspects and ignore the negative ones, making it difficult to choose which of them is best and almost impossible to combine them in the hope of retaining what is good about each of them and ignoring the rest.

It is not my intention to argue what I think the church should be, or be like. I have no desire to rake over past quarrels or to advocate a particular way forward to the exclusion of anything else. My aim is more modest than that. I want to look at the four classical marks of the church and examine where we stand in relation to them today. I then want to outline some of the problems that will need to be addressed under each heading, and challenge us to think how we might tackle them. History shows us that consensus will be difficult to achieve, and that well-meaning attempts to bring the church into line with Biblical teaching will probably do no more than produce a series of new denominations, each one claiming to be more faithful to the Word of God than the others. I do however want to peer into the future as far as we can and take a look at the challenges we all face, whatever our particular background or ecclesiastical allegiance might be.

Perfection is unattainable and the danger that we may find ourselves in a position that none of us wants is very real. When Oliver Cromwell invaded Scotland in 1650 he tried to avoid battle at Dunbar by asking the Scots, in the bowels of Christ as he put it, to consider that they might be mistaken. Of course, by that he meant that they should have the good sense to agree with him. Neither side was prepared to concede the possibility of error on their part or admit that their opponents might have something worthwhile to say, and so the issue was settled—temporarily and unsatisfactorily as it turned out—by force of arms. I hope that we can avoid that outcome today, and I believe that we shall do so if we can come to a common mind about where we are and humbly seek the LORD's help as we consider together how we might go forward from here. So let us begin.

2. 1 Cor 14:40.

Unity

We believe that the church is one. That is the first and most basic statement of ecclesiology that we have. The church is one because it is the body of Christ, and he became incarnate only once. The church is one because it is the bride of Christ, and he is not a polygamist. The church is one because, as the Apostle Paul told the Ephesians, there is only one LORD, one faith and one baptism.[3] Around the heavenly throne all Christians will be united in wonder, love, and praise. Jesus told his disciples that in his Father's house there are many mansions, but despite the jokes that occasionally circulate about this, nobody seriously thinks that we can seal ourselves off in one of those mansions and ignore whoever might be in the others. As the ancient theologian Origen observed many centuries ago, the ark of salvation may have three decks, just as Noah's ark did, but even if places on the upper deck are reserved for those who are especially close to Jesus, as Origen thought, the ship contains every kind of animal, and all will be brought safely to the other shore. Predestination is God's decision, not ours—those who are saved will all be washed by the blood of the one Lamb slain from before the foundation of the world, whose names are written in the one book of life.[4]

Those are the principles on which all Christians are agreed, but how far does it tally with the perception of most people in actual practice? On the one hand, at a time when Christianity seems to have ever less influence in its historic homelands and is under threat of persecution in various parts of the developing world, the sense and even the practice of unity across Christendom seems to be stronger than it has been for many centuries. On paper, our denominations preserve the memory of past conflicts, but with few exceptions, these play little part in the lives of ordinary Christians today. Institutions may find it hard to merge because their polities are different, and the vested interests of their personnel often stand in the way. Devotional practices, particularly those that distinguish Protestants from Roman Catholics or Eastern Orthodox, frequently diverge to the point where they divide people from one another and are barriers to practical unity. Theologians are always ready to wage battle over points of doctrine and many of them find argument more congenial than agreement. But beyond these things there is a deep sense that whatever differences Christians have, we are all on the defensive in a world that has turned against God. We

3. Eph 4:6.
4. Rev 13:8.

all have to confront those who have either rejected Christ outright or who have reduced him to dimensions that pervert the message of his gospel. When confronted with this reality, our internal disputes often fade into the background, even if they do not entirely disappear.

It is not difficult to see that in some spheres, pan-Christian ecumenism is already taken for granted. Bible translation, for example, is almost always a collaborative effort with no noticeable denominational or doctrinal bias. Translators may disagree about some of their methods and choice of words, but these are usually professional disputes among linguists, not theological or ecclesiological problems. This situation is reflected in theological colleges and seminaries, where students are regularly made aware of the entire range of thought on a wide variety of issues. Very rarely would any lecturer ignore or dismiss a book simply because its author was Catholic, Orthodox or Protestant–ordinands and seminarians are expected to become familiar with different points of view and in most cases will use books, like commentaries on the Bible for example, that come from sources outside their own tradition. The world of scholarship is generally free of denominational bias and theological students of many different backgrounds study together, often in inter or non-denominational settings.

At a more popular level, worship services across the spectrum are much more similar now than they once were, with only a few traditional Protestants and Catholics, as well as the Eastern Orthodox, resisting the trend. Everybody sings the same hymns, devotional literature circulates widely across denominations, and many lay people worship wherever they feel most at home, regardless of the ecclesiastical label the particular congregation wears. At times it seems to them that denominationalism is the province of the clergy and a few obsessive fanatics who stand out precisely because they are so odd. Pockets of traditionalism survive here and there but they are declining as younger people move away and seek fellowship wherever they can find it. This sort of practical ecumenism is now very common, and on the whole its effects are more positive than negative. Old quarrels are put aside, secondary matters are increasingly seen for what they are, and people tend to concentrate on the essentials. To some this appears to be a kind of dumbing down that obscures important doctrines, but people who think that way are in the minority. The process of homogenization is not yet complete, but we have come a long way in the past century and there is no going back now.

Of course, divisions still exist, but for the most part, they are of a different kind from what was common in the past. At the risk of oversimplification, I would say that they fall into two main categories—external authority and internal spiritual experience. The question of external authority is one that takes us back at least as far as the Reformation and even beyond that. Speaking in the most general terms, the main dividing line here is between the living *magisterium* of the church and the deposit of faith found in the Holy Scriptures. There used to be a fairly clear distinction between the approach of Roman Catholic and Eastern Orthodox churches on the one hand, and that of most Protestant churches on the other, but things are not that simple nowadays. Rome and the East continue to believe that ultimate authority lies with the church hierarchy—in the Roman case, primarily (though not exclusively) with the Bishop of Rome, and in the East with councils of the church. But in recent times, popes have been known to reproach Protestants who ordain women on the ground that they have gone beyond the authority of Scripture, something that they claim they cannot do, and the Eastern churches have not managed to hold an authoritative council since 787, which makes it hard for them to decide on any question that has arisen since then.

Protestants retort that Rome and the East have frequently and quite openly ignored the teaching of the Bible and added many things to the requirements of faith that Jesus and his disciples never taught, but although this appeal to *sola Scriptura* makes sense to them, it does not persuade either Catholics or Orthodox. Their response to Protestant claims is to say that the Spirit who inspired the Scriptures is alive and guiding the church into fresh revelations, which can go well beyond the ancient texts without actually contradicting them. Thus, Catholics can argue that there is no contradiction between the compulsory celibacy of the clergy today and the fact that the Apostle Peter, supposedly the first bishop of Rome, had a wife. In their view, doctrine has developed over time, so what was acceptable for Peter is no longer permitted to his successors. Of course, that could change if a fresh revelation were to come along, particularly where the question is one of tradition, not dogma. Compulsory clerical celibacy is not an immutable doctrine but is subject to revision, as are many other practices of a similar nature. No Catholic would ever agree that the Bible could be set aside by papal decree, but in the final analysis it is the pope who determines how the church must interpret it and to supplement its teaching where necessary.

This traditional position is well known, but what is often not perceived so clearly is that many Protestant churches have developed a living *magisterium* of their own that is not all that different from the Roman position. Synods, general assemblies, and even theological committees set up by particular denominations have taken it upon themselves to pronounce on important matters of doctrine, regardless of what their confessions of faith or other founding documents might say. The ordination of women is a case in point, and now we are similarly confronted with the claims of same-sex marriage advocates. In both cases, proponents of change have had to argue that the Bible does not prevent them from introducing such novelties, even if they must admit that it does not encourage them either. The tension is usually resolved by saying that the Bible is a book of its time and can no longer be applied in the way that it originally was, something that even conservative Protestants are forced to admit to a limited extent. The result is that significant numbers of church people no longer accept the Scriptures as their supreme authority in matters of faith, and so division of one kind or another is inevitable.

Conservative Protestants, and particularly those in mixed denominations, often appeal to the concept of the invisible church, which goes back at least as far as the Reformation, and which can be found in different guises throughout Christian history. This says that the wheat and the tares grow together until the harvest, that the visible church on earth is a mixed bag of true believers and others, who belong to it in body but not in spirit. True believers are identified by their spiritual experience, which brings us to the second great question that confronts us when we seek to ground the unity of the church in some overarching principle. Those who have known personal conversion, the indwelling presence of the Holy Spirit and the transformation that he brings, recognize each other and share in fellowship. This includes a strong element of orthodox doctrine, but that is not the essential thing.

The reason for that is that it is possible to hold to classical orthodoxy on paper without knowing it as a living experience, just as it is possible to know the LORD Jesus Christ in spirit without being well-read in doctrine. In this second case, those who have been converted are expected to learn the doctrine and to profess it—if they fail to do so, their *bona fides* will be questioned and they may find themselves excluded from a fellowship to which they do not really belong. In practice this is how Evangelicals operate most of the time. We may be involved in mixed denominations, but our true allegiance is to those who are like-minded, wherever they may be found. We are not doctrinal minimalists, but hold to orthodoxy in theology plus vital experience in our lives. However, if we see the latter in someone from a different church or denomination, we usually accept them on the basis of that and overlook differences of doctrine, as long as they are of secondary importance. This principle extends across all Protestant denominations and even to Roman Catholics and Eastern Orthodox whom we do not exclude from our fellowship purely on the basis of their formal church allegiance.

Looked at in this way, we can say that the ecumenical church of the future has already arrived. Barring a few residual barriers here and there, most of us circulate freely among congregations, fellowships and parachurch organizations that share our basic outlook, and conflict is rare. In many places independent churches have sprung up that avoid denominational entanglements, though they are usually more dependent on existing formal structures than they realize. Many of their ministers have received their training in denominational theological colleges, and to that extent they are somewhat parasitic. But except in cases where a minister leaves an existing denomination and practices deliberate sheep-stealing from established congregations, hostility is rare. Some refugees from mixed churches make their way to independent congregations and may feel a certain bitterness towards those whom they have left behind, but that is seldom encouraged by the leaders of the independent churches to which they have gone. For the most part, people take their own decisions, and everybody learns to live with that, which is probably the best we can hope for in the circumstances. church splits often leave hard feelings behind, but over time these tend to diminish, and spiritual, if not institutional, unity can be allowed to prevail.

There seems to be little doubt that spiritual affinity wins out over institutional connections whenever the unity of the church comes up for discussion. We see this most clearly when people move from one locality to another and start to look for a "good church" to go to. In a few cases this may mean a congregation belonging to the same denomination as the one they are leaving, but most of the time, one suspects, that is a secondary consideration. What really matters is the quality of the preaching, the soundness of the teaching and the vibrancy of the fellowship on offer. If they are satisfactory, denominational allegiance is liable to be overlooked. The result is that for more and more people, it is the local congregation that represents the universal church, and it is there that worshipers expect to find the fulness of gospel ministry.

It is not my purpose to recommend congregationalism as the way of the future, and like every other system of church government, it has weaknesses as well as strengths. Rather, what I would say is that in our present circumstances, and given the challenges that we now face, Christian unity is more likely to be worked out in that way than in any other. Fewer people nowadays can be brought to accept decisions taken by a wider and more impersonal church body—if someone does not like a woman minister or same-sex marriage, he or she is likely to go elsewhere, to a place where his or her views will be more congenial. We already know how hard it is for institutional churches to practice any kind of discipline, but we should not pay too much attention to aberrant clergy. The truth is that the power of lay people to vote with their feet has never been greater than it is today, and it is the spiritual bond that unites them to fellow believers. This does not make pastors and teachers redundant, but it puts whatever authority they may exercise on a different basis. Those who lack the authentic seal of the Holy Spirit will either lose their congregations or create churches that will not be accepted by others as fellow-workers in the Kingdom of God. What already happens in practice will probably become the norm, making it necessary for believers to discern where they belong and putting the onus on them to make sure that the congregation does not lose its zeal for the LORD.

To ensure the maintenance of a godly church unity in the future, teachers will have to restructure their approach to the faith, concentrating on the essentials and keeping controversial issues in their place, as far as this can be done. Human nature assures that there will always be disagreements of one kind or another, and some of these will continue to divide us, but it will be the duty of church leaders in the future to make a clear distinction between what really matters and what is less important, insisting on agreement about the former while leaving room for different opinions about the latter. In a sense we shall find ourselves back in the seventeenth century, when Puritan ministers were faced with a similar challenge, but too often failed to rise to it. History seldom repeats itself exactly, but perhaps a pattern is there, and our grandchildren will be able to revisit the fundamental principles and take a course different from the one that our ancestors either chose or were forced by the circumstances of their time to follow.

Holiness

When it comes to the question of the church's holiness, we find that a very different dynamic has been at work in the past generation. One of the main complaints of the Reformers in the sixteenth century was that the church had lost a sense of its own holiness and had allowed itself to be corrupted by the surrounding world. Contrary to what many Protestants have been taught to believe, the Roman Church did not ignore this criticism. On the contrary, as it launched what is usually known to us as the Counter-Reformation, the need for the church to manifest practical holiness was top of the agenda. Abuses were rooted out and a new spiritual discipline was imposed on the clergy. There was even a new religious order, the Society of Jesus, that was founded to be a kind of salvation army—the Jesuits were the shock troops of the new dispensation who would demonstrate by their dedication to the cause all the virtues of military-style self-discipline. It was a strategy that worked better than anyone could have imagined, and that shaped the understanding of holiness in the Roman fold at least until the Second Vatican Council in the 1960s. The discipline imposed on the clergy and the religious was naturally stricter than what was applied to the laity, but the latter did not escape. From eating fish on Fridays to weekly confession followed by penance and communion, Catholics were trained up in a pattern whose ultimate goal was sainthood, even if few achieved it in this life.

Protestants could not compete with this. They had their own ideas about holiness, to be sure, and did what they could to implement them. Old superstitions were swept away, and church members were encouraged to become educated, reading the Bible and putting it into practice as best they could. Whereas spiritually-minded Catholics had to get away from society and join monastic communities in order to work out their vision of holiness, their Protestant counterparts believed that it was their duty to put their principles into practice in the world, by running honest businesses, bringing up godly children and making sure that even the humblest of occupations was sanctified as a calling from Almighty God, to whom every believer would have to give account on the day of judgment.

This Protestant concept of holiness transformed society in ways that are still evident. We have only to compare Northern with Southern Europe, Northern with Southern Ireland, or North with South America to see what a difference this could (and did) make. But as time went on, this kind of transformational holiness gave way to something else, which in important respects was closer to the experience of lay Catholics than to the early gen-erations of Reformers. From the late eighteenth century, when the Evan-gelical revival was at its height, there developed a legalistic kind of holiness teaching that began with the Wesleys and continued with little alteration until the 1950s and even later. It was a teaching that laid a heavy emphasis on personal behavior—no drinking, no dancing, no card playing, and so on—and that became the object of much ridicule in the nineteenth and early twentieth centuries, when its superficial interpretation of "godliness" came to be seen as little more than hypocrisy. That judgment was unfair, but it made a powerful impact, reducing the concept of "holiness" to a form of pseudo-piety and giving the word "puritan" a bad (and historically quite inaccurate) name.

It is fair to say that this form of so-called "holiness" is no longer domi-nant in Protestant circles, just as its Catholic counterpart seems to have vanished from sight as well, but the legacy of both has been profound and mostly negative. As the old strictures have been discredited and have disap-peared, so too has the concept of holiness itself. The problem for most of us today is not that we have the wrong idea about holiness, but that we have no concept of it at all. To many people even the word "holy" sounds archaic, as in the expression "holier-than-thou." The Bible says that all Christians are saints, called to live out the holy life that is the true mark of our profession, but who would dare stand up in front of a congregation and proclaim that they are holy people, even if it is theologically correct to do so? It sounds both pretentious and undesirable, and so for the most part, we pass over it without comment.

This is a disaster for the church. What it means in practice is that we have become chameleons, blending in with our environment to the point where we can no longer be readily detected as believers in Christ. The church of the future must change its whole approach to holiness if it is to make a serious impact on the world around us. The first thing we have to do is recover the Biblical meaning of the word "holy." In scriptural terms, holiness is an attribute of God and indicates his presence. Strictly speaking there are no holy things or holy places—there are only holy people because it is in people, and not in inanimate objects, that God dwells.[5] Furthermore, all God's people are holy. The term has nothing to do with their merits or

5. It is true that the word "holy" is sometimes used with respect to particular objects or places, but this is by extension. The things or places are not holy in themselves, but only because God told his people to set them apart and promised to reveal his presence in and through them.

behavior, but with the decision of God to dwell in and among them. Indeed, we could go further and say that the Bible would never have been written if God's people had lived up to their calling to be holy. It is precisely because they did not achieve this, and could not achieve it, that God gave them the law and the promise of the gospel.

Holiness is not something we earn or aspire to; it is something that has been given to us because of who we are. The biblical calling is for us to work out our salvation with fear and trembling, not as we once were in Adam but as we now are in Christ.[6] If we start with that understanding, all legalism, all anxiety, and all despair at our sense of constant failure will be excluded. Instead, we shall have renewed minds, which is the key to living out what it means to be holy. A renewed mind will see the world for what it is and will mark its distance towards it. We cannot go out of the world—Jesus and Paul both remind us of that.[7] We must live in the circumstances in which we have been placed, but we must rule over them and not let them control us.

Prescription is difficult because circumstances vary so much, but Christians must always be constructively critical of their surroundings. I say "constructive" because it is very easy to be negative, and if we stop there, we are no better than the world around us. We must always remember that our world is a precious gift from God and that we are called to be stewards of it. But it is that very stewardship that must make us critical—if we spot weeds growing in our garden, we root them out, not because we hate them but because we want to preserve the beauty of what we have been given. Philosophical arguments about the fundamental goodness of weeds as creatures of God, or the need to be tolerant of what we do not like, are a waste of time. We do not know why weeds exist, and it may be that they have some purpose of which we are unaware, but we know that they do not belong in our patch. The holy gardener discerns this and takes the necessary action.

Tending a garden is relatively easy, but protecting the world we live in is another thing altogether. We must have the mind of Christ to spot what is wrong, and the power of his Holy Spirit to do something about it. True holiness is more than just knowledge—it is action on the basis of the knowledge that we have. In recent years there has been a renewed interest in medieval monasticism as a possible response to the secularism of the modern age. Some people think that Christians should withdraw into hermitages or

6. Phil 2:12.
7. John 15:19; Rom 12:2; 1 Cor 5:10.

small communities where they can live without being contaminated by the cares of the world. This is a delusion. Trying to escape may be attractive, but as monks throughout the ages have discovered, they take the world with them into the monastery and cannot do otherwise. Self-isolation is not the key to holiness, and we must resist that temptation. Engaging with the world is difficult. It requires skill and it requires grace. Can we recover these gifts and apply them in today's context?

This is the challenge before us. The early church conquered the world because it stuck to its principles and did not allow itself to be seduced by outside influences. Today it is all too often the case that the church apes the world, though it often does so badly, and too late to make a difference. We have become followers when we should be leaders. Pastors and theologians are not equipped for this task and should not try to deal with matters outside their sphere of competence. What we need are inspired lay people in all walks of life, men and women with the knowledge and expertise to apply the Christian principles that they have learned from their pastors to the tasks set before them. Holiness is an individual commitment, but it is also a collective enterprise, and it is an open question how far we have risen to the challenge. Too often we have retreated into our pious world of specifically Christian activities and done little or nothing to encourage front-line engagement with the surrounding culture, with the result that the latter threatens to overwhelm us. Here, more than anywhere, we see how acute the need is to rethink what the church is called to be. Let us hope and pray that the Spirit of God will lead us into the fulness of the holiness that is the great gift of his presence in and among us.

Catholicity

What is the catholicity of the church? This is a particular problem for Protestants because we have to recognize that at the time of the Reformation, the church in Western Europe broke up. That was not the Reformers' intention, but as it became clear that universal reform was impossible and that local churches could only be changed with the co-operation of secular rulers, the creation of national churches with little or no communion with each other was almost inevitable. It was those who rejected reform who clung to the ancient notion of the church's catholicity, so much so that they became—and have remained—identified with that to a degree that is not true of anyone else. We must admit that their claims, though often disputed, have some justification. At the same time as Protestants were breaking away from Rome, the remaining Catholics were evangelizing across the world—in the Americas, in Africa and in Asia. A worldwide church did in fact come into being in the sixteenth century, but it was Roman Catholic. Protestants were not totally indifferent to foreign missions, but did not really get going with them until nearly three hundred years later. By then Catholic missions could be found on every continent. Some were more successful than others and the way in which catholicity was imposed—by introducing the Latin mass in completely alien contexts, for example—may be criticized, but an effort had been made and its legacy can still be seen in many places today. Until the reforms of the 1960s, it was possible for a Roman Catholic to attend mass anywhere in the world and take part in it more or less intelligently, because the outward form was virtually identical everywhere.

Protestants, with their emphasis on translation into the mother tongue, were less able to do this, though the basic forms of worship and many of the hymns are often recognizable. This is not genuine indigenization, but neither is it a form of Western imperialism, as many modern critics have claimed. Many Christians in the so-called majority world are perfectly happy with what they have received from Western missionaries and some of them look on attempts to embrace the local culture with deep suspicion. They do not want to embrace practices that seem to them to be covered in the paganism from which they have been delivered, and it is not right for Westerners burdened with post-colonial guilt feelings to try to insist that they should think differently about this. Indigenization has to come from below, and there is a real danger that well-meaning outsiders may end up appearing as latter-day imperialists, which is the very thing that they most object to.

The spread of Christianity across the world in recent times is undoubtedly a good thing, but it creates problems for the church that must be recognized and dealt with. The first and most fundamental of these is the need to maintain standards of doctrinal orthodoxy. If the message preached in far-away places turns out to be something different from the faith once delivered to the saints because of misguided attempts to adapt it to a local culture, the universality of the gospel will be compromised. Whether we like it or not, the Son of God came to the Jewish people at a particular moment in their history. The message he proclaimed was communicated against the background of Graeco-Roman civilization, using concepts that made sense in that context. That process led to controversies that split the church and that required decades of intense debate to resolve. We may regret some of the twists and turns to which this led, but we cannot escape from their legacy. For better or worse, we have inherited certain ways of thinking about our faith that cannot easily be changed without running the risk of introducing heresy by the back door. Roman Catholic missionaries in seventeenth-century China who tried to graft the gospel onto that country's ancient ancestor cults found that out to their cost, and the more recent appearance of syncretistic religions in places like Korea and the Congo are reminders that this phenomenon is by no means dead. However desirable indigenization may be it cannot be pushed to the point of losing contact with the roots of our faith.

At the same time, we must also face the fact that some Western churches have tried to move away from historic orthodoxy by adopting beliefs and practices derived from post-modern Western culture, and that too is a denial of catholicity. The idea that people today are somehow more sophisticated than our ancestors were and that it is no longer right, or even possible, to accept traditional beliefs on sin and salvation, is a conceit that denies the communion of saints. The apostle Paul was well aware that he preached a gospel that was considerably more detailed than the revelation that God had given to Abraham two thousand years before, but he recognized that Abraham was the founder of our faith and that in spite of everything, there was no fundamental difference between what the Hebrew patriarchs believed and what the early Christians were proclaiming. If that was true of them, how much more must it be true of us now? The passage of time cannot alter an eternal message, and the saints militant here on earth must never forget that a significant portion of the church's membership is already enjoying the triumphant rest of the Kingdom of Heaven. Catholicity extends to time as well as to space because it transcends the created order, being the expression in the finite world of a reality that in its essence lies beyond it.

The time dimension is all too easily forgotten, especially in our modern, throw-away world. We have a rich inheritance of medieval and early modern church buildings because our ancestors built for eternity, what will future generations say about us? What legacy will we bequeath to them? Do we even think about this? A deep knowledge of the past is necessary if we are ever to have a long-term perspective for the future. None of us knows when Christ will come again, and we must live each day as if it were our last, but at the same time we must guard the deposit of faith and hand it on to those who will come after us, even if the end is approaching.

But for all the importance of time, there is no denying that space now claims priority. Our medieval ancestors did not think much about that, but the modern world is increasingly interconnected, and it is no longer possible for developments in one place to go completely unremarked elsewhere. We have learned to our cost that a virus that first appears in a market in Wuhan can soon threaten the entire world, and that individual, supposedly sovereign states, can do nothing about it. News travels fast and the impact of distant events is felt almost immediately. Some things go unreported in the media and are therefore largely ignored, but this does not stop them from affecting us. Bad government and persecution in little-known places produces floods of refugees who try to save themselves by migrating in our direction. We cannot absorb them all, but neither can we abandon them to their fate. It is only by winning their countries over to our way of thinking that this problem can be solved, but globalization on anything other than a Christian basis would be a disaster from which we would all suffer.

For the church there is no alternative to catholicity. Heretical books and delinquent pastors in Western countries, not to mention churches that promote immoral lifestyles in the name of "love," can do untold harm to Christians elsewhere. We hear reports of how those in Muslim-majority countries may be persecuted because of the acceptance of things like same-sex marriages in Western countries. The increasing use of English as a universal language, while it may make life easier for us, carries with it responsibilities. If British or American Christians are seen to be supporting groups and ideas that are incompatible with the teachings of Christ, this will quickly become known around the world and the message of the gospel may be compromised as a result. The political interventions of American evangelists in particular are extremely unhelpful in this regard, and our inability to discipline them is frustrating, to put it mildly. The fact is that too many Western Christians are blind to the effects that their words and deeds might have elsewhere and carry on as if the outside world does not exist. It does, and sooner or later, it will come back to haunt us if we are not careful.

Finally, catholicity extends to every aspect of human life and culture. We understand this when it comes to indigenization of the gospel in the developing world, but may be less sensitive to it in our own context, which continues to influence that world to a disproportionate extent. How far we can embrace ideas and practices that come from outside the church is controversial, and there is no easy answer to it. We feel it most acutely in the realm of music. Can Christians adopt or adapt new and unfamiliar musical styles for our worship? Churches divide over this question, but it has to be asked and answered on an almost daily basis. What should we do about new technologies and the often complex issues associated with them? The rapid advance of ever-increasing specialization makes it harder to develop a comprehensive world view that can encompass all aspects of our lives. Breadth of vision will lead to superficiality if it is pressed too far, but over-specialization in narrow areas has its dangers too, especially when the bigger picture, or catholicity, is lost sight of. The church has to recover an all-encompassing theological vision that can moderate and contextualize the findings of those who have great expertise, but in highly circumscribed fields. Never has a Christian world view—catholicity again—been more necessary than it is today, and it is here that the pastors and teachers of the church face their greatest challenge. Does the Bible speak today, and if it does, how? We must move away from a fundamentalism that clings naively to an outdated past and get back to the fundamentals, or basic principles of God's revelation, which need to be re-expressed for the world in which we are now called to live. It may be the most urgent task facing us as Christians today.

Apostolicity

What does apostolicity mean today? Officially. the Roman Catholic Church maintains that the Bishop of Rome is the living apostle, the direct successor of Peter, the chief of the apostles and the inheritor of his power and authority. Other Christians do not accept that, and it is increasingly questioned within the Roman fold itself. The notion that anyone can speak infallibly about anything runs counter to the scientific understanding of reality, where everything is at least potentially falsifiable, and statements to the contrary tend to be ignored. Protestants have traditionally regarded the Bible as infallible, but what that means in practice is hard to pin down and the variety of interpretations that circulate on just about everything makes an infallible consensus seem illusory. It may be possible to defend the view that the New Testament represents the teaching of the apostles, but how systematic or comprehensive that teaching is is a matter of ongoing dispute. Even those who accept it in principle find it hard to define in practice, and it is extremely difficult to work out what the apostles would have said or done in situations that were unknown to them. Would they have supported *in vitro* fertilization, for example? Would they have insisted on keeping bodies clinically alive on life-support machines when there is no hope of recovery? These, and a thousand other questions like them, cannot be conclusively answered on the basis of the New Testament alone, and disagreements are bound to arise. Unfortunately, the fault lines tend to run along levels of education—those who know most about the subjects usually appear to be more "liberal" in the way that they handle them, while their opponents often make an emotional case that is painfully short of scientific knowledge.

Of course, even a cursory glance at the New Testament will show us that Christians have always been mocked for their faith by the intelligentsia and denounced as dangerous troublemakers by the conventionally religious. That is unlikely to change, and we must get used to it. Martyrdom is more likely than popularity as the apostles themselves knew only too well. To be apostolic is to recognize that and accept it—fame and honor, if they come at all, will most likely arrive long after our deaths. But that is no reason to lose heart. The example of the apostles is there before us and gives us hope. What do we need to make that hope come alive in our generation?

First of all, there must be unswerving dedication to the gospel doctrines revealed in Scripture. Unless they are our foundation, there is no hope that what we build on top of it will stand the test of time. Compromise on basic principles is simply not possible, and we must be prepared to accept that refusal to bend will cost us friends and possibly even our lives. Then too, we must be single-minded in our devotion to Christ. The apostle Paul was often discouraged and spent years in prison, sometimes merely because the secular authorities had forgotten about him and let him languish there. What must have been going through his mind during those apparently wasted years? As far as we can tell from his writings, his determination never wavered. Whether he was speaking to kings or to his prison guards, Paul had the same message for everyone. The Savior of the world had come and called all people everywhere to repent and believe. It was simple and straightforward, but resistance was strong. Even King Herod Agrippa II who was almost persuaded to become a Christian never quite made it, much to Paul's distress. He really wanted to see people saved and never took his eye off that prize. Are we as apostolic as he was in our own commitment to mission?

Comfortable Christianity is not apostolic Christianity, but it is the prison in which most of us are trapped. We forget that the blood of martyrs is the seed of the church because we do not want to be martyrs, but when we look around the world. we see that it is where faith is on the line that the church is growing. It would be perverse for us to invite persecution, but can we expect to grow and prosper without it? If the world is truly opposed to our message. then there should be some evidence of that from the way it reacts to us. If we are allowed to live in peace, is that because we have nothing to say that would disturb anybody? The Protestant Reformers knew what it was to suffer for their beliefs, and we honor them for it, but are we prepared to follow their example?

Here we have reached the limits of where a conference or a lecture can take us. There are some churches that have a sign on the way out that says "You are now entering the mission field." One of the interesting things about the first apostles is that while they stuck together during their discipleship training with Jesus, they tended to disperse once the gift of the Holy Spirit was given to them at Pentecost. They did not all leave Jerusalem immediately, of course, and Peter, James, and John at least were still there when Paul was converted and went to meet them.[8] But Paul had no intention of staying in Jerusalem, and was always looking for new fields of mission where he could be a pioneer in ministry. As for the other apostles, we know next to nothing about them, though legends that may contain elements of truth tell us that some may have gone as far as India, preaching the gospel as they went. The lesson for us must surely be that we are called to mission, but none of us can say for sure where that will take us.

An apostolic church is a church that walks by faith and not by sight, trusting in the sovereign and Almighty LORD as it goes. In every generation, revival has come when men and women of God have seen the parlous state of the world around them and been moved by the Holy Spirit to do something about it. Simeon and Anna spent long years in the temple, waiting for the Messiah to come, but when Joseph and Mary turned up with him in their arms, they did not hesitate to respond.[9] The boy Samuel lived in a time when the word of the LORD was scarce and there was no open vision, but when God spoke to him he listened, even though he had to be prompted by the unfaithful Eli, who represented the religious establishment of his day.[10] The long catalogue of saints in Hebrews 11 is a reminder

8. Gal 2:9.

9. Luke 2:25–38.

10. 1 Sam 3:1–18.

of how God has chosen the foolish things of this world to shame the wise.[11] The key, it always seems to me, is what the writer slips into verse thirty-four: "whose weakness was turned to strength." We cannot be apostles on our own, but only in the strength and power of Almighty God.

Let me conclude with some wonderful words that Samuel Rutherford wrote to Robert Campbell as both men were awaiting their fate after the collapse of the Puritan Commonwealth:

> The Lord calleth you, dear brother, to be still 'steadfast, unmoveable and abounding in the work of the Lord.'[12] Our royal kingly Master is upon his journey, and will come, and will not tarry. And blessed is the servant who shall be found watching when he cometh. Fear not men, for the Lord is your light and salvation. It is true; it is somewhat sad and comfortless that you are alone. But so it was with our precious Master; nor are you alone, for the Father is with you. It is possible that I shall not be an eyewitness to it in the flesh, but I believe he cometh quickly who will remove our darkness, and shine gloriously in the Isle of Britain, as a crowned King, either in a formally sworn covenant, or in his own glorious way, which I leave to the determination of his infinite wisdom and goodness. And this is the hope and confidence of a dying man who is longing and fainting for the salvation of God.[13]

Go forth in peace, to love and serve the LORD. In the name of Christ, amen.

---

11. 1 Cor 1:27.

12. 1 Cor 15:58.

13. Smith, *Letters of Samuel Rutherford*, II, 70, 484.

4

Calvin on the Church

Why Is It in *Institutes* Book 4?[1]

STEPHEN WILLIAMS

The Issue

THOSE OF US WHO were inducted into Calvin's *Institutes* by the stately Henry Beveridge translation of 1845 were intrigued by the discrepancy between what was promised in a preliminary account of its "Method and Arrangement" and what was delivered in the course of its text. Said account was authored by Kaspar Olevianus, and inserted between Calvin's "Epistle to the Reader" and the Table of Contents. Calvin, Olevianus informs us, handles the knowledge of God and of ourselves by "simply" adopting "the arrangement of the Apostles' Creed." taken as quadripartite, the Spirit occupying Calvin's third and the Church the fourth book.[2] Right enough, working through the *Institutes*, we are in the swim of the Creed as Calvin concludes its second book, methodically taking us through the creedal

---

1. In its original version, this essay was very heavily footnoted with reference to both primary and secondary literature. For the most part, I have dispensed with these here, in order to allow the argument of the essay to stand out in bolder relief.

2. Calvin, *Institutes of the Christian Religion*, 27–30.

clauses from "crucified, dead and buried" to "from whence He shall come to judge the living and the dead."

Then the surprise. The order in the Apostles' Creed is, of course: Spirit, church, communion of saints, forgiveness of sins, resurrection of the body and the life everlasting, but whether we take the Creed as quadripartite or tripartite, Calvin abandons its topical order. He separates the creedal "*ecclesia*" and "*communio sanctorum*" from the Spirit by treating forgiveness and resurrection in connection with the Spirit in the third book, so that they precede *ecclesia* and *communio*, which are duly assigned to the fourth book. Why? At the beginning of book four, the Apostles' Creed features, as it did at the end of book two. In 4.1.2, Calvin remarks on the impropriety of using the preposition "in"—"I believe *in* the church"—and shortly afterwards (4.1.3), refers to the creedal: "communion of saints." Subsequently, and still in 4.1, he grants the propriety of speaking of forgiveness *after* and not *before* ecclesiology, as does the Apostles' Creed, though he himself does not do so structurally (4.1.20, 27).

Calvin was not responsible for what Olevianus said. Although this final Latin edition of the *Institutes* has been labelled "the 'credal' *Institutio*," Calvin does not tell us that its structure will be tightly ordered to the Apostles' Creed, and more than one proposal has been offered for how exactly it is structured. Nonetheless, Olevianus piques our curiosity, for the Gospels announce that Jesus will baptize with the Spirit, and after his death, resurrection, and ascension, he pours out his Pentecostal Spirit to constitute publicly the new people of God, the New Testament church. In that context, forgiveness of sins and the hope of resurrection are the subject of apostolic proclamation. If it is merely noteworthy that Calvin does not follow this trajectory, after ending book two with the session of Christ, it is a positive jolt to find that when the church is visited in book four, it is set forth under the rubric: "The External Means Or Aids By Which God Invites Us Into The Society Of Christ And Holds Us Therein." The opening sentences place two issues on the table immediately. "Since . . . in our ignorance and sloth (to which I add fickleness of disposition) we need outward helps to beget and increase faith within us, and advance it to its goal, God has also added these aids that he may provide for our weakness."[3] (I stick to Battle's translation, though it is not altogether satisfactory at this point).[4] So, firstly, how is the

---

3. Calvin, *Institutes*, 4.1.1. From now on, references to the text will frequently be provided in the body of the paper.

4. In the words I have quoted, it looks as though Calvin uses first the word "helps"

church just an "aid"—an aid to personal spiritual development? Supposing we were told that Joshua, Samuel, and company thought theologically of Israel as an "aid" to their personal spiritual development, their personal faith—what would we say? Is the church located in book four because Calvin views Christian religion individualistically?

Secondly, and I linger longer here, what is the significance or implication of Calvin's adoption a few sentences later of the familiar patristic designation of the church as our "mother?" It is not just one designation amongst others; it is apparently a rubric under which he treats the church in book four, something of a hermeneutic for his ecclesiology. He has in mind the visible church: "[B]ecause it is now our intention to discuss the visible church, let us learn even from the simple title 'mother' how useful, indeed how necessary, it is that we should know her" (4.1.4.) Calvin cites Gal 4:26: "The Jerusalem above is free, and she is our mother." He soon reverts to talk of motherhood in Galatians 4 (4.2.3), and, before that, he has told us that "there is no other way to enter into life unless this mother conceive us in her womb, give us birth, nourish us at her breast, and, lastly, unless she keep us under her care and guidance until, putting off mortal flesh, we become like the angels" (4.1.4).

As a matter of exegesis, it is scarcely possible to interpret the "mother" of Gal 4:26 as the visible church. It is the language of children, not of maternity, that Paul applies to the church in Galatians: the Galatians are "children of promise" (28), "children of the free woman" (31), the children of Sarah, the mother of Israel, so children of the covenant of promise, the maternity belonging not to the church below, but to Jerusalem above. Consistently with reference to the heavenly Jerusalem in both Hebrews (12:22; see too 11:10, 16) and Revelation (3:12; 21:2, 9–10), the pilgrim church, comprising the children of Zion, born from above, is not identical with the heavenly Jerusalem. Granted the complexity of Paul's treatment of allegory in Galatians 4 and different ways of interpreting the relevant verses in Galatians, nevertheless, Calvin's exegesis is in trouble, even though the claim

---

and then, synonymously, the word "aids" to refer back to the "helps." But the word "aids" is supplied by Battles himself. Calvin at this point simply says "these things." Of itself, this is materially unproblematic, as Calvin's meaning remains correctly represented. However, the impression is conveyed that Calvin is repeating in the sentence the word which Battles has translated as "aids" in the title of book four. Calvin is not. It is the ablative form of the word *adminicular*, which Calvin uses in the title, and which Battles translates there as "aids." The word Calvin uses in the sentence in question in the *text* is the ablative form of *subsidia*, a word which is not in the book title. To complicate life still further, the editorial title of 4.1 gives us the typographically errant "aims" instead of "aids."

that the heavenly Jerusalem above is, indeed, the visible church prior to the Parousia, lay deep in the patristic and medieval exegetical background to Calvin's interpretation.

This is not to deny the theological propriety—or, indeed, the exegetical possibility—of designating the church as our mother on the basis of *other* biblical materials. Nonetheless, we must ask why Calvin assigns to this (*mater ecclesia*) designation of the visible church its prominent role in book four. In his remarkably enduring and invariably rewarding survey of the church in the New Testament, Paul Minear considered ninety–six images of the church, and the *mater fidelium* is all but completely absent from, and anything but central in his account.[5] So does the early emphatic vocabulary of motherhood indicate that Calvin regards the church not just as having the features of an institution, but *primarily* as an institutional structure, "church" being defined in maternal terms in view of its nourishing leadership, of which Calvin will make so much in Book four, and attracting more theological attention than its nourished membership? If so, does a questionable institutionalism, accompanying a misplaced individualism (notions which, in another context, can be at loggerheads), explain the assignment of the church to book four?

Indeed so, it has been alleged. If we want to hear it straight from the modern Reformed household, Emil Brunner is our man. Brunner averred that what explains the order of doctrinal arrangement in the *Institutes* was Calvin's mistaken identification of the *ekklēsia* of the New Testament with the institutional church of history. In truth, the New Testament *ekklēsia* is a fellowship in Christ and in the Spirit.

"Never did it occur to an apostle that the *Ekklesia*, the fellowship of Christian believers, the true people of God of the New Covenant, might be regarded simply as a means to an end, and even at that a purely 'outward' means, an *externum subsidium fidei.*"[6] So says Brunner in *The Misunderstanding of the Church.* His book began with the prefatory words: "What is the Church? This question poses the unsolved problem of Protestantism." and the first sentence of the first chapter alights on Calvin's *Institutes.* Calvin conceives of faith individualistically, and of the church institutionally, rather than as being intrinsically a fellowship. *Prima facie*, Calvin's individualism is modified by his view of the church as invisible. However, this is not an effective mitigating factor, since an invisible church is not a

5. Minear, *Images of the Church in the New Testament.*
6. Brunner, *The Misunderstanding of the Church,* 9–10.

fellowship, but a *numerum electorum*, an "aggregate." as Brunner puts it elsewhere.[7]

Brunner was not isolated in the ranks of modern Reformed theologians. Barth served up a slither of sympathy.[8] When Pannenberg explored "*The Place of Ecclesiology in the Structure of Dogmatics*" in his *Systematic Theology*, he drew special attention to Hendrikus Berkhof, amongst modern Reformed theologians.[9] Berkhof is "one of the few theologians to discuss the problem of the ordering of the church before individual appropriation of salvation."[10] Turning directly to Berkhof, we find him both critical of and sympathetic to Brunner's appraisal.[11] On the one hand, *mater ecclesia* "sounds far from individualistic!," so Brunner oversimplifies. On the other hand, Brunner "does not speak as he does without reason," for Calvin's observations that our ignorance, sloth, and fickleness cause God to bring the church to our aid "give the impression that Calvin sees the external organization of the church as a concession of God in view of our poor and sinful nature." Accordingly, "the total picture of Calvin's ideas is not quite clear." Berkhof reckoned that what accounts for the tension in Calvin's account is that "the Reformed Church is the daughter of the Catholic Church type and the mother of the Free Church type. She has affinities with both."[12] In effect, while talk of the motherhood of the church belies the title of book four, talk of the church as an outward help is suited to it.

---

7. Brunner, *The Christian Doctrine of the Church*, 20.

8. While critical of much in Brunner's ecclesiology, Barth agreed with his "conjecture that no apostle would ever have thought of the community merely as an external means to serve a quite different end—the sanctification of individual Christians," and he asks whether Calvin could possibly have appreciated the full and proper dimensions of "mother church" if he could come to speak of the church only in book four and, even then, as one of the *externa media vel adminicula* whereby we are called into fellowship with Christ, Karl Barth, *Church Dogmatics*, IV/2, 615. For criticism of Brunner, see 616 and 679–86, and for later criticism of Calvin's "mother church" as restrictive, relatively neglecting the church as the "community for the world," see Barth, *Church Dogmatics*, 766–67.

9. Pannenberg, *Systematic Theology*, 21–27. Brunner is mentioned too.

10. Pannenberg, *Systematic Theology*, 23 n.70.

11. Pannenberg was referring to Berkhof's *Christian Faith*, but although Berkhof does allude to Brunner there, he also takes up Brunner's interpretation of Calvin in an earlier work which I cite here, *The Doctrine of the Holy Spirit*, 47–49, from which my subsequent quotations from Berkhof are taken.

12. In *Christian Faith: an Introduction*, Berkhof describes what Calvin does with these alternative ecclesiologies as a "going back and forth," 342.

As a good biblical theologian, I reckon two witnesses—both from the Reformed tradition, to boot,—sufficient to instigate an investigation into Calvin on the charges of individualism and institutionalism. I am accenting my question as follows: "What is 'the Church' doing *in book 4*?" So, first: is Calvin's ecclesiology in the *Institutes* individualist? If so, does that either explain or contribute to an explanation of what the church is doing in book four?

Individualism

Ploughing through the *Institutes*, we should be unlikely on the basis of its first two books to indict Calvin confidently on the charge of individualism, as formulated by Brunner. True, the self, knowledge of which is urged upon us, is not placarded as an essentially relational self- relational in terms of fellow-humans. True, the sustained discussion of sin and human bondage which takes us deep into book two, before broaching knowledge of the Redeemer, may provisionally portend an individualistic concentration on grace later. Nonetheless, arriving at the sixth chapter in book two, where we learn that fallen humans should seek their redemption in Christ, the Christological-soteriological exposition is markedly ecclesiological. God preserved the Old Testament Church in the form of the children of Israel, and "promised to David" that he "would be through the hand of Christ the deliverer of the church" (2.6.4). Of course, as long as we are approaching the question of individualism on Brunner's terms, the mere vocabulary of "church" does not overthrow his claim, because he held that talk of the invisible church privileges individualism. Calvin has informed us in his "Prefatory Address" that the question of whether the church is necessarily visible is a leading point of contention with Rome. Admittedly, then, bare reference the "church" proves little. It is not always possible to know whether the visible is included where Calvin speaks of church in the first two books.

However, moving onto book three, suspicion of individualism is aroused, and not just on account of our Brunner-sensitized antennae. It comes to its sharpest focus when Calvin deals with "The Christian Life." Calvin aside, the first thing to say theologically about the Christian life is that it is corporate, ecclesial life in the Spirit. We are ready to hear that after Calvin's talk of the ascension and session of Christ; but the Spirit who enters at the beginning of book three is not the public, Pentecostal Spirit who constitutes the post-ascension *ekklēsia* on the foundation of a missionary apostolate, but one who operates "secretly" to generate individual faith.

Yet, this is just one side of the matter. Aspects of the Christian life have already been treated in book two in relation to the law (2.8). Faith and obedience to law presuppose and function within the covenant community of Israel and New Testament Church alike. We are immediately reminded at the beginning of 3.1 that Christ is head of the church and later told that "[h]e was raised by the Father inasmuch as he was Head of the church" (3.25.3). Although attention is frequently drawn in book three to individual faith, it is also drawn to the new covenant community. The desideratum of ecclesial fellowship can be expressed in strong terms (3.4.6). The longest chapter in the *Institutes* is on prayer, "the chief exercise of faith," and the clearly corporate nature of faith emerges in it (3.20). As far as book three goes (and it turns out to apply to book four as well), Alasdair Heron was right: "Much more indicative of his [Calvin's] true position than the setting of the individual believer over against the community of the church is the insistence running through both of these books that church and individual alike depend wholly upon Christ."[13]

By the time, then, a very thin and narrowly-focused eschatology has brought book three to its conclusion, while suspicion of individualism *may* linger, if we have worries about what Calvin has done with pneumatology, eschatology, and ecclesiology, we may yet wonder whether the problem lies elsewhere. We shall certainly be a long way into book four before it is impressed on us that Jesus is he who baptizes his people with the Spirit, in fulfilment of the Old Testament promises, but whether or not this will turn out to have anything to do with individualism must remain an open question at this point.

By the time we have arrived there, Calvin has explicated what was portended in the "Prefatory Address" by informing us that the word "church" may be used in two senses: the invisible inward and the visible outward. Book four is about the visible outward. This is our *subsidium*, our "aid." So distant does talk of *mater ecclesia* appear to be from any *externum subsidium* that we are tempted to ask whether Calvin *does* call the visible church an *externum subsidium* in so many words. Might it be rather the *governance* of the church, including its preaching function, and the sacraments which are the *subsidia*? However, without these you do not, for Calvin, have a visible church in any, let alone a true, sense. To conceive of

13. Heron, *The Holy Spirit*, 104.

a visible church without proclamation, governmental structures and sacra-ments is impossible; they belong to the definition of a visible church.[14] So the visible church is formally an *externum subsidium*.

Calvin is strong on the invisible church. Does that spell individual-ism? If it does, it is not necessarily because individualism is the object of his disproportionate theological affection. Consider the days of Elijah. Calvin believed that, under the regime of medieval Catholicism, as at the time of Elijah, the true church lacked a visible form, yet God certainly did not lack a church. If the invisibility of the church means a lack of corporate manifestation, this is because the church has been corrupted, not because individualism has been courted. Theologically, then, is Calvin's invisible church a case of God preserving faith at the expense of fellowship? Not necessarily. Let us put a *prima facie* case for Calvin here. Even if we take a contrary position to his and maintain that "church" is never so used in Scripture that "invisible" is an adjective suitably attached to it, we might still defend it as a theologically permissible phrase to describe the unity in Christ of true believers, just as long as its use in that way did not trammel or weaken anything that we *should* say biblically and theologically about the visible church. This is not an idle permission. As long as presumptively true believer has spiritual dealings with presumptively true believer, would not the word "fellowship" be appropriately used, even if institutional corrup-tion robbed that fellowship of its visible corporate expression, and, if the fellowship, then the "church?" Even if our answer is: "no." Calvin's church is not in the same position as Calvin's Israel. Calvin believed that God wills not the return of the days of Elijah, but a visible church—a remnant, but visible. As far as possible, the visible church must be the true church of the elect, but although a church can possess the characteristics of a true church, tares will still be found therein. There was election within election in Israel, but as the inner election, that of the remnant, was of an invisible company, so the visible church of the New Testament is different.

It seems that Brunner's allegation, then, that invisibility does not miti-gate individualism, is insecure. Yet, the question of individualism may still arise if we ask about the connection between election and invisibility. Our answer to it depends on how we read Calvin on election and predestina-tion—whether his focus is on the election and predestination of the com-pany or of individuals into a company. If the latter, it is Calvin's doctrine of

14. Perhaps it is not technically impossible, but a church lacking these things would resemble a society without government or institutional structure.

election, not his concept of invisibility *per se* which advances individualism. However strongly Calvin believed that God willed the remnant Reformed Church or churches to be visible, as long as its membership did not coincide exactly with those whom God has chosen for salvation, he generally preferred not to apply the designation "elect" to a visible body which may contain reprobates. From the standpoint of New Testament terminology, we might quarrel with him here; if the New Testament Church is a remnant church, it is a corporate entity which can be described in terms applied in the Old to external Israel. Had Calvin conceded this, it is conceivable that ecclesiology would have been treated and perhaps located differently. But that is speculative.

Our solid ground is that, in book four, the visible church is an aid—but a necessary aid. It may be there on account of our weakness, but as long as we are in the body, we are weak, human; unlike angels, who need no aids, we need the church. Of course, that way of putting it preserves an individualistic interpretation of Calvin. And from this point of view, it cannot easily be dismissed. Book four consistently offers support for it, so that even if we have concluded that the concept of the invisible church does not entail individualism, we may still conclude that Calvin's treatment of the visible church does. There are passages, notably in connection with the LORD's Supper, "the bond of love" (4.17.38, 44), which so laud the importance of ecclesial, communal, loving fellowship, that we might well be tempted to banish all suspicion of individualism, especially if we imagine the weekly participation in the eucharist which Calvin wanted. And yet, his whole discussion of the sacraments is governed by his initial statements on it, which is that they are all about strengthening believer's faith. It is a *corporate* strengthening of faith, of course, but the accent is not on the fulfilment of the human person in relationships.

Berkhof is right: although Brunner exaggerated, the accusation of individualism was not groundless when applied to Calvin's formulations in the *Institutes*. On the one hand, Brunner focused too narrowly on the relevant terminology (*media, adminicula, subsidia*) rather than interpret it according to the substance of Calvin's account in book four, and too narrowly on portions of rather than on the whole text of the *Institutes*. On the other hand, although even sympathetic commentators have found Calvin's terminology here something of a stumbling-block, and suggested implicitly that we judge his ecclesiology by its substance rather than the rubric under which he developed it, we cannot dismiss Calvin's categorically descriptive language about the church as an "aid" as a lapse from high humanistic literary standards. He sustains the language of "aid" in Book four and means what he says. Nothing more than God's power is *absolutely* needed to build up His people. "God," as he says elsewhere, "might Himself have performed" the work of edification, "if he had chosen; but He has delegated it to the ministry of men," thus instituting maternal nourishment as well as paternal power.

Berkhof thought that what accounted for the tension which he found in Calvin was his combination of a traditional, institutional view of the church and a free church approach. This judgement is apparently premised on the belief that a free church approach is individualistic, and this certainly should be challenged. It is a matter which I must by-pass. As for whether Calvin's individualism, such as it is, accounts for the location of the church in Book four, it seems to me that we must return the verdict: "Not proven." This is emphatically so when we keep in mind Calvin's context. In pondering what the church is doing in book four, rather than featuring in book three as the first item in the exposition of pneumatology, we are in danger of reading the *Institutes* too much in context-free terms of our own theological expectations of dogmatic order and too little in light of Calvin's day. What is the point of exalting fellowship and community if we have no idea what the Christian faith is *about*? We have to know what salvation is, what faith is, before we speak of its fellowship. According to Calvin, the tragedy and corruption of the medieval church lay in the hindrance to the salvation of individuals which it provided. Misunderstanding itself and the need of the people, it had to be put right by a proper account of the human condition. "Instead of an experience of God, Rome offered an experience of the church."[15] To have dealt with church and sacraments before faith would have been to perpetuate the medieval error regarding the way that we receive the grace of Christ—to the destruction of our souls. Back in 1536, the Latin title of the first edition of the *Institutes* described it as *Containing almost the Whole Sum of Piety and Whatever It is Necessary to Know in the Doctrine of Salvation*. Not to have prioritized the relationship of the individual to God would have been a first-order dereliction of religious duty for Calvin, and undermined his motive for writing the *Institutes*. What does God require of *me*? is the question we should all be asking. The answer is that I should be saved. If that is individualism, is it not also Christianity, some will protest? It would little further Reformation to be told, first, that

15. McDonnell, *John Calvin, the Church, and the Eucharist*, 109.

what is deficient in the Roman Catholic Church is a lack of loving fellow-ship, and emphasize *ekklesia* before getting onto faith. So, it all looks from Calvin's point of view.

Calvin's thought had both an intrinsic theological impulse and a par-ticular polemical expression. It is not clear to me that we can categorically decide that the church is in book four because of individualism without meticulously distinguishing these two strands in the *Institutes*. It is a task too big for here and now.

Institutionalism

What, then, of institutionalism? Initially, I broached this question in con-nection with Calvin's appeal to Galatians 4. In applying the language of maternity to the visible church, he was, broadly speaking, adhering to the Western, rather than to the Eastern patristic tradition. Cyprian was for-mative here and where Augustine, who also spoke of mother church, is ubiquitous in the *Institutes*, Cyprian turns up conspicuously in book four after a couple of cameo appearances earlier. His formulation, "You cannot have God for your Father if you have not the Church for your mother" is almost reproduced at the beginning of book four (4.1.1). Cyprian is favor-ably referenced throughout much of that book. Indeed, Calvin has been called "the Protestant Cyprian" of the sixteenth century.[16]

Cyprian's attribution of motherhood to the church did not rest on an exegesis of Galatians 4:26 (nor am I suggesting that this was the case with Calvin everywhere outside the *Institutes*). Clearly, a description of the church as an *externum subsidium* would have been entirely incomprehen-sible to Cyprian; equally clearly, he is anything but individualistic. But is his not classical and original Western institutionalism? The bishops constitute the heart of and binding force in the church, do they not? If we substitute a presbyterian for an episcopal order, is Calvin not just entering here into Cyprian's inheritance?

Calvin twice quotes at relative length words from Cyprian's *De Unitate Ecclesiae* where, "following Paul," Cyprian "derives the source of concord of the entire church from Christ's episcopate alone" (4.2.6; see too 4.6.17). Although Calvin has no need to mention it, these words occur at or around the point at which Cyprian makes his celebrated reference to the church as our mother and, on the second occasion that he quotes them, Calvin

16. Whale, *The Protestant Tradition*, 154; cf. 161.

refers to the beauty of Cyprian's description of the church.[17] Rightly so. In these passages, Cyprian conveys a sense of the visible church in its communal, historical, institutional, and mystical aspects which surely set the standard for the theological unity—not to mention spiritual warmth—of any account of the visible church regulated by the thought of the church as mother. More striking still than Cyprian's institutional emphasis is his emphasis on the bonds of love. Cyprian's correspondence, frequently cited by Calvin, sustains this note, including in those letters specifically cited by Calvin. Thus, in Cyprian's writing, there is both a warmth and an integration of all the elements mentioned above which are even more striking than and which pervade his institutional ecclesiology. Only a perusal of Calvin's correspondence and sermons, *inter alia*, will show how he reads in comparison with this, but our sensitivities to what goes on in book four, when Calvin dwells on the governmental structures of the church, are honed by a glance at Cyprian. Calvin ascribes motherhood to the church in closest connection with the leader's discharge of their responsibilities. What is of interest is the ensuing maternal profile.

Book four is distinctive in that Calvin studiously turns to church history to make his point. His ecclesiology is set against the background of the one (Western) church that hitherto has existed in major institutional form and is largely shaped by his anti-Roman polemic. However, this does not sufficiently explain Calvin's theological preoccupation with the governance, as opposed to the lay life, of the church, even if it is the government of the Roman Church which bears the principal responsibility for its corrupt state in the medieval centuries. The reason why Calvin devotes half the chapters of this book to the governance and officers of the church is that he regards ministry as "the church's chief sinew, indeed its very soul" (2.7) "by which believers are held together in one body" (3.2). Although he makes extensive use of other parts of Ephesians (and, of course, of Scripture), Paul's description in Ephesians 4 of the gifts of leadership given by the ascended Christ to the church is pivotal in Calvin's ecclesiology. Even though the leadership of the church is given so that its members may be nurtured, Calvin devotes a huge proportion of the expository space assigned to the *ekklēsia* to its leadership. For the true church is subject to Word and Spirit and its leaders are the preachers of the Word. "[T]he church is built up solely by outward preaching" (4.1.5; cf. 3.4.14). "Doctrine," Calvin says elsewhere, "is the mother by whom God begets us" and "preaching is the mother who

---

17. For the first reference to the church as mother, see Bévenot, *De Unitate Ecclesiae*.

conceives and brings forth, and faith is the daughter who ought to be mindful of her origin."[18] Most comprehensively: "[T]he Church of God is not only begotten by means of holy and godly pastors, but . . . its life is also cherished, nourished, and confirmed by them to the end."[19]

Sobering as it is to be reminded of this, when considered as a piece of dogmatics grounded in biblical theology, Calvin's ecclesiological attention to leadership is disproportionate. The New Testament church is a new community to which God has given leaders, but to concentrate on the nature of leadership is a case of the hierarchical tail wagging the ecclesial dog. If we confine ourselves simply to Ephesians, it is after exalting Christ's headship over his body, the new humanity which constitutes the household of God, and the function of the church in making God's "manifold wisdom . . . known to the rulers and authorities in the heavenly places" (3:10), that Paul explains how its governance works to ensure its flourishing. The nature of the church is explained in Ephesians 1–3. But let us not be a-historical: given the contextual constraints on Calvin's exposition in the shadow of sixteenth-century Roman Catholicism (and Anabaptism, for that matter), we should not expect Calvin to produce a dispassionate theological treatment, *De Ecclesia*. Further, let me heavily underline that this paper is *not* on Calvin's ecclesiology *per se*. I am not assuming that Calvin's *Institutes* gives us a comprehensive or balanced account of his doctrine of the church, nor am I assuming that Calvin's ecclesiology should be deduced simply on the basis of what he wrote and not also from his practices. Even the most cursory look at what Calvin says elsewhere about the church will show that the *Institutes* is far from saying it all.

But we must also ask whether questionable exegesis in the *Institutes* contributes to a skewed emphasis. Calvin takes Romans 12:8, which describes the gifts of exhortation, contribution, leadership, and merciful action—as "*certainly*" (my emphasis) about public offices in the church (4.3.9). It is the *apostles* who are called "the light of the world" and "the salt of the earth" in the Sermon on the Mount (4.3.3). In the same year as Calvin produced this final Latin edition of the *Institutes*, he prepared the *Confessio Fidei Gallicana*. Unsurprisingly, as in the *Institutes*, Calvin arrives at the

---

18. See Calvin, *Commentary on Galatians*, on 4:24, and Calvin, *The Second Epistle of Paul to the Corinthians and the Epistles to Timothy, Titus and Philemon*, on 2 Cor 13:5.

19. Calvin, *Isaiah 59—Jeremiah 32:20* on Jer 3:15.

church after treating justification, faith, and the Spirit; but when he does arrive there, he leaps to talk of the pastors, not of the fellowship.[20]

Calvin surely understands the church visible in excessively institutional terms. Specifically, it is too hierarchical; hence the appellation "aristocratic" which has been used of Calvin's view of the church, and which invites far-reaching comparison with the traditions of Swiss republicanism embodied in the ecclesiological tradition stemming largely from Zwingli. The most straightforward way of making this point is to say that the institutional aspect encroaches too much on the church as community, although the suggestion is not that community and institution should stand in theological tension. We have to eschew insularity in addressing this point: if we quit the realm of theology and church, most of us take for granted that civil community requires institutions, and easily imagine institutions that enable community to flourish. If we couch matters in slightly tighter theological terms, congenial to the Reformed—and not only the Reformed—tradition, we shall go beyond "community" to say that the principle of the life of the ecclesial *organism* is somewhat eclipsed in Calvin's ecclesiology in practice in the *Institutes* by the interest in leadership. This means that, theologically, Calvin's pneumatology, for a start, needs some adjustment.

However, does this state of affairs account for the location of the church in book four? Well, if we flee historical context for a moment and take refuge under the wings of anachronism, we should not leap to an affirmative answer. Let Herman Bavinck be our landing-place. When, in the *Prolegomena* to his dogmatics, Bavinck described book four of the *Institutes* as "trailing behind" the rest, he conveyed the impression, without actually saying it, that Calvin failed to accord to ecclesiology the significance due to it.[21] In a later volume, he noted the case for treating ecclesiology before soteriology—naturally so, because he described "The Outpouring of the Holy Spirit" in ecclesiological terms, straight after discussing the humiliation and exaltation of Christ.[22] Specifically, he indicated that the dogmatically proper notion of the church as an organism, and not an aggregate of individuals, invites this reversal of Calvin's order.

---

20. For the text, see Schaff, *The Creeds of Christendom*, 356–92. The relevant chapter is 25.

21. Bavinck, *Reformed Dogmatics*, vol. 1: *Prolegomena*, 101, in his section on "Order in Reformed Dogmatics."

22. Bavinck, *Reformed Dogmatics*, vol. 3: *Sin and Salvation in Christ*, 499–508.

Yet, Bavinck will not himself accept the invitation. For one thing, establishing the theological place of the covenant of grace—which he believes can sensibly precede Christology in dogmatic order—"has the advantage that these theologians have in mind when they give priority to the doctrine of the church."[23] For another, the proposed reversal could mistakenly upgrade the theological importance of the institutional church by confusing it with the body of Christ. Bavinck does not tell us why, if the church were talked about before individual salvation, we could not simply make clear that we were talking about the church as the body of Christ, an organism primarily, and not an institution. Presumably, the reason is that this would separate talk of the church as body from talk of the church as institution, with talk of individual salvation sandwiched in between, something which would make for messy dogmatics. But then, does not the treatment of ecclesiology after individual salvation provide a mirror-image disadvantage? At all events, when Bavinck arrives at ecclesiology, the result is that sanctification and perseverance, for example, have been treated before the church.[24]

This is no idle digression. Bavinck's dogmatics, produced in an historical context much different from that of Calvin, shows that if we deny the church the status of external means and emphasize instead its organic dimension, it does not predictably follow that we shall assign to it a dogmatic location at variance with that of Calvin. Whether or not we agree with his theology, Bavinck gives us reason to say that a purified pneumatology and ecclesiology are not bound to promote ecclesiology *out of* book four of the *Institutes*. What I think we can say is that when the visible church is viewed in such heavily institutional-hierarchical terms as Calvin views it, that might be sufficient to keep it *in* book four after dealing over the course of three books with the theological truth which God purposes to protect by the means now laid out in book four.

I have seized on the language of "organism" because it is congenial to the Reformed (though not exclusively to the Reformed) tradition, but the organism in question is dynamic, and so the question also arises of whether Calvin's institutionalism eclipses a sense of ecclesial dynamic in book four as well. Theologically, the question of eschatology, which I earlier mentioned fleetingly in connection with pneumatology, impinges directly on the question of ecclesiological substance here. The eschatology of book

---

23. Bavinck, *Reformed Dogmatics*, vol. 3, 524.
24. Bavinck and Bolt, *Reformed Dogmatics*.

three is not only thin; it is also not strongly connected with the Spirit. Ronald Wallace observed that:

> [i]n speaking of the union between Christ and His people Calvin can speak, *with reservations*, of the Holy Spirit as bringing Christ *down* into the lives and hearts of His people. He seems to prefer to speak of the Holy Spirit as raising men *up* from earth to Heaven, there to dwell with Christ and there to partake of Christ.[25]

The effect of bringing the Spirit down to earth and making the eschatological connection would have been to shift the balance of ecclesiological exposition from constitutive institutional structure to dynamic pilgrimage.

Comprehensively speaking, the call for more emphasis on the organic is a call for the re-shaping of pneumatology; the call for the re-shaping of pneumatology is a call for a fuller eschatology; the call for a fuller eschatology is a call for greater attention to the dynamic forces in ecclesiology; and we could complete the circle by saying that the call for eschatological dynamism is integrated into a call for the organic to characterize ecclesiology as much as, indeed, more than, institutional thinking. A missionary dynamic, what's more. Brunner was again onto something with his insistence on connecting ecclesiology with mission. What is lacking in Calvin's ecclesiology may thus account for its status in book four.

Aside from what was noted about ministerial corruption in the Roman Church, is there a contextual justification for Calvin's hierarchical institutionalism, as in the case of his putative individualism? Not manifestly. In 1526, Luther wrote in relation to the form of divine worship:

> If one had the kind of people and persons who wanted to be Christians in earnest, the rules and regulations would soon be ready. But as yet I neither *can* nor *desire* to begin such a congregation or assembly or make rules for it. For I have not the people or persons for it.[26]

Calvin's erstwhile mentor, Martin Bucer, took this aspiration seriously, broadening it when he briefly sought to establish *ecclesiolae in ecclesia, Christlichen Gemeinschaften* in Strasbourg—relatively small groups of the committed faithful who would give mutual pastoral help and aid the designated leaders in pastoral and teaching leadership. Although this was

---

25. Wallace, *Calvin's Doctrine of the Christian Life*, 20. While he states the point in general terms, he documents it only with reference to Calvin on the LORD's Supper.

26. "The German Mass and Order of Service" in Lehmann, *Luther's Works*, 53–90; 64.

not the success story of the Reformation, it was one evidence that Bucer had a stronger sense of the church as community and its bonds of love than Calvin displays in the *Institutes*, though he (Bucer) was strong on the institutional nature of the church. In vacant or in pensive mood, I toy gratuitously with the notion that, had it been given to Bucer to write a *Loci Communes* or an *Institutes*, he would have ordered his *oeuvre* differently from either Melanchthon or Calvin, and treated ecclesiology immediately after pneumatology. We shall never know, and it is just as well; the product would have been four times as long as the *Institutes* and twice as hard to read.

More soberly, we must look to Zurich as well as to Strasbourg for something which Calvin does not, in his *Institutes*, say: love is an internal mark of the church. In his first sermon in chapter five of *Decades*, on the *sancta catholica ecclesia*, Bullinger mentioned the internal *notae* of love, faith and communion with Christ and Spirit. Calvin sometimes adds "the right hearing" to "the right preaching" of the Word as a mark of the church, along with the proper administration of the sacraments, and presumably where right hearing embraces obedience and not just comprehension, love enters the scene as a mark of the church. Shortly before adverting to Cyprian on episcopacy as the bond of concord, Calvin observes in the *Institutes* that "communion is held together by two bonds, agreement in sound doctrine and brotherly love" (4.2.5). Yet doctrine is more prominent than love in that role.

Grounded Bullingerian ruminations and waking Bucerian dreams aside, is there anything more than an historical exercise at stake in asking about the location of ecclesiology in the *Institutes*? Is not tinkering around with sixteenth-century dogmatic order an irrelevant indulgence in Covid days? "Yes" to the first and "no" to the second question. However we describe the theological genre of the various editions of Calvin's *Institutes*, his final one (in Latin and French) has been widely received in the churches as a form of systematic theology. In Calvin's case, that is taken to be a biblical theology, and in his prefatory letter to the reader of the *Institutes* Calvin made the celebrated observation to the effect that it was designed as a guide to the reading of Scripture. One commentator expounds this last edition under the rubric: "Christianity according to Calvin: *The Message.*"[27] What Calvin made in it of the institutional nature of the church matters greatly

---

27. McGrath, *A Life of John Calvin*, chap. 8.

today not only in the Western world but in an extra-Western context such as, for example, contemporary China.[28]

Contemporary Reformed appropriation of Calvin must take into account what is happening with ecclesiology in the *Institutes*, particularly in connection with pneumatology. Covid-19 introduced to many in the West a question long familiar in another form to members of persecuted churches, about the possibility of fellowship without a regularly constituted assembly. The more ecclesiological weight is borne by Spirit and organism, the more we shall be ready to amend external institutional form; the more we emphasize the latter, the less properly flexible we shall be. For instance, whatever our views on on-line eucharist, it is a cause of dismay when churches in the tradition of Calvin have opposed it on the grounds that it could not be celebrated according to a stipulated institutional form. But I stop there, before my reveries on the order of Bucerian dogmatics are joined by reveries on whether Calvin would have sanctioned on-line communion.

---

28. See Chow, "Calvinist Public Theology in Urban China Today," 158–75, especially 171–72.

5

Faith and Sacraments, especially Baptism
A Dialogue with Roman Catholicism[1]

A. N. S. Lane

Introduction

AFTER THE *JOINT DECLARATION on the Doctrine of Justification* was signed
in 1999, I entered into an email exchange about it with Richard Rex, a
conservative Roman Catholic professor at Cambridge. He argued that
the Declaration failed to engage with a vital difference between Roman
Catholicism and Protestantism, the centrality for the former of the sacramental system. In response I cited the fact that the pope's representative
had signed the *Joint Declaration* and felt that I had got the better of the
argument. Further reflection, however, persuades me that he was right
about this being a fundamental divide, perhaps more significant than rival
theories of justification.

---

1. I am grateful to Dennis Tamburello and Richard Price for their help with setting
out the Catholic position, but neither of them is to be held responsible for the way that
I have expounded it. I am also grateful to Gordon Margery, Chris Castaldo and Gerald
Bray for comments on earlier drafts of the paper.
   All Bible quotations are taken from the ESV, which is appropriate given that this
version is approved by the Roman Catholic Church in a number of English-speaking
countries, including Britain and India.

The present chapter focuses especially on Evangelical and Roman Catholic teaching, in the light of Scripture, and Catholic teaching is treated as a dialogue partner. Many Evangelicals and many Roman Catholics are seeking to move beyond the polarizations of past years, and to find a satisfactory way of holding together the roles of faith and the sacraments. To some extent they share a common aim, albeit beginning from very different starting points.

What is a sacrament? Historically, theologians have often begun by setting out a doctrine of the sacraments, and have then applied this doctrine in turn to each individual sacrament. For example, in Book four of his *Institutes* Calvin first defines a sacrament (chapter fourteen), and then applies this definition to baptism (chapters fifteen and sixteen) and the LORD's Supper (chapters seventeen and eighteen). This approach is logical, but mistaken. The New Testament teaches much about the practice and doctrine of baptism and the eucharist; it says nothing about the concept of a sacrament. There is no explicit doctrine of the sacraments in the New Testament. If we wish to arrive at such a doctrine (a perfectly legitimate aim) we must start by working out a doctrine of baptism and of the eucharist. We can then ask what these have in common, and go on to develop a doctrine of the sacraments. The proper procedure is to start with what is clear (baptism and the eucharist, about which there is a body of biblical teaching) and only then proceed to that which is not clear (the concept of a sacrament, about which there is no biblical teaching).

In Reformation times a sacrament was defined as a "visible Word" (following Augustine) and there were debates about the relation between Word and sacrament. This contrast makes some sense when considering the eucharist/LORD's Supper, but much less sense when considering baptism. There the issue is not how baptism relates to the Word, but how it relates to faith. Calvin's doctrine of the LORD's Supper concerns the respective roles of faith and partaking of the sacrament.

I want to start by looking briefly at the relationship between Word and sacrament in worship, before focusing on the question of the relationship between faith and baptism in the process of Christian initiation.

Word and Sacrament

The central act of worship illustrates well the divide that we are discussing. It is hardly controversial to claim that Roman Catholic worship is centered on the sacraments in general and the Eucharist in particular. By contrast, for the majority of Protestants it is the sermon that is central to the service and the other elements of the service (e.g., choice of hymns) are often built around it. Putting it differently, while Catholics may debate the importance of having a homily at mass, Protestants are more likely to be debating how often to celebrate communion and in which context.[2] For most Protestants a main Sunday service without communion would not be unusual; one without a sermon would be.

In this context, it has been said that ultimately for Catholics all means of grace reduce to the church, while for Protestants all means of grace reduce to the Word. Related to that, Karl Rahner referred to the church as the "fundamental sacrament,"[3] and Vatican II described the church as the "universal sacrament of salvation."[4]

Peter Fransen, in an article on "Sacraments Signs of Faith" concludes by seeking to hold preaching and the sacrament together: "There is no sacrament without the announcement of the Gospel of salvation, and there is no real preaching of the Gospel which does not prepare, accompany and perfect the sanctifying activity of the sacraments."[5] Such unifying pronouncements are commendable, but do not of themselves remove the real differences that remain.

We turn now to our main topic: the relationship between faith and baptism.

Relationship between Faith and Baptism

How does one become a Christian? Is it by faith or by baptism or by both?[6] We will start by considering those offering one-sided answers—that we become Christians either by faith not baptism, or by baptism not faith.[7]

2. A debate that my own church was having at the time when this paper was being written!

3. Rahner, *The Church and the Sacraments*, 11–19. Cf. International Theological Commission. *The Reciprocity between Faith and Sacraments*, 73 §78: "Grundsakrament".

4. Vatican II, *Lumen Gentium* 7:48 in Abbott, *Documents of Vatican II*, 79. Cf. *Catechism of the Catholic Church*, §1118.

5. Fransen, *Sacraments: Signs of Faith*, 31–50.

6. For the need for both, see "Baptism, Eucharist and Ministry Baptism," in Leith, *Creeds of the Churches*, 3:8.

7. Baillie, *Baptism and Conversion*, 13–15 sets out the polarized views and after reviewing different approaches sets out his "Attempted Conclusion" (41–48). His book is

Those who hold such views do not generally deny that both faith and baptism are called for, though there are a few like the Salvation Army and the Quakers who do not practice baptism at all. Our question is not "Should we both believe and be baptized?" but "What is it that makes us a Christian?"

While we will focus on the relation between baptism and faith, this is part of a broader issue of the relation between the inner and the outer, the former embracing repentance as well as faith. At times our sources will force us to bring repentance explicitly into the picture.

Faith or Baptism?

Only Faith

That Christian initiation involves both faith and baptism is widely held these days, but not all agree. In particular, the majority of Evangelical *practice* points in a different direction.

In a recently published chapter, I compared the New Testament pattern of initiation with the evangelistic practice of British Evangelicals in the 1960s, in the current century, and in online materials.[8] For the 1960s, books by Billy Graham, John Stott, Michael Green and David Watson were examined, as well as the much-used booklet *Journey into Life*. In this material the need for repentance and faith is clear, but baptism plays no part in the process of becoming a Christian. For the current century the much-used enquirer's courses *Alpha* and *Christianity Explored* were examined, together with two popular booklets. These are no clearer on the role of baptism. The online resources equally ignore baptism.

The upshot is that whatever Evangelical theologians may say, the practice of evangelism largely reduces becoming a Christian to repentance and faith at best, often just to an unbiblical phrase such as "invite Jesus into your heart." Baptism plays no role, though it may be mentioned as something to do later. Baptism, like reading one's Bible, is something a Christian should get around to, but it does not play a role in *becoming* a Christian.

Particularly noteworthy is the example of Michael Green. In the text of his racy evangelistic book *Man Alive*, he draws attention to the role of baptism in Christian initiation, but when we come to the business end of the book, where the reader is invited to respond to the gospel, baptism

---

written in a setting where infant baptism is the norm.

8. Lane, "Becoming a Christian," 11–28.

disappears from the picture and conversion reduces to repentance and faith.[9] The better-rounded theology of the body of the book has unfortunately not worked through to the initiatory step of commitment at the end. Twenty years later, as a New Testament scholar, he wrote a book about baptism, which develops more fully the positive view of it found in the body of *Man Alive*.[10] Also, in a response to the first draft of my published chapter, he affirmed the role of baptism in initiation, and commented: "I have myself baptized people immediately on profession of faith as part of Christian initiation, and done so both in the river, the sea, and by affusion."[11] Gordon Kuhrt pointed out to me that Stott and Green both wrote their evangelistic books when they were relatively young and that they developed their theology over the years.

Why is baptism thus overlooked or marginalized?[12] First, there are a number of more practical reasons:

- In the sixties the majority of the populace had a Christian background, and would have been baptized as babies. At that stage the main emphasis was on bringing nominal churchgoers or christened non–churchgoers to a living faith.

- In modern times evangelism has often become separated from church life, taking place through para-church organizations such as Christian Unions. One effect of this has been to sideline the church—and even more the sacraments.

- Billy Graham in particular was concerned to avoid "divisive" issues in order that his preaching of the gospel would reach as wide an audience as possible. This is probably a contributory motive for his failure to mention baptism, although he could simply have urged his readers to make sure they were baptized according to the way of their particular church. Nicky Gumbel explicitly mentions his concern to avoid controversial teaching on infant baptism.

- All of the literature reviewed mentions the need to join a church. It could be argued that the authors assume that baptism will be covered at this stage. There may be some truth in this, but the fact remains that these authors do not portray baptism as being part of Christian

9. Green, *Man Alive*, 21, 52, 92–96.

10. Green, *Baptism*, 45–57.

11. Email of 11 August 2004.

12. See Lane, *Becoming a Christian*, 24–25.

initiation, and their clients would have no reason to suppose that it has anything to do with *becoming* a Christian.

Behind all these practical considerations lies a fundamentally theological one. there was and is a very widespread belittling of the sacraments among British Evangelicals. For many, "low church" meant (and still means) an extremely low view of baptism. Why is this? There are a number of reasons.

The indiscriminate baptism of the children of those no longer going to church or having any intention of providing their children with Christian nurture led to millions of baptized unbelievers and many nominal Christians. In that context reliance upon baptism was often seen as something to be combated.

There was also a reaction against those (about to be considered) who taught that it is simply by baptism that one becomes a Christian. Evangelists were motivated by the fear that people would imagine that they are true Christians just because they have been baptized, and attend church.

Beyond that, some play down baptism because it is regarded as just a ritual. Ironically, those who hold that view often effectively replace baptism with an Evangelical ritual, whether the "altar call" or praying a "sinner's prayer."[13]

Most British Evangelicals simply do not consider baptism an aspect of Christian initiation. In the New Testament, by contrast, baptism is part of the gospel message. Indeed, in the "Great Commission" of Matthew 28:19–20 baptism is commanded but faith is not even mentioned! For the majority of British (and other) Evangelicals, unlike the New Testament writers, baptism has no place in the gospel message.[14] Much Evangelicalism is fundamentally non–sacramental, thereby departing both from the New Testament and from historic Christianity, including not just the Early Church Fathers but also the Reformers.

---

13. The Salvation Army claims that its "enrolment" or "swearing-in" procedure is equivalent to baptism, see Susan K. Wood, "Baptism" in Wainwright., and McPartlan. *Oxford Handbook of Ecumenical Studies*, 241–56, 240–41.

14. For example, the account of the gospel in the Lausanne Covenant makes no mention of baptism. I am grateful to Gordon Margery for pointing this out.

Only Baptism

If Evangelicals have often tended to airbrush baptism out of the process of *becoming* a Christian, Catholics at times have tended to do the same for faith. Fransen accuses the fifteenth-century Catholic Church of "'mechanical' interpretation of the '*opus operatum*'" and of "quasi-magical practices . . . which started the Reformation."[15] The Reformers duly reacted against this view of the sacraments, leading to the Council of Trent hardening and narrowing the Catholic position in reaction against the Protestant *sola fide*. This happened because they were "driven by the psychological laws which, whether we like it or not, govern every passionate stage of controversy."[16] He criticizes the way in which the one-sided polemical anathemas of Trent came to be seen as exhaustive definitions. The result is that "the later controversies of decadent scholasticism on sacramental causality brought the idea of a sacrament, as it was taught in the catechisms and pulpits and as it was carried out in the practice of so many Christians, dangerously close to a 'magical rite.'"[17]

The effect on catechisms that he mentions can be seen in a catechism, with a 1951 *Imprimatur*, that I bought in Ireland in the early 1970s. This has a chapter on "The Sacraments in General," whose eight questions stress the efficacy of the sacraments, with no mention of faith or any human response other than the need to "receive them worthily," in which case they "always give sanctifying grace."[18] The next chapter is on "Baptism and Confirmation" and there is a strong emphasis on what baptism does: it cleanses from original sin, remits actual sins, makes us children of God, members of the church and heirs to the kingdom of heaven. And what do we need to do? Forgiveness requires true sorrow for our sins. Salvation is possible for those dying without baptism if they have "perfect contrition, which is called Baptism of desire." There is no mention at all of faith.[19] So what is the role of faith according to the catechism? It is one of the three theological virtues which are bestowed by sanctifying grace and consists in believing those truths revealed by God.[20] It is sanctifying grace that makes us Christians

---

15. Fransen, *Sacraments*, 34.

16. Fransen, *Sacraments*, 33.

17. Fransen, *Sacraments*, 35–36.

18. *Catechism of Catholic Doctrine*, 77–78 chapter 23, qq. 332–39.

19. *Catechism of Catholic Doctrine*, 79–80 chapter 24, qq. 340–45.

20. *Catechism of Catholic Doctrine*, 37 chapter 10, qq. 127–29.

and children of God.[21] And how do we acquire it? The principal means is prayer and the sacraments.[22] So Christians should have faith, along with hope and love, and faith consists in believing the truths of revelation, but it has no part to play in becoming a Christian. Faith, like loving one's neighbor, is something a Christian should get around to, but the catechism gives it no role in *becoming* a Christian.

An anecdote can serve to illustrate this approach. Some years ago, I was talking with an older Roman Catholic man who was lamenting the fact that none of his children had remained practicing Catholics. He commented that he had made the mistake of thinking that going through the rituals (i.e., the sacraments) was enough. He had failed to get them to embrace the faith inwardly. If he had been an Evangelical, he might have said that his children needed to be converted. Putting it differently, those who once would have grown up to become nominal Christians are these days more likely to become lapsed Christians.

The Jesuits once used to say, "Give me a child until he is seven years old and I will give you the man." Those, whether Catholic or Evangelical, who these days rely upon that for the transmission of the faith to their children are liable to have a rude awakening.

Having looked at those who polarize the issue, who hold that one becomes a Christian either by faith or by baptism, we will now turn our attention to those who hold that it is by faith *and* baptism that one becomes a Christian. We will look first at the New Testament, then at the Early Church (AD 100–500). After a digression to consider two related issues we will turn to the *Catechism of the Catholic Church* and to a more recent Catholic document on the reciprocity between faith and sacraments.

Faith and Baptism in the Early Centuries

In the New Testament

How does one become a Christian? What does the New Testament have to say? I have argued elsewhere that from the Day of Pentecost, Christian initiation involved repentance, faith, baptism and receiving the Spirit.[23] This is what we see in Acts, and it is borne out by the Epistles. For our present

---

21. *Catechism of Catholic Doctrine*, 35 chapter 9, qq. 117–19.
22. *Catechism of Catholic Doctrine*, 35 chapter 9, q. 122.
23. Lane, *Sin and Grace*, 93–103.

purposes we can concentrate on faith and baptism especially. Baptism was not a later development but always took place on the same day as conversion, with one exception. The Philippian jailer was baptized the same hour of the *night* (16:33)![24]

The second point to note is that in the New Testament baptism is not purely symbolic and declaratory.[25] It will come as no surprise to hear that the New Testament attributes salvation to faith. The devil snatches the word from the hearts of people "so that they may not believe and be saved" (Luke 8:12). And of course, Paul's response to the Philippian jailer's query about salvation was, "Believe in the LORD Jesus, and you will be saved" (Acts 16:31). Finally, Paul states that we have been saved by grace, through faith (Eph 2:8). But salvation is also attributed to baptism. Peter bluntly states that "baptism . . . now saves you . . . through the resurrection of Jesus Christ" (1 Pet 3:21). Paul tells Titus that God "saved us, not because of works done by us in righteousness, but according to his own mercy, by the washing of regeneration and renewal of the Holy Spirit" (Titus 3:5). This is less clear than the Peter passage, but the "washing of regeneration" probably refers to baptism.

There are other passages that attribute salvation to both faith and baptism. The longer ending of Mark contains the statement that "whoever believes and is baptized will be saved" (16:16).[26] Paul states that "if you confess with your mouth that Jesus is LORD and believe in your heart that God raised him from the dead, you will be saved. For with the heart, one believes and is justified, and with the mouth one confesses and is saved" (Rom 10:9–10). The verbal confession probably refers to baptism, in line with the practice that we see in Acts.

Union with Christ is attributed especially to baptism. Paul states that "as many of you as were baptized into Christ have put on Christ" (Gal 3:27). Being baptized into Christ means being baptized into his death, and being buried with him by baptism so that, as he was raised from the dead, we might walk in newness of life (Rom 6:3–4). But it would be wrong to see this as happening without faith. Immediately before stating that the

24. To preempt any pedants, I should mention that Paul's baptism had to await the arrival of Ananias three days after Jesus appeared to him (Acts 9:9–19).

25. For more on this, see Lane, *Sin and Grace*, 114–23, which draws especially upon Beasley-Murray, *Baptism in the New Testament*, 263–305.

26. The longer ending of Mark may not be part of the original Gospel, but at the very least expresses an early Christian viewpoint. See Black, *Perspectives on the Ending of Mark* for different views on this.

baptized have put on Christ Paul tells the Galatians that they were all children of God through faith (3:26). While we are buried with Christ in baptism, we are also raised with him through faith (Col 2:12). Likewise, in Romans Paul expounds justification by faith in chapters three to five, then turns to baptism in chapter six. The faith described in chapters three to five is a faith that expressed itself in baptism; the baptism described in chapter six is the baptism that came at the point of conversion. Paul could glide naturally from faith to baptism because the two went together, and were not separate, as we see in Acts.

Forgiveness is also tied to baptism. John's baptism was a baptism of repentance for the forgiveness of sins (Mark 1:4). Peter, likewise, on the Day of Pentecost, called upon his hearers to "repent and be baptized . . . for the forgiveness of your sins" (Acts 2:38). And Ananias called upon Paul to "rise and be baptized and wash away your sins, calling on his name" (Acts 22:16). But forgiveness, like union with Christ, is also tied to faith. "Everyone who believes in [Jesus] receives forgiveness of sins through his name" (Acts 10:43).

This New Testament teaching makes no sense while we think of faith and baptism as separate, as alternative ways to salvation. From that starting point we are forced to choose between salvation by faith or salvation by baptism, but in the New Testament faith was expressed in baptism and baptism was the outward expression of faith, as we see in Acts. From this perspective it does make sense to talk of salvation by faith and baptism, as in Mark 16:16. That is why Paul can talk both about salvation though faith and about salvation through baptism. For New Testament Christians, baptism was the decisive turning point. This is still true today for converts from Islam and Judaism, who often when asked for the date of their conversion will point to their baptism. It is when one of their number is baptized that Jews and Muslims regard them as having become Christians, not when they merely talk about believing in Jesus.

Saying that we become Christians by faith and baptism is the easy part; the harder part is saying what happens if only one of these is present. What of those with faith without baptism? There is not much relating to this in the New Testament for the simple reason that converts were baptized immediately, so it was not an issue, but there are three relevant passages. The thief on the cross (Luke 23:40–43) is often cited but is not strictly relevant. How is his situation different from other circumcised Jews dying under the Old Covenant? Furthermore, a Lutheran colleague of mine was taught as a child that he was in fact baptized—by Jesus spitting at him! Secondly, after stating that "whoever believes and is baptized will be saved," Mark adds that "whoever does not believe will be condemned" (16:16), with no mention of baptism. The implication is that baptism is less crucial than faith. Finally, Paul refers to the Old Testament example of Abraham, who was justified by faith before being circumcised. His circumcision served as a "seal" of the righteousness that he had already received (Rom 4:9–11). A parallel can be seen with the not-yet-baptized.

What about those who have baptism but no faith? This is not answered explicitly, but the account of Simon Magus in Acts 8:9–24 is relevant. Simon was baptized but proceeded to offer the apostles money in order to be able to bestow the gift of the Spirit. Peter responds, "You have neither part nor lot in this matter, for your heart is not right before God. Repent, therefore, of this wickedness of yours, and pray to the LORD that, if possible, the intent of your heart may be forgiven you." This is not baptism without at least some sort of faith since we are told that "even Simon himself believed," but it is an indication that it is possible to receive the outward sacrament without the inner reality and that such baptism is not salvific.

In the Early Church (AD 100–500)

How did the early Christians understand the significance of baptism? From the very beginning baptism was seen as *effective*, i.e., actually doing something. Giving someone baptism, like bestowing nationality on them,[27] makes a real difference, so must it be given with care. In particular, it was seen as bestowing regeneration and the forgiveness of *past* sins. Baptism was seen as necessary for salvation because "unless one is born of water and the Spirit, he cannot see the kingdom of God" (John 3:5). In his *First Apology*, Justin Martyr states that those who repent, believe, and choose to be born again receive the forgiveness of *previous* sins. He states that through baptism they are born again, citing John 3:5.[28] Irenaeus, writing towards the end of the second century, states that through baptism we are made clean and are spiritually born again, also citing John 3:5.[29]

As we see from Justin Martyr, it is to those who repent, believe, and choose to be born again that baptism is given. The process of catechetical

27. I am grateful to Gerald Bray for this analogy.

28. Martyr, *First Apology* 61 *Ante-Nicene Fathers*, 1:183.

29. *Ante-Nicene Fathers*, Fragment 34, 1:574.

preparation for baptism, developed especially in the third and fourth centuries, was geared to inculcating faith and repentance. The reciprocal nature of faith and baptism was nicely spelt out by Basil the Great: "Now faith and baptism are two ways of salvation that are naturally united with each other and indivisible. While faith is perfected by baptism, baptism is established by faith, and each is carried out by the same names" (i.e., Father, Son, and Holy Spirit).[30]

Cyril of Jerusalem gives an account of baptism in the fourth century in his *Catechetical Lectures* 3 and 20, given to catechumens before and after their baptism respectively.[31] Baptism is clearly seen as effective, as bestowing forgiveness of sins, the gift of the Spirit, new life, adoption as children of God and union with Christ (3:2–4, 12–15; 20:6). Salvation requires both outward baptism with water and inner reception of the Spirit, according to John 3:3, 5.

Baptism is given to those who repent and believe (3:2). But what about those who receive baptism without faith? "He that is baptized with water, but not found worthy of the Spirit, does not receive the grace in perfection" (3:4). There is a blistering attack on those who, like Simon Magus in Acts 8, come to baptism without true repentance, without believing from the heart, and who clearly do not receive the benefits of baptism (3:7).

What about faith without baptism? "If a man be virtuous in his deeds, but does not receive the seal by water, he shall not enter into the kingdom of heaven" (3:4). Cyril goes on to mention the case of Cornelius, who in Acts 10 received the Spirit before his baptism. His comment is that his soul was born again by faith and then the body partook of grace by the water (3:4). But "born again by faith" does not apply to those who do not get baptized. Cyril is clear that neither baptism without repentance, nor repentance without baptism suffices.

But what about catechumens who die before receiving baptism, the classic case of someone run over by a bus (or chariot) on their way to baptism? There is no salvation without baptism, except for martyrs (3:10). So, Cyril acknowledges the baptism of blood, as it is usually called, but makes no mention of the baptism of desire. Why not? I don't imagine that Cyril would have thought that Cornelius would have been lost had he died of a stroke just before Peter baptized him. But that was not the burning issue in

---

30. Basil the Great, *On the Holy Spirit*, 59.

31. *Nicene and Post-Nicene Fathers*, 7:14–18, 147–48. In my quotations I have modernized this translation.

Cyril's time. Following the conversion of the Emperor Constantine, there was a flood of "converts" as it suddenly became politically expedient to be a Christian. The problem then arose that people were signing up as catechumens preparing for baptism, but forever putting off being baptized and thereby becoming subject to church discipline. They were trying to get the best of both worlds, claiming the name of Christian whilst remaining free of church discipline. A number of fourth century fathers urged such folk not to delay their baptism, since if they died without being baptized, they would not be saved.

Augustine, in his *Baptism, against the Donatists* 4:21:29–25:33, also discussed the situation of faith without baptism and vice versa, more systematically than Cyril.[32] Salvation is made complete by both baptism and conversion of heart (33). But what about those having one without the other? It depends whether the other was missing because of lack of opportunity or because of pride or contempt (32). Simon Magus was baptized but "was puffed up with an unclean spirit," not the Holy Spirit (29). By contrast, baptized infants who die (31–33) and the thief on the cross (30–33) are both saved, "God in either case filling up what was *involuntarily* wanting." But if either is missing *intentionally*, there is no excuse (33). Cornelius was filled with the Holy Spirit before his baptism, but he would not have been saved if he had gone on to *refuse* baptism (29, 32). Abraham likewise was justified by faith without the sacrament (circumcision), but that was because the sacrament had not yet been commanded, not because he neglected it. "Circumcision was added afterwards as the seal of faith" (32). So, baptism and conversion of heart (including faith) are both required, and there is no salvation for those despising either, but salvation is not denied to those denied the opportunity of one or the other.

Augustine was converted in August 386 but not baptized until Easter 387. What was his status between these two events? In his *Confessions* he states that it was at his baptism that he was born again.[33] We shall return to this question at the end.

The baptized were not guaranteed final salvation. Because baptism was seen as obtaining forgiveness for past sins only, post-baptismal sins were a problem, leading many in due course to delay baptism until late in life so as

---

32. *Nicene and Post-Nicene Fathers*, First Series, 4:459–62. Origen, like Cyril and Augustine, contrasts Simon Magus and Cornelius, see Origen of Alexandria, *Homilies on Numbers*, 3:2 (p. 9).

33. Augustine, *Confessions*, in *Nicene and Post-Nicene Fathers*, 9:3:6, 9:6:14.

to maximize its effect. Salvation could be lost by serious moral lapse, such as the famous trio of murder, adultery, and apostasy. It could also be lost by lapse in faith, especially heresy or schism. Faith was increasingly identified with doctrinal orthodoxy. The main way that faith was linked with baptism was the profession of the creed.

The Two Elephants in the Room

Infant Baptism

Some may have noticed that I have so far failed to discuss a large elephant in the room—infant baptism. The evidence is very clear that in the third and fourth centuries people were baptized at many different ages, including at birth. Adult believer's baptism was the norm, but infant baptism was practiced alongside it. Most significantly, different theologians had different ideas about what was expedient but none, not even Tertullian, suggested that either baptizing one's children or not doing so was actually wrong. I have argued elsewhere, on the basis of this, that it is most likely that this variety of practice goes back to apostolic times.[34]

Until the fourth century children fit into the existing pattern of convert's baptism, whether by being baptized or by being enrolled as catechumens. By the fifth century, with the conversion of the Roman Empire, adult baptism was becoming rarer and infant baptism becoming the norm. The significance of the efficacy of baptism changes as instant convert's baptism becomes delayed convert's baptism and eventually infant baptism. This shift encouraged a more mechanical view of the effects of baptism, now separated from conversion. That is illustrated by a story told by Augustine. In his Manichee years a friend became seriously ill, and his concerned Catholic parents had him baptized while he was unconscious. When he came round Augustine joked with him about this, but having been baptized he now rebuked Augustine. Augustine and his friend shared the assumption that baptism made a difference, even if one is unconscious at the time.[35]

The change whereby infant baptism becomes the norm, combined with a view of baptism as efficacious, radically changes the relation between faith and baptism. It was not for nothing that David Wright wrote a book

---

34. Lane, "Did the Apostolic Church Baptise Babies?, 109–30. For shorter versions of the argument, see Wright, *Baptism: Three Views*, 144–63; Lane, *Sin and Grace*, 124–35.

35. Augustine, *Confessions*, 4:4:8.

entitled *What has Infant Baptism done to Baptism?*[36], though he was more concerned about how indiscriminate infant baptism had caused many Evangelicals to deny the efficacy of baptism. The remedy is to see adult believer's baptism as the norm and infant baptism as the exception. Calvin in the sixteenth century perceptively understood this, expounding baptism in general before turning specifically to infant baptism.[37] This point is widely recognized today by Catholic theology.[38]

Infants were seen to be born again in baptism. For many Evangelicals this would seem to imply that baptized infants are guaranteed final salvation, but that is not how it would have been seen. Regeneration was seen more like the sowing of a seed, which needs to germinate and mature to bear fruit, the planting of a new life, which may or may not grow to salvation. Baptism did not cover post-baptismal sins.

The Definition of Faith

There is another elephant in the room—smaller and easier to overlook but still very significant. Until now I have referred to faith without asking what people might mean by that term. This is important as when people understand different things by the word, apparent agreement can be illusory, as also can apparent disagreement. There are a number of different meanings to consider.

- Faith as giving assent to correct doctrine. This is the sort of faith that James brands as insufficient on its own (2:14–19). Catholic theology has tended to operate with this definition. Faith at conversion is often seen as giving assent to the truths of revelation, as found in the creed for example. Naturally, Catholics insist that *this* faith alone does not suffice for justification, a point with which the Reformers concurred.

36. Wright, *What has Infant Baptism Done to Baptism?*

37. Calvin, *Institutes of the Christian Religion*, 4:15 and 4:16. For a discussion of the relation between the two chapters, see Wright, *Infant Baptism in Historical Perspective*, 226–37.

38. In the Catechism of the Catholic Church (see below), baptism is routinely linked with faith, while infant baptism warrants only a brief mention (§§1250–52, cf. 1231, 1282). See also Yarnold, "The Sacraments of Christian Initiation", 242–58. 248. In 1972 the patristic process of the catechumenate was revived in the Rite of Christian Initiation of Adults.

- Scholastic theology differentiated between unformed and formed faith, using categories of Aristotelian philosophy. Unformed faith is intellectual belief, and this faith becomes "formed" by love: *fides caritate formata* (faith formed by love). The Reformers objected to this concept on the grounds that it effectively leads to the claim that we are justified by love. At the Regensburg Colloquy (1541) the agreed Article 5 on justification affirmed justification *sola fide*, but those Catholics who objected to this put it around that because saving faith is formed faith, we can say that we are justified *sola caritate*.[39]

- Although the Reformers were mostly unhappy with the idea of *fides caritate formata*,[40] for the reasons just given, none of them believed that saving faith could exist *without* love and good works. Calvin, for example, stated that "we confess with Paul that no other faith justifies 'but faith working through love' [Gal. 5:6]."[41] Again, "we dream neither of a faith devoid of good works nor of a justification that stands without them."[42] We are not justified *by* love or works, but nor are we justified *without* them.

- For the Reformers the key element of saving faith was trust in Christ for one's salvation. Interestingly, the Council of Trent defines hope, in a manner remarkably similar to the Reformers' definition of saving faith, as being "confident that God will be propitious to them for Christ's sake,"[43] while at the same time rejecting the idea that confidence that one's sins are forgiven belongs to faith.[44]

- When Evangelicals say that we become Christians by faith they normally have in mind a faith that is inseparable from repentance, a faith that has some cognitive element and involves trust, but which would bring no salvation to the one who professed it but was unwilling to undergo a moral transformation.[45]

---

39. Lane, *Regensburg Article 5 on Justification*, 42–44, 259–62.

40. Bucer was ready to accept the term (Lane, *Regensburg Article 5 on Justification*, 185).

41. Calvin, *Institutes,* 3:11:20.

42. Calvin, *Institutes,* 3:16:1.

43. *Decree on Justification*, chap. 6 (my trans.).

44. *Decree on Justification*, chap. 9, can 12–14.

45. For a rounded account of faith that sees it as involving commitment and conversion, see Ratzinger, *Introduction to Christianity*, 88.

Faith and Baptism:
Two Contemporary Catholic Documents

In this section we will look at two contemporary Roman Catholic documents, before making some concluding observations.

Catechism of the Catholic Church (1994)[46]

The Catechism repeatedly refers to the sacraments as "sacraments of faith," the term twice appearing in headings (§15, 1122). "The sacraments are sacraments of faith, drawing their origin and nourishment from the Word" (§1122). They "not only presuppose faith, but by words and objects they also nourish, strengthen, and express it. That is why they are called 'sacraments *of faith*'" (§1123).[47]

The Catechism also repeatedly affirms the efficacy of the sacraments (e.g., §1131). They "make present efficaciously the grace that they signify" (§1084). "Celebrated worthily in faith, the sacraments confer the grace that they signify. They are *efficacious* because in them Christ himself is at work" (§1127). As the Council of Trent teaches, they act *ex opere operato*, so (quoting Thomas) "the sacrament is not wrought by the righteousness of either the celebrant or the recipient, but by the power of God." "Nevertheless, the fruits of the sacraments also depend on the disposition of the one who receives them" (§1128). In short, "What faith confesses, the sacraments communicate" (§1692).

So how do we become Christians? The Catechism repeatedly states, in a variety of ways, that this is by faith and baptism (§§14, 167, 2017 and below) and baptism is repeatedly called the "sacrament of faith" (§§1236, 1253, 1992).[48] Faith and baptism both play a role in the process of initiation, of conversion:

---

46. See Yarnold, "Sacraments of Christian Initiation," 242–52. Quotations from the Catechism are taken from the 1997 edition, which incorporates modifications in the Latin typical edition. All emphases in quotations are from the Catechism and most are not found in the 1994 edition. Biblical references in footnotes have been inserted into the text in brackets.

47. Quoting Vatican II, *Sacrosanctum concilium* 59.

48. Lest one get too excited by this, the last of these cites the Tridentine *Decree on Justification* chap. 7, which calls baptism the sacrament of faith and states that without faith no one has ever been justified.

From the time of the apostles, becoming a Christian has been accomplished by a journey and initiation in several stages. This journey can be covered rapidly or slowly, but certain essential elements will always have to be present: proclamation of the Word, acceptance of the Gospel entailing conversion, profession of faith, Baptism itself, the outpouring of the Holy Spirit, and admission to Eucharistic communion. (§1229)

The proclamation of the Word of God enlightens the candidates and the assembly with the revealed truth and elicits the response of faith, which is inseparable from Baptism. Indeed Baptism is "the sacrament of faith" in a particular way, since it is the sacramental entry into the life of faith. (§1236)

Jesus calls to conversion. This call is an essential part of the proclamation of the kingdom: "The time is fulfilled, and the kingdom of God is at hand; repent, and believe in the gospel" (Mark 1:15). In the Church's preaching this call is addressed first to those who do not yet know Christ and his Gospel. Also, Baptism is the principal place for the first and fundamental conversion. It is by faith in the Gospel and by Baptism (Cf. Acts 2:38) that one renounces evil and gains salvation, that is, the forgiveness of all sins and the gift of new life. (§1427)

Faith and baptism together lay hold of various benefits:

- Salvation (Mark 16:15–16) (§§977. 1427).

- Forgiveness of sins (§§977, 1427).

- Regeneration, being born again of water and the Spirit (John 3:3–5) (§782, 2790).

- Justification. We are "justified by faith in Baptism" (§§818, 1271. Cf. §§1266, 1992). Interestingly, non-Catholics are also justified by faith in baptism and "put in some, though imperfect, communion with the Catholic Church"[49] (§§818, 1271. Cf §838).

- Membership of the church (§782).

It is in the light of these repeated statements that we should interpret those passages in the Catechism that attribute things to baptism, without (at that point) mentioning faith:

---

49. Quoting Vatican II, *Unitatis redintegratio* 3.

- Purification from sins (Acts 2:38) (§1262); forgiveness of original and actual sins (§§1263, 2520).

- Regeneration or new birth (John 3:5) (§§694, 784, 1212–13, 1215, 1262, 1692, 2345, 2783. Cf. §1212).

- Being made a new creature (2 Cor 5:17) (§1265).

- Becoming children of God (§1692).

- Justification (§2813).

- Union with Christ (§§537, 1694, 2472, 2565).

- Incorporation into the church, the Body of Christ (§§1267–69, 2782), citing 1 Corinthians 12:13 and other passages.

What are we to make of this? First, to attribute things to faith and baptism together in one place and to baptism alone in another is to do no more than the New Testament does. Just as things are attributed to baptism alone in some places, so also in other places things are attributed to faith, with no mention of baptism (§§1709, 1715, 1814–16). In both cases we should assume that the reference is to faith joined with baptism. Secondly, adapting what David Wright said of *Baptism, Eucharist and Ministry* to the Catechism, "We balk at the indicatives of [the Catechism] when it is the indicatives of the New Testament that truly bother us."[50] The New Testament indicatives that he is referring to are statements like "all who have been baptized into Christ have put on Christ" (Gal 3:27).

So how does the Catechism correlate the efficacy of faith with that of baptism? Sometimes faith is portrayed as preceding baptism, either explicitly or by implication (§§14, 167, 784, 818, 838, 1253, 1271). But elsewhere faith is presented as itself a fruit of baptism. The baptized receive "sanctifying grace, the grace of *justification*: —enabling them to believe in God, to hope in him and to love him" (§1266, cf. §§1253–54). There is no contradiction here. It is comparable to the way in which the Holy Spirit works in us to lead us to conversion, and then afterwards dwells in us.

What about those who have faith without baptism? The position of the Catechism is nuanced. "For believers the sacraments of the New Covenant are *necessary for salvation*" (citing the Council of Trent) (§1129). Again, "Baptism is necessary for salvation for those to whom the Gospel has been proclaimed and who have had the possibility of asking for this sacrament (Cf. Mark 16:16). The Church does not know of any means other than

50. Wright, *Infant Baptism in Historical Perspective*, 369.

Baptism that assures entry into eternal beatitude." But, on the other hand, *"God has bound salvation to the sacrament of Baptism, but he himself is not bound by his sacraments"* (§1257). In particular, "for *catechumens* who die before their Baptism, their explicit desire to receive it, together with repentance for their sins, and charity, assures them the salvation that they were not able to receive through the sacrament" (§1259. Cf. §1281). (Although, to be fair, this refers to desire for baptism, repentance, and charity, but not in so many words to faith.)

This generosity is extended even to infants who die with neither faith nor baptism. "As regards *children who have died without Baptism*, the Church can only entrust them to the mercy of God, as she does in her funeral rites for them. Indeed, the great mercy of God who desires that all men should be saved, and Jesus' tenderness toward children which caused him to say: 'Let the children come to me, do not hinder them,' (Mark 10:14) allow us to hope that there is a way of salvation for children who have died without Baptism" (§1261).

What about baptism without faith? The most obvious example of this is infant baptism. This should not be denied to children as it brings new birth and "the priceless grace of becoming a child of God," manifesting the "sheer gratuitousness of the grace of salvation" (§1250). It encapsulates "the preparatory stages of Christian initiation in a very abridged way" and needs to be followed by a *"post-baptismal catechumenate"* (§1231). As regards faith, the child is baptized in the faith of the church (§1282) and for children and adults alike "faith must grow *after* Baptism" (§1254).

> Baptism is the sacrament of faith (Mark 16:16). But faith needs the community of believers. It is only within the faith of the Church that each of the faithful can believe. The faith required for Baptism is not a perfect and mature faith, but a beginning that is called to develop. The catechumen or the godparent is asked: "What do you ask of God's Church?" the response is: "Faith!" (§1253)

The Reciprocity between Faith and Sacraments in the Sacramental Economy

I think someone must have alerted the Vatican to the fact that I was giving this paper and they decided to get in a pre-emptive strike. Earlier this year the International Theological Commission published a document entitled

The Reciprocity between Faith and Sacraments in the Sacramental Economy.[51] While the catechism contains much material relevant to our topic, as we have seen, this document is actually focused on it. It was prompted especially by the issue of "baptized non-believers" demanding the sacrament of marriage (§3). The whole document argues, as the title indicates, for the reciprocity of faith and sacrament. It highlights the same polarization that I have mentioned, between a "ritualism devoid of faith" and a "privatization of the faith, reduced to the inner space of one's own conscience and feelings" (§9, cf. §10), or, more succinctly, between "subjectivist privatization and ritualism" (§51, cf. §71). It traces the philosophical undergirding of the divide between faith and sacrament from medieval Nominalism through to post-modernity (§§4–6).

The document correctly argues that in the New Testament, "conversion, the human response to the proclamation of the Gospel, seems inseparable from the sacramental rite of baptism" (§81). And so, as with the catechism, "baptism is the sacrament of faith par excellence" (§82). In response to the Reformers Trent clearly affirmed the efficacy of the sacraments (§66). But for the sacrament to be fruitful, "the recipient must believe both in the content (*fides quae*) and existentially (*fides qua*) that which Christ gives him sacramentally through the mediation of the Church" (§68). "Celebration of a sacrament without faith is meaningless, because it contradicts the sacramental logic that underpins the divine economy, which is constitutively dialogical" (§11). Conversely, "faith itself has, in its very essence, a natural tendency to express itself and nourish itself sacramentally" (§78).

The document examines the role and nature of faith. Faith is "the most apt means to receive the offer of salvation" (§1). "Since the personal relationship with the Trinitarian God is already lived with faith, faith leads to salvation and eternal life" (§78). Quoting the Catechism of the Catholic Church (§150), "faith is first of all a *personal adherence* of man to God" (§1). Faith is repeatedly called a personal relationship with the triune God (§§7, 49, 78; cf. §14). This is significant as probably the most common reason given by those who turn from Catholicism to Evangelicalism is the desire for a personal relationship with God.[52]

Different types of faith are mentioned.

---

51. All emphases in quotations from this document are from the original.

52. Castaldo, *Holy Ground.*

- The distinction between unformed and formed faith is set out, with the latter being described as faith "molded by a personal and loving relationship with Christ" (§62).

- The document also expounds the distinction between implicit and explicit faith. "It is not necessary that simple believers know how to give a detailed intellectual account of Trinitarian or soteriological developments" (§53). On the other hand, as Thomas Aquinas maintained, "all the baptized are obliged to believe explicitly the articles of the Creed" (§54).

- There is recognition of the value of "incipient faith," an imperfect faith that is still developing, and "finds some difficulty in adhering to the totality of the contents that the Church holds as revealed" (§45).

- Finally, what sort of faith is required for baptism? As baptism is the door of entry, faith at that point "does not have to be perfect, but initial and eager to grow" (§84).

Throughout the document there is the concern to combat the twin dangers of ritualism devoid of faith and of a privatized faith which does not come to sacramental expression. As the latter danger is found among Evangelicals it is worth focusing more on that. The document stresses that "Christ . . . cannot be accepted *only* invisibly or privately" (§58). "The Reformation has exerted an influence that is hardly overestimated on the supremacy of the individual act of faith over the confession of ecclesial faith" (§50). This Reformation approach includes an emphasis on faith as appropriating grace and equating faith with assurance of salvation. The document states that this subjunctivization has of late influenced Catholicism, with the result that "faith is described less as confession than as a personal relationship of trust (faith in someone), and, at least tendentially, is opposed to doctrinal faith (faith in something)" (§50). The impression is given that while this Reformation influence is dangerous, e.g., in the equation of faith with assurance of salvation and the belittling of doctrinal faith, it has at the same time left its mark on this document, as with the recurring affirmation that faith is a personal relationship with God.

There is much in this document to commend it to those Evangelicals who are also concerned about a privatized, non-sacramental faith. That does not mean that there are no remaining differences, especially on the question of the definition of faith.

Conclusion

In the light of what we have seen, how should we regard the relation between faith and the sacraments in general, faith and baptism in particular?
I will answer that in two ways, first by considering some analogies and secondly by talking of two stories.

Analogies

How can we hold to salvation by faith, and yet also affirm the efficacy of
the sacraments? Two analogies come to mind. The Baptist theologian A.
H. Strong regarded baptism as purely symbolic and used a singularly inept
analogy to make his point. He described baptism as a symbol of an already
existing union, like a wedding service![53] This analogy might have more appeal in an age where many couples cohabit before getting married, but that
is hardly what Strong had in mind. The point about a wedding, whether in
a church or in a registry office, is that two individuals enter as single people
and emerge as a married couple. On any reckoning a wedding is not just a
symbol of an already existing union but itself creates a new form of union.

Secondly, consider a graduation ceremony. Undergraduates leave the
ceremony as graduates. Their status has changed. Of course, the ceremony
would have no value if you somehow gained entry despite not having quali-
fied for it. On the other hand, technically you are not a graduate until after
the ceremony, or some equivalent process for those who choose to graduate
in absentia. Arising from this, there is one clear effect of baptism. Baptism
brings membership of the church, the people of God.[54] For the great majority of churches baptism is a precondition of church membership and of
taking communion.[55] One could argue that this is the one empirically veri-

---

53. Strong, *Systematic Theology*, 946.

54. Interestingly, Richard Price, a Roman Catholic priest, tells me that what Catholic
laity "see as the sole and essential fruit of baptism is that it admits into the fellowship of
the Catholic Church. It is this sharing of Christian living and worship with other Christians, enabled by baptism, that is seen as the essence of being a Christian" (in an email
of May 13, 2021).

55. Baptism, Eucharist and Ministry Eucharist 2 (Leith, *Creeds of the Churches*, 619).

fiable benefit of baptism[56]—at least for those churches that take the New Testament seriously.[57]

Two Stories

The New Testament talks about being a Christian in two different ways. The first story tells how we become Christians by faith, repentance and receiving the Spirit. These are all inward and none of them is visible to others. The second story is about the outward manifestation. Faith leads to confession of faith and baptism, and thereby membership of the visible church. Repentance leads to the fruit of repentance in a changed life and good works. The reception of the Spirit leads to outward manifestations as fruit of the Spirit and as gifts of the Spirit. So, there are two different stories to tell. The first concerns the inward reality; the second concerns its outward manifestation.

There are two opposite errors to avoid. The first is to assume that the two stories are identical—that everyone who professes faith and is baptized has true faith, that everyone who professes repentance has genuinely repented. The New Testament warns against this error, as in the case of Simon Magus. Jesus refers to those performing charismatic miracles whom he *never* knew (Matt 7:21–23). There is the recognition elsewhere that not all who profess to be Christians are genuine. "They went out from us, but they were not of us; for if they had been of us, they would have continued with us. But they went out, that it might become plain that they all are not of us" (1 John 2:19). As Paul put it, "the Lord knows those who are his" (2 Tim 2:19), implying that the rest of us do not always know.

Augustine developed the concept of the "invisible church." He distinguished between the "visible church," the mixed body that we see, and the "invisible church," the body of true Christians.[58] The visible church consists of those who profess to be Christians, i.e., those who are baptized and in good standing. Among these are both genuine Christians and nominal Christians, those without true faith or true love. The invisible church is

56. Some might claim the same for the gift of the Holy Spirit, but that is not indisputable.

57. For a discussion of the empirically verifiable effects of infant baptism in particular, see Quick, *The Christian Sacraments*, 172, 175–76.

58. Origen, in contrasting Simon Magus and Cornelius, makes a similar distinction, citing Rom 9:6 (Origen, *Homilies on Numbers*, 3:2).

invisible only in the sense that its boundaries are known to God alone. There was no suggestion that one might belong to the invisible church *instead of* the visible church. The idea, rather, was that the boundaries of the true church are invisible to us, but known to God who reads people's hearts. No membership list is infallible because we cannot see people's hearts, only their outward actions. As Archbishop James Ussher put it, whilst we judge the heart by the actions, God judges the actions by the heart.[59]

It is wrong to assume that the two stories always coincide, that everyone who professes faith is genuine. It is equally wrong to treat the two stories as if they were unconnected, as if all that mattered is the inward story. It is inward faith that is crucial, but genuine faith will always lead to outward manifestation, in baptism, in words and actions. It is inward repentance that is crucial, but genuine repentance always leads to "fruit in keeping with repentance" (Matt 3:8). It is belonging to the invisible church that is crucial, but that is not a substitute for belonging to the visible church. Some Christians try to be more "spiritual" than the New Testament. Outward observances without the inner attitude of the heart are condemned throughout the Bible. But the Bible does not support the opposite extreme, an inner change that is not expressed outwardly and physically. We are physical as well as spiritual beings and the gospel addresses us at the physical as well as the spiritual level.

Baptism belongs to the outward story. Being baptized is of itself no guarantee that one has the inward reality. We must not fall into the error of assuming that all who have been baptized are certainly saved. But the outward is also important, and no one who declines baptism has the right to claim to be a genuine Christian.

The Role of Delayed Baptism

Finally, what about the person who, like Augustine, is baptized seven months after coming to faith? What does their baptism do? We have already argued that believer's baptism should be seen as the norm, and infant baptism as (theologically) the exception. This principle can be taken one step further. Theologically, instant convert's baptism (as in Acts) should be seen as the norm and baptism after an interval as (theologically) the exception. This means that we should build our understanding of the significance

---

59. Cited by Richard Snoddy in *The Soteriology of James Ussher*, 160. See also 1 Sam 16:7.

of delayed baptism on the New Testament teaching about instant convert's baptism, not start from today's experience of delayed baptism and build our theology of baptism on that. Two suggestions can be made. As with Abraham's circumcision, delayed baptism can be seen as a *seal* on the righteousness already received by faith.[60] Secondly, as we have seen, baptism opens the door to membership of the visible church.

---

60. As suggested by Augustine himself see *Baptism, against the Donatists* 4:24:32; *Nicene and Post-Nicene Fathers*, 4:461.

6

The Church as a Learning Community

Andrew D. Clarke

Introduction

IN THE 1960 INAUGURAL volume of the *Journal of Religious History*, an Ancient Historian from New Zealand, based at the University of Sydney, published the first of a short series of two articles entitled, "The Early Christians as a Scholastic Community."[1] Edwin Judge's core thesis was that the earliest Christ followers primarily understood themselves to be communities of learning. Whilst it might be assumed that communal worship dominated the agenda of these groups, it is remarkable that so little is known about either their organization of gatherings for worship, their practice of welfare or indeed the missional exploits of members and even leaders of these earliest Christian communities. They certainly did engage in cultic and social welfare activities,[2] but Judge argued that the historical record, insofar as it can be reconstructed from the New Testament sources, suggests a far greater community focus directed towards teaching and learning.

---

1. Judge, "The Early Christians as a Scholastic Community," 4–15; Judge, "The Early Christians as a Scholastic Community: Part II," 125–37. Cf. Judge, "Higher Education in the Pauline Churches," 23–31.; and Judge, "On This Rock I Will Build My *Ekklesia*." 619–68, 633–36. Cf. also Harland, "The Most Sacred Society," 207–32.

2. Judge, "Early Christians as a Scholastic Community," 8.

During his rich academic career now spanning more than seven decades, Edwin Judge has gained a reputation for the unconventional, and for challenging stereotypes. It is perhaps consistent with this pattern that his construction of churches as scholastic communities has not been subsequently adopted by social historians of the New Testament. Instead, other models of community organization—including the family,[3] the synagogue,[4] voluntary associations,[5] philosophical schools, and mystery religions— have been more assiduously, and in many cases more fruitfully, developed.[6]

Twenty years after that earlier publication, Judge was invited by the editors of the same journal to return to his thesis and address it once again.[7] In doing so, he recognized the potential there was to misunderstand his choice of the term "scholastic" as a key descriptor.[8] Nonetheless, this return to the topic gave rise to no significant revision to his position. Rather, Judge reaffirmed his challenge to the competing reconstructions of early Christian social identity, using the proverbial statement that "wellestablished assumptions cast an illusion of light."[9]

There may be a temptation first to overstate Judge's case, and then find fault with it. However, for the avoidance of doubt, he did not suggest that there were no similarities to other contemporary, first century models of community organization. However, for Judge, an early Christian emphasis on learning had been a marked distinctive. It is what set them apart from other groups. This would have been apparent not only in their own writings, but also to outsiders whose curiosity might have driven them to locate the nature or character of these small groups. He argues:

3. Hellerman, *The Ancient Church as Family.*

4. Burtchaell, *From Synagogue to Church.*

5. Kloppenborg, *Voluntary Associations in the Graeco-Roman World*; Kloppenborg, *Christ's Associations*; Ascough, *Paul's Macedonian Associations*; Harland, *Associations, Synagogues, and Congregations.*

6. Clarke, *Serve the Community of the Church.*

7. Judge, "The Social Identity of the First Christians," 201–17.

8. Cf. Smith, *Pauline Communities.*

9. Judge, "Social Identity of the First Christians," 201. These assured conclusions included the assumption that the earliest Christians were predominantly drawn from the socially depressed strata of society, and uninterested in, perhaps incapable of, pursuing learning as a core focus. Significant historical interest in the social location of the New Testament communities by German, British and North American scholars during and following the 1980s has, indeed, succeeded in overthrowing this particular illusion, which had been at the heart of Deissmann's ideological reading of the earliest Christians as a homogeneous group of uneducated believers.

> While the ultimate objective may be communion with God, the means to this end are distinctly intellectual: the correct interpretation of the law and the prophets, or the comprehension of the message of the gospel, such are the immediate objects . . . There are other sides to the picture, of course, but the view that must have been commonly taken is that of a school of disciples under the instruction of a rabbi, or a devout sect committed to the study and preservation of the law, or finally of a society formed to attend upon the teaching of a travelling preacher.[10]

Judge offers an imaginative contextualization of this learning context with the description of "*talkative, passionate and sometimes quarrelsome circles* that met to read Paul's letters over their evening meal."[11]

However, in terms of reception history, during the following three decades, Judge's fundamental proposal still did not attract significant attention. That is until 2009, nearly fifty years after that inaugural volume of the *Journal of Religious History*, when Claire Smith submitted her doctoral dissertation, also in Sydney. In it she explicitly tested Judge's model, by addressing "the place and practice of educational activities" in three of the Pauline communities. Her particular contribution lies in looking at the *practice* of teaching, as evidenced in four Pauline letters. Her findings are that "these communities were 'learning communities' in which educational activities fundamentally shaped individual and community life, and where the goals of, and relationships within the communities dialectically impacted the educational activities . . . all believers were learners."[12]

However, Smith's over-riding portrait is of communities in which learning is principally fostered through the medium of delivered instruction. This picture emerges from a detailed study of the many verbs of teaching in texts addressed to these three Pauline communities.[13]

In reprising Judge's work, Smith helpfully clarifies that he had not intended to suggest by his description of "scholastic communities" that a

10. Judge, *The First Christians in the Roman World*, 136.

11. Judge, "Social Identity of the First Christians," 212 [italics mine]. This cameo will be explored further below.

12. Smith, *Pauline Communities as "Scholastic Communities,"* 1 (cf. p. 6). The last phrase that "all believers were learners" warrants further exploration below.

13. Smith focuses on as many as fifty-five different words, reflecting nine distinct semantic domains: "core-teaching," "speaking," "traditioning," "announcing," "revealing," "worshipping," "commanding," "correcting," and "remembering." Smith is aware of the criticism established most vocally by James Barr regarding the widespread misunderstanding of how words work and where the meanings of words are located.

system of schooling, especially the formal education of children, had been in place. Indeed, apart from the Household Codes in Ephesians and Colossians, the New Testament texts notably pay little attention to the place of children within these communities. Rather, Judge's essential focus had been on the education of adults[14] (that is, in recent parlance, andragogy, rather than pedagogy). Thus, "teaching was a constituent part of Christian ministry, and learning was an essential part of Christian experience."[15]

Together, Judge and Smith consider that the New Testament, whether as a whole, or in part, presents prime evidence that the earliest Christian believers ordered and understood themselves to be communities of instruction. Whilst Judge framed his picture by means of social historical tools, Smith's focus is primarily exegetical, and revolves around Paul's use of particular vocabulary that describes or presupposes instruction.

Beyond testing and establishing Judge's construction, one further contribution made by Smith is her contention that "community" was part and parcel of the educational process within these groups. She states that these churches were being encouraged to adopt "a dialectic process through which the community was shaped by teaching activities, and, reciprocally, those teaching activities were shaped by the community."[16] This dialectical and communitarian character of learning is especially interesting; and yet tantalizingly Smith gives it very little specific attention in her monograph. Indeed, readers might be forgiven for overlooking this seam in her findings altogether, and instead draw the conclusion that teaching was, to all intents and purposes, exclusively of the lecture format—that is, the prior learning of the teacher is orally presented to groups of pupils. In the latter part of this article, I shall take this notion of a dialectical process, and substantiate it further. In so doing, I shall challenge Smith's relative focus on teaching over learning by exploring how additional semantic domains, occurring extensively across the New Testament, including the Pauline letters, shed light on other contexts for learning, that were widely adopted within these first communities. A key element of this entails learning *in* community, even *from* that community. In some cases, these additional contexts are only known because attention is drawn to them as a consequence of this

14. Smith, *Pauline Communities as "Scholastic Communities,"* 3.

15. Smith, *Pauline Communities as "Scholastic Communities,"* 3. Judge, "The Conflict of Educational Aims in New Testament Thought," 32–45, draws a stronger, although he determines still inadequate, parallel with ancient philosophical schools.

16. Smith, *Pauline Communities as "Scholastic Communities,"* 379.

approach being pursued to a fault. That is, the corrective statements of Paul presuppose, and then directly address, the excessive manner or tone of some of these communitarian learning contexts.

Discipleship

First, however, I shall consider how the gospels and Acts frame allegiance to Christ in terms which promote the continuing formation of all, and this not simply by means of formal education—a regular program of instruction of pupils (that is a subset of believers) at the hands of appointed, even anointed, teachers.

The dominant term in each of the canonical gospels for a Jesus follower is "disciple." It is clear, although popularly overlooked, that, over time, the meanings of words routinely evolve, diverge and even become disconnected from their earlier roots. For example, the literal resemblances between the English words "disciple" and "discipline" suggest some connection. However, while an overlap in meaning was once transparent, it is now incidental, and has largely disappeared.[17] Accordingly, it is not normally considered that discipline is primarily a distinctive of disciples; nor that disciples are especially defined either by their self-discipline or by being subject to the discipline of their teacher.[18] Nonetheless, the academic subject pursued by a teacher and pupil may be described as a discipline. Contemporary usage, including in Christian contexts, does not obviously reflect any necessary connection between the two terms "disciple" and "discipline," nor even, I suggest, between "disciple" and an over-riding commitment to instruction. Education, even formation more generally, is now the dominant motif of neither of the words "disciple" nor "discipline." However, both words share a common Latin root, most probably in the verb *discere*, "to learn."[19]

17. Cf. *Oxford English Dictionary Online, ad loc,* which argues that early English usage of "discipline" referred to the tuition or training of pupils/disciples.

18. For more detailed discussion of the history of the word "discipline," especially in ecclesiastical contexts, see Clarke, "Lexicography and New Testament Categories of Church Discipline," 129–51.

19. Cf. Varro, *On the Latin Language,* 6.62; although the root of the syllable -*ip*- in *discipulus/disciplina* is less certain. Cf. Lewis, and Short eds, *A Latin Dictionary. Revised ed. ad loc,* who present *discipulus* as a contraction of *disco* ("I learn") and *puer* ("boy"), or *pupillus* ("orphan"), reflecting a one-time association between the child and his education; and Glare, *Oxford Latin Dictionary, ad loc,* who suggests the alternative

In ancient Greek the noun for pupil (μαθητής; also "student" or "apprentice," that is, one who learns)[20] and the verb "to (cause to) be a pupil" (μαθητεύω) predominantly apply to one who is under instruction, or is subject to learning at the hands of a teacher.[21] Specifically, in some ways similar to the Latin analogy, these two Greek words which describe the identity or focus of a pupil/disciple shared a more resilient connection with the verb, "to learn" or "to be taught" (μανθανεῖν) than does the word "disciple" in later English translations of the New Testament.[22] Furthermore, the μαθητής was typically expected to have a respectful relationship towards a particular teacher or teaching. By extension, the denotation "disciple" may presume elements of being an "adherent," or even a subservient "follower."[23]

I shall explore this more specifically first in the gospels and then in the book of Acts.

"Disciple" in the Gospels

A pupil-teacher relationship between Jesus and his followers is clearly presented in all four of the canonical gospels. Furthermore, a number of verses support the notion that there was a pedagogic focus to that bond: Matt 11:1 describes Jesus "*instructing* (διατάσσω) his disciples." The request to Jesus by a representative of his disciples, in Luke 11:1, is specifically to "*teach* us to pray, as John *taught* (διδάσκω) his *disciples*." The Pharisees, in

---

construction, *dis-* + *capio* + *-ulus*. *Oxford English Dictionary Online, ad loc.* notes that "Some modern scholars favor a derivation from an unattested verb **discipere* 'to grasp mentally' (< *dis-* prefix + *capere* to take, seize: see capture n.)."

20. Cf. this focus on instruction (of the Christian disciple) in the reference by the second century Apologist, Theophilus of Antioch (3.17): "It behoved, therefore, that he should the rather become a scholar (μαθητής) of God in this matter of legislation, as he himself confessed that in no other way could he gain accurate information (μανθάνω) than by God's teaching (διδάσκω) him through the law. And did not the poets Homer and Hesiod and Orpheus profess that they themselves had been instructed (μανθάνω) by Divine Providence?"

21. The noun is commonly found in Diogenes Laertius, *Lives of the Philosophers*. Josephus refers to Elisha as Elijah's μαθητής, but also having disciples in his own right. Joshua was similarly described as a disciple of Moses. Philo uses the term "disciples of God" (*Sacr.* 7), or "disciples of the only wise being" (*Sacr.* 64, 79). Cf. also *Det.* 66.

22. E.g., Matt 9:13; 11:29; 24:32; Phil 4:11; 1 Tim 5:4, 13; Acts 23:27; Rev 14:3.

23. Cf. the bold assertion in Matt 8:19, "*Teacher*, I will *follow* you wherever you go"; and the statement in John 1:38 that a group of individuals had chosen to *follow* Jesus, and accordingly addressed him as a *teacher*.

talking to Jesus' disciples, specifically ask in Matt 9:11, "Why does your *teacher* (διδάσκαλος) eat with tax collectors and sinners." Similarly, in John 18:19, the High Priest questions Jesus "about his *disciples* and his *teaching*" (διδαχή).[24] The disciples are as likely to refer to Jesus as "teacher" as any other title (cf. Mark 13:1).[25] In other words, inasmuch as a child has a parent, and a slave has a master, so a disciple (μαθητής) presupposes a pupil-teacher relationship. Furthermore, the goal of both pupils and slaves is to emulate their teacher or master. This much is not contentious. Thus:

> A disciple (μαθητής) is not above his teacher (διδάσκαλος), nor a servant above his master. *It is enough for the disciple* (μαθητής) *to be like his teacher* (διδάσκαλος), and the servant like his master (Matt 10:24–25b; cf. Luke 6:40).[26]

In addition to this notion of instruction, there are further connotations that might reasonably be assumed in ancient Jewish references to "disciple," if not in recent English usage. The expectation that a teacher might have disciplinary authority over his disciples is reflected by the Pharisees as they remonstrate with Jesus: "Teacher (διδάσκαλος), rebuke your disciples (μαθητής)" (Luke 19:39). This is also apparent in the Aramaic loanword "rabbi," equivalent to the Greek title "teacher," and often used as a term of address.[27] The role spans aspects both of the teacher (cf. John 1:38; 3:2) and the master.[28] This conjunction is not surprising, and reflects the respected status of the teacher, who would not only educate, but might also routinely issue commands.[29] Accordingly, the title "rabbi" was highly prized, even by

24. Cf. also Jesus "teaching his disciples" (διδάσκω) in Mark 9:31.

25. Even those who were not Jesus' disciples would address him as "teacher," whether in actual or feigned respect (Matt 22:16).

26. Cf. also Jesus' instruction to his disciples that they must report: "The *Teacher* says, My time is at hand. I will keep the Passover at your house with my *disciples*" (Matt 26:18; cf. also Mark 14:14; Luke 22:11).

27. Judge, "Early Christians as a Scholastic Community," 9–11, who argues that, more than a Messiah (which, perhaps in part as a consequence of Jesus' reluctance to draw attention to this, became more widely recognized after his death), Jesus was understood by his contemporaries as a rabbi. While many disputed his position as a prophet, even his detractors accepted that he was a teacher.

28. Cf. also the juxtaposition of "teacher" and "LORD" in John 13:13–14. This partially parallels some school contexts in which "sir" might be used in English.

29. One person recognizes that, as a teacher, Jesus can be expected to issue commands (Luke 12:13; cf. also Luke 19:39). The statement of the sons of Zebedee is, consequently, all the more audacious, as it inverts the normal teacher/pupil relationship: "Teacher, we want you to do for us whatever we ask of you" (Mark 10:35).

those who may not be deserving.[30] Rabbi is especially found in the Fourth Gospel as a term of address on the lips of those who regarded themselves as Jesus' disciples (John 4:31; 9:2; 11:8), but it is also used by John's disciples of their teacher (John 3:26).

On a number of occasions in the gospels, Jesus is portrayed as an especially effective teacher;[31] while in others, it is clear that his pupils are so dull and foolish that they repeatedly fail to grasp his otherwise remarked upon teaching.[32] In ways that are surprising from a pedagogical perspective, Jesus sometimes frames his teaching in ways that are deliberately opaque—and this approach is reinforced by those occasions when his disciples express confusion, his teaching generates discussion, and they have to seek further clarification.[33] The final section of this article will demonstrate that a deliberate intention to incite discussion is central to a pedagogical approach that is used or reported across the New Testament. The goal may well be to incite a process of learning, as opposed simply to the articulation of answers. This more oblique approach will likely distinguish "those who have ears to hear," from those who are unprepared to engage in reflection and exploration. (The motif of "ears to hear," in the sense of a readiness or ability to be attentive, occurs widely across Old and New Testaments).[34]

It is apparent that, for a first century audience, the most appropriate designation for this relationship was that of the pupil-teacher; and the most common designation of Jesus' followers in the gospels is consequently that of "pupils" or "students." Further, the historic formation of disciples impinged not only on their understanding and entailed intellectual assent. It also required the lived-out adoption of developing understanding, evidenced by an ever more authentic, but never completely achievable, emulation of their teacher ("a disciple does not exceed his teacher," Matt 10:24),

30. Cf. the contrast prescribed between the scribes and Jesus' disciples in Matt 23:1–12.

31. Cf. John 3:2, in which Nicodemus is said to recognize that Jesus is apparently "a teacher sent from God," on account of his miracles; or Mark 1:22, in the synagogue at Capernaum, where Jesus is contrasted with the scribes, on account of his authority.

32. Cf. especially the developing portrait of the disciples in Mark's gospel.

33. A principal example of this is Jesus' widespread use of the parable, not as an accessible story by which to present a simple truth, but as a puzzling picture, which confuses his hearers and prompts both questions and debate. I shall discuss further this notion of learning by means of generating debate, rather than simply by providing answers.

34. Cf. Deut 29:4; Ps 115:6; 135:17; Isa 6:10; 32:3; Jer 5:21; Ezek 3:10; 12:2; 40:4; 44:5; Matt 11:15; 13:9, 15–16, 43; Acts 28:27; Rom 11:8.

often by means of strict obedience. That is, this kind of pupil learning addressed formation in ways that were wider than simply the acquisition of intellectual knowledge.

"Disciple" in Acts and the Epistles

While "disciple" in the gospels most often designates this didactic relationship between the earthly Jesus and his select number of chosen pupils (principally the Twelve), in the post-ascension setting of Acts the term is used much less frequently, and it additionally tends to have a broader referent.[35] The Twelve are now often termed apostles, rather than disciples.[36] When Luke does use the category "disciple" in his second volume, it is largely as a general and collective term for the believers,[37] whether in Jerusalem, Judea, Syria, Asia Minor or Achaia,[38] and occasionally for an individual believer.[39] Thus, the relationship of teacher/pupil, where Jesus is the incarnate

35. While the frequency of usage of μαθητής and μαθητεύω is higher in John's gospel (cf. especially John 20–21) than in Matthew or Mark, it is significantly lower in both Luke and Acts. Cf. also Acts 11:26. This distinction between the Twelve and the rest of the disciples is seen in Acts 6:2.

36. In regard to the Jerusalem Council, the apostles are grouped with the Jerusalem elders, cf. especially Acts 15:2, 4, 6, 22–23; 16:4.

37. The term ἀδελφός is most common, especially in speech, and refers sometimes to fellow believers and at other times fellow Jews. The word ἅγιος (often translated "saint") is also occasionally used as a collective term for believers in Jerusalem and Judea (cf. Acts 9:13, 32, 41; 26:10). The present participle of πιστεύω (πιστεύοντες, "believers"; Acts 2:44; 5:14; 13:39 [singular]; 15:5 [perfect participle]; 19:18 [perfect participle]; 21:25 [perfect participle]; 22:19) and the adjective πιστός ("believer"; Acts 10:45 [plural]; 16:1, 15) is sometimes used. (The verb, πιστεύω, "I believe," is widespread, marking the transition to faith).

38. Cf. Jerusalem (Acts 6:1–7; 9:1, 26); Joppa (Acts 9:36 [μαθήτρια, "a female disciple"]); Lydda (Acts 9:38); Tyre (Acts 21:4); Caesarea (Acts 21:16); Damascus (Acts 9:10, 19, 25); Syrian Antioch (Acts 11:26, 29; 14:28); Lystra (Acts 14:20; 16:1); Pisidian Antioch (Acts 13:52); Ephesus (Acts 19:1, 9, 30; 20:1); Achaia (Acts 18:27).

39. Acts 9:10, 26; 16:1; 21:16. Cf. also the New Testament *hapax legomenon* μαθήτρια, "female disciple," in Acts 9:36, as a description of Tabitha/Dorcas in Joppa. Following the Evangelists, the early Apologists predominantly use "disciples" in reference to the Twelve. However, there are exceptions: Justin, in *Trypho* 35, describes himself as a disciple, in that he is one who, not only confesses Christ and is called a Christian, but also is among those who are "of the true and pure doctrine (διδασκαλία) of Jesus Christ"; and Irenaeus 3.12.5, 9, who refers to disciples as the post-ascension followers of Christ, in similar vein to Acts; and Irenaeus 2.32.4, who also describes his contemporary believers as disciples; and Irenaeus 10:1, where he refers to the disciples of the apostles.

teacher,[40] is less obviously in the frame, and the term "disciple" has a lower profile. Nonetheless the described setting surrounding the term "disciples" in Acts is not infrequently one of teaching and learning, directed towards some measure of continuing formation.[41]

Whilst Luke continues occasionally to use "disciple" to describe these post-ascension believers, should it be regarded as significant that neither the noun "disciple," nor the verb "to make a disciple," occurs in the New Testament letters or Revelation? In this context, the preferred collective terms for Christians are "saints" (in the sense of, those who are sanctified); "believers" (that is, those who have faith in or display commitment to Christ); or, most commonly, "brothers" (used generically of those who share a fictive, sibling relationship in Christ). These terms mark initiation into and affiliation to a group, expressed by subscription or adherence to a shared set both of beliefs and practices. It appears that the dominant term in the gospels, which Luke continued to use in his second volume—a word that had been used to reflect ongoing formation—had been substituted by a number of terms that focus on the established status of Christians as sanctified brothers and sisters, who expressed faithfulness towards Christ. The earlier emphasis on Jesus as teacher has become diluted.

Even without this language of discipleship, however, it has been noted that Judge and Smith have argued that contexts for teaching continued to be of paramount importance in the post-ascension New Testament communities, not least in the Pauline mission. My next question, motivated in part by the comparatively recent shift in educational notation from an emphasis on teaching to one on learning, is whether the New Testament sources offer evidence as to *how* teaching continued to be conducted in these new ecclesiastical communities. How indeed was learning achieved?

---

40. Note Luke's prologue, in which his former book is framed as an account of "what Jesus *began* to do and teach" (Acts 1:1). It may be that Luke is here introducing Acts as a description of how Jesus continues his ministry as teacher—from his ascended vantage point—and thus his followers are those who continue to learn from Jesus, and warrant their designation as disciples.

41. Cf. Acts 6:2, 7; 9:19, 26, 38; 11:26; 13:52; 14:20–22, 28; 18:23, 27; 19:1, 9; 20:1, 30. Note that, on one occasion, a group of "disciples" appears to be affiliated to Saul/Paul, rather than to Jesus (cf. Acts 9:25—cf. John's disciples).

Disputation

I have already noted Claire Smith's important finding that the earliest Christian communities were significantly characterized by an expectation that brothers and sisters would learn in response to directed instruction. Consistent with this, I have elsewhere argued that persuasion, or the use of rhetoric, was commended by Paul as a key tool both for him and for local leaders in these communities.[42] However, I have also previously argued that a further important means of community influence should be by means of the visible, accessible, modelled life of the leader. Paul highlights this characteristic in his use of the motif of imitation.[43] On these bases, it is clear that Christian brothers and sisters were to be learners, and they pursued this both through formal instruction, in the manner of persuasive teaching, and through a combination of observation and emulation.

In this final section, I shall draw attention to a further feature of community formation, which has been neglected in reconstructions of the Pauline communities—and yet, this feature is evident not only in his letters, but also more widely across the New Testament canon. As with the tool of imitation, it is a context for learning that is not dependent on formal, didactic delivery.[44] Once this element is identified in the text, it soon becomes clear that it is by no means an insignificant characteristic of intercourse in early Christian gatherings. This element both supports and importantly nuances Smith's suggestion that learning was an activity pursued as a community.

I introduce this element by returning to Edwin Judge's colorful cameo of "*talkative, passionate and sometimes quarrelsome circles* that met to read Paul's letters over their evening meal."[45] Judge here offers little further support for this description; but it conjures scenes of dynamic debate, of questioning, of doubt, and of group exploration. This would be in marked contrast to the unchallenged reception of authorized content delivered by the uninterrupted voice of an appointed teacher. In a later publication, Judge paints a vivid scene "of lively social intercourse [in which] there was neither solitude nor mystery, no shrine, no statue, no cult, no ceremony, no offering . . . Instead there was talk and argument, disturbing questions

---

42. Clarke, *A Pauline Theology of Church Leadership*, 159–72.

43. Clarke, "Be Imitators of Me," 329–60. Cf. also Clarke, *Pauline Theology of Church Leadership*, 173–82.

44. Cf. the term δημηγορέω in the setting of a public address (Acts 12:21).

45. Judge, "Social Identity," 212 [italics mine].

about belief and behaviour (two matters of little concern to religion in antiquity), conscious changes to accepted ways, and the expectation of a more drastic transformation soon to come."[46]

I shall show that this dynamic of debate and challenge was not a characteristic only of interactions directly with Paul, but also of community dynamics in his absence, and furthermore of the earlier interactions with and around Jesus, recorded across the gospels.

Many studies have fruitfully explored the grounds and heated nature of social and theological dissension within a significant number of the Pauline communities.[47] However, it has not been widely noted that a dynamic of discussion, debate and questioning, when not dissolving into discord, might also have been regarded as a socially normal, potentially productive and valued context for learning—a medium, which was invited and fostered by both Jesus and Paul.

Across the New Testament corpus, a number of overlapping semantic domains is used with notable frequency. Together they embrace notions of discussing, discerning, exploring, disputing, arguing, quarrelling, questioning, and reasoning. They certainly surface on occasions of internal doubt and reflection, that is in reference to the turning over of one's own thoughts;[48] but they also arise in contexts of open, even animated, community debate.

As many as twenty-nine words (predominantly verbs and nouns, but also adjectives and adverbs) reflect this mode of interaction, and together they occur across seventeen books of the New Testament, on at least 147 occasions.[49] These are widely distributed, but predominantly located in the

---

46. Judge, "Cultural Conformity and Innovation in Paul."

47. Williams, *Enemies of the Cross of Christ.*; Peterlin, *Paul's Letter to the Philippians*; Finney, *Honour and Conflict in the Ancient World.*

48. Mark 7:21 (Matt 15:19); Luke 1:29; 2:35; 5:22; 6:8; 12:17; 24:38; Rom 1:21; 1 Cor 3:20; Jas 2:4.

49. διαλογίζομαι (16 occurrences), "to reason, question, discuss, consider, discern" (Matt 16:7–8; 21:25; Mark 2:6, 8; 8:16–17; 9:33; 11:31; Luke 1:29; 3:15; 5:21–22; 12:17; 20:14); διαλογισμός (14 occurrences), "thought, thinking, opinion, discussion, argument, reasoning, doubt, quarreling" (Matt 15:19; Mark 7:21; Luke 2:35; 5:22; 6:8; 9:46–47; 24:38; Rom 1:21; 14:1; 1 Cor 3:20; Phil 2:14; 1 Tim 2:8; Jas 2:4); διαλέγομαι (13 occurrences), "to dispute, discuss, argue, reason" (Mark 9:34; Acts 17:2, 17; 18:4, 19; 19:8–9; 20:7, 9 [Paul engaged in a talk]; 24:12, 25; Heb 12:5; Jude 1:9); διακατελέγχομαι (1 occurrence), "to refute" (Acts 18:28).

συζητέω (10 occurrences), "to argue, question, dispute, discuss" (Mark 1:27; 8:11; 9:10, 14, 16; 12:28; Luke 22:23; 24:15; Acts 6:9; 9:29); ζήτησις (7 occurrences), "search,

four gospels, Acts, the so-called Pauline Hauptbriefe and the Pastoral Epistles. That is, in terms of both occurrence and spread, this is not a marginal phenomenon; indeed, it was a distinctive feature of both the pre-ascension followers of Jesus and the subsequently formed communities of Christ followers. Significantly, it emerges as a characteristic of the ways in which Jesus communities engaged in learning. In modern pedagogy, this would be framed as a form of active learning.

Drawing attention to a number of these instances here may be sufficient to suggest that an extensive and detailed exploration could helpfully nuance and prove the rule.[50]

---

debate, discussion, question, controversy" (John 3:25; Acts 15:2, 7; 25:20; 1 Tim 6:4; 2 Tim 2:23; Titus 3:9); ζήτημα (5 occurrences), "dispute, question, controversy" (Acts 15:2; 18:15; 23:29; 25:19; 26:3); ἐκζήτησις (1 occurrence), "speculation, controversy" (1 Tim 1:4).

ἀπολογέομαι (10 occurrences), "to defend oneself, answer, excuse [someone]" (Luke 12:11; 21:14; Acts 19:33; 24:10; 25:8; 26:1–2, 24; Rom 2:15; 2 Cor 12:19); ἀπολογία (8 occurrences), "defence" (Acts 22:1; 25:16; 1 Cor 9:3; 2 Cor 7:11; Phil 1:7, 16; 2 Tim 4:16; 1 Pet. 3:15); ἀναπολόγητος (2 occurrences), "without excuse" (Rom 1:20; 2:1).

ἀνακρίνω (16 occurrences), "to examine, judge, question" (Luke 23:14; Acts 4:9; 12:19; 17:11; 24:8; 28:18; 1 Cor 2:14–15; 4:3–4; 9:3; 10:25, 27; 14:24).

ἀντιλέγω (11 occurrences), "to speak in response, speak against, object, deny, oppose, contradict, be argumentative" (Luke 2:34; 20:27; 21:15; John 19:12; Acts 4:14; 13:45; 28:19, 22; Rom 10:21; Titus 1:9; 2:9); ἀντιλογία (4 occurrences), "contradiction, lawsuit, controversy, dispute, hostility, rebellion" (Heb 6:16; 7:7; 12:3; Jude 1:11).

ἔρις (9 occurrences), "strife, quarrelling, dissension, rivalry" (Rom 1:29; 13:13; 1 Cor 1:11; 3:3; 2 Cor 12:20; Gal 5:20; Phil 1:15; 1 Tim 6:4; Titus 3:9); ἐρίζω (1 occurrence), "to strive, challenge, quarrel" (Matt 12:19).

στάσις (3 occurrences), "argument, dissension" (Acts 15:2; 23:7, 10).

συμβάλλω (3 occurrences), "to ponder, confer, converse, consider, compare" (Luke 2:19; Acts 4:15; 17:18).

διαλαλέω (2 occurrences), "to discuss, talk about" (Luke 1:65; 6:11).

παροξυσμός (2 occurrences), "sharp disagreement, encouragement" (Acts 15:39; Heb 10:24 [vocally inspire]).

λογομαχέω (1 occurrence), "to fight or quarrel about words" (2 Tim 2:14); λογομαχία (1 occurrence), "dispute about words" (1 Tim 6:4).

ἀναντίρρητος (1 occurrence), "undeniable, indisputable" (Acts 19:36); ἀναντιρρήτως (1 occurrence), "without objection" (Acts 10:29).

φιλονεικία (1 occurrence), "argument, dispute, contentiousness" (Luke 22:24); φιλόνεικος (1 occurrence), "argumentative" (1 Cor 11:16).

ἀντίθεσις (1 occurrence), "contradiction" (1 Tim 6:20).

διαπαρατριβή (1 occurrence), "constant arguing" (1 Tim 6:5).

θυμομαχέω (1 occurrence), "to be very angry" (Acts 12:20).

50. Another phrase that is consistent with this thesis of mutual engagement in learning is based around the word ἀλλήλων, in the context of mutual exhortation; e.g., "able to instruct one another" (Rom 15:14); "comfort one another, agree with one another"

Matthew presents Jesus responding to a question of the chief priests and elders by proactively posing his own question of his detractors, and then awaiting the results of their collective discussion (Matt 21:23–26).[51] In Mark, the warm reception of Jesus' teaching in the synagogue at Capernaum, followed by his exorcism of an unclean spirit, was evidenced by those in the congregation questioning (Mark 1:21–28).[52] A developing narrative theme in Mark's gospel is the way in which Jesus directly and increasingly attracted adverse engagement in argument with his opponents, as in his exchange with the Pharisees in Mark 8:11.[53] Some of that disputing attracted the admiration of onlookers and prompted further questions, which Jesus entertained (Mark 12:28–34).[54] During the mountainside descent of Peter, James, and John following the Transfiguration, Mark suggests that some of the disciples came away with profound questions, but had been sworn to secrecy, so they kept these to themselves, rather than divulging them beyond this select group (Mark 9:9–10). However, this did not prevent them from raising particular questions directly of Jesus about the coming of Elijah (Mark 9:11–13).[55] An interesting practice here, then, is teaching that is frequently prompted by the questions of others, whether those questions were constructively or obstructively raised. In addition, Jesus is also occasionally presented as preferring to avoid, or side-step, the opportunity to respond to posed questions, perhaps in order to motivate learning by means rather of asking his own questions.

(2 Cor 13:11); "addressing one another" (Eph 5:19); "teaching and admonishing one another in all wisdom" (Col 3:16); "encourage one another and build one another up" (1 Thess 5:11; cf. also 4:18); "exhort one another" (Heb 3:13); "stir up one another . . . encouraging one another" (Heb 10:24–25); "confess your sins to one another and pray for one another" (Jas 5:16).

51. "'The baptism of John, from where did it come? From heaven or from man?' And they discussed it among themselves (διελογίζοντο), saying, 'If we say, "From heaven," he will say to us, "Why then did you not believe him?"'" (Matt 21:25).

52. "And they were all amazed, so that they questioned among themselves (συζητεῖν), saying, 'What is this? A new teaching with authority! He commands even the unclean spirits, and they obey him'" (Mark 1:27).

53. "The Pharisees came and began to argue (συζητεῖν) with him, seeking from him a sign from heaven to test him" (Mark 8:11).

54. "And one of the scribes came up and heard them disputing with one another (συζητούντων), and seeing that he answered them well, asked him, 'Which commandment is the most important of all?'" (Mark 12:28).

55. "So they kept the matter to themselves, questioning (συζητοῦντες) what this rising from the dead might mean. And they asked (ἐπηρώτων) him, 'Why do the scribes say that first Elijah must come?'" (Mark 9:10–11).

In Acts, Luke repeatedly highlights hostile disputation, from outsiders, as in some members of the synagogue of the Freedmen, together with some Cyrenians, Alexandrians, Cilicians and others from Asia Minor, who together opposed Stephen (Acts 6:8–10).[56] On occasion, however, this debate is generated from those who, initially at least, are positively disposed to Paul. In Rome, local Jewish leaders, respond to accounts of the new sect being spoken against, by inviting the apostle to present his views (Acts 28:22).[57] In a context of theological tension and uncertainty, some Judeans were presenting teaching about the status of the Mosaic law. Both Paul and Barnabas engaged in heated debate with them—an exchange which soon prompted the Jerusalem Council (Acts 15:1–2).[58] Luke also presents the synagogue as a context in which Paul would regularly "reason (διαλέγομαι) from the Scriptures"—a term that may embrace the exchange or interchange of views.[59] It may well have been that this was through a process of debate and refutation, as in the instance of the eloquent Apollos in Corinth.[60] Having "received the word" eagerly, the Beroean Jews resorted to "examining/questioning (ἀνακρίνοντες) the Scriptures daily to see if these things were so" (Acts 17:11). This suggests a context of communal engagement—a pouring over the Scriptures together. In one particular context, recounted apparently by an eyewitness, an unfortunate listener falls asleep, to his cost, whilst Paul engaged somewhat at length, both in a presented talk (παρέτεινέν τε τὸν λόγον, Acts 20:7), but also in extended conversation or argument (διαλεγομένου) with a group of believers (Acts 20:9).[61]

Turning to the New Testament letters, Paul frequently castigates that discussion can regress into harmful hostility. It is one matter to disagree and consequently to explore together, but quite another to quarrel, especially in

56. "Then some of those who belonged to the synagogue of the Freedmen (as it was called), and of the Cyrenians, and of the Alexandrians, and of those from Cilicia and Asia, rose up and disputed with (συζητοῦντες) Stephen" (Acts 6:9).

57. "But we desire to hear from you what your views are, for with regard to this sect we know that everywhere it is spoken against (ἀντιλέγεται)" (Acts 28:22).

58. "And after Paul and Barnabas had no small dissension and debate with them (στάσεως καὶ ζητήσεως), Paul and Barnabas and some of the others were appointed to go up to Jerusalem to the apostles and the elders about this question" (Acts 15:2).

59. Cf. Acts 17:2, 17; 18:4, 19; 19:8–9.

60. ". . . he powerfully refuted (διακατελέγχομαι) the Jews in public, showing by the Scriptures that the Christ was Jesus" (Acts 18:28).

61. "On the first day of the week, when we were gathered together to break bread, Paul conversed with them, intending to depart on the next day, and he prolonged his speech until midnight" (Acts 20:7).

the presence of those who are weak in faith (διαχρίσεις διαλογισμῶν, Rom 14:1).[62] The Corinthian Christians are especially presented as having an unhealthy reputation for this (1 Cor 1:11; 11:16). However, it has been recognized as characteristic of the Pastoral Epistles that it is to Timothy and Titus that some of the strongest and most widely repeated warnings are given.[63]

On a more positive note: the ability to reason constructively with others about one's faith is commended in 1 Pet 3:15.[64]

In concluding this section, I return to one of my opening statements, that very little is known about the nature, format or practices of the earliest Christian gatherings. One element that emerges here, however, is evidence of a widespread element of dialogue, debate, discussion, even disagreement, which may indeed be regarded as culturally characteristic—a contextually accepted practice in which the understanding of the early Christ followers was both challenged and took shape. Such a dynamic would be consistent with Paul's prescriptive statement that not only acknowledges, but encourages, a limited number of vocal contributions from all those present. However, aware that the interplay between divergent voices can, indeed did, get out of hand, he specifically warns the Corinthian believers that their interactions should be done without interruption and in an orderly fashion.[65]

Conclusion

A few caveats should be noted. My proposals here have focused on some descriptions that have been neglected in scholarly reconstruction of the earliest Christian groupings—namely that these were learning communities. Whilst I have suggested that they are significant, and perhaps even dominant, this is not to deny, first, that other parallel models of community organization were also helpfully promoted or embraced in the first century. Secondly, a focus on learning does not preclude the importance of other aspects of community life that were fundamental to the identity of these early Christ followers. Thirdly, drawing attention to discursive, even disputatious, contexts for learning neither overlooks that this frequently

62. Cf. also Phil. 2:14 (διαλογισμῶν).

63. 1 Tim 1:4; 6:4, 20; 2 Tim 2:14, 23; Titus 1:9; 2:9; 3:9.

64. "in your hearts honour Christ the Lord as holy, always being prepared to make a defence to anyone who asks you for a reason for the hope that is in you; yet do it with gentleness and respect" (1 Pet 3:15; cf. also Col 4:3–4).

65. 1 Cor 14:26–33.

regressed into unhelpful, perhaps harmful, hostility, nor that other, more regulated contexts for instruction also took place. However, recourse to the lecture presentation is not presented as a remedy to the risk of heated disagreement.

7

A Review of Tom Greggs's *Dogmatic Ecclesiology, Volume 1, The Priestly Catholicity of the Church*

T. A. NOBLE

THE PRIESTLY CATHOLICITY OF *the church* is the first volume of a projected three-volume work on ecclesiology by Tom Greggs, Marischal Professor of Divinity at the University of Aberdeen. David Fergusson commends it as "a theologically rich ecclesiology," and Susan Durber of the World Council of Churches' Commission on Faith and Order describes it as "a timely contribution" and "a truly exhilarating read." Tom Greggs is obviously planning ahead since he gives us a ground plan for the projected three volumes in a "Chart of Prospective Chapter Topics" (lxi).

To grasp the project as a whole, I shall first give some detailed attention to the introductory material in "How to Read This Book" and in the Preface. I shall then attempt a synopsis of the book, adding some comments and finish the review with some questions for discussion.

Introductory: "How to Read This Book" and the Preface

The very first claim made in "How to Read This Book" is that this is a "Protestant ecclesiology" and that means being true to the insights of the

Reformation churches, not to offer a blueprint or comment on questions of polity, but "to reflect on [the church's] place theologically within the broader account of God and God's ways with the world" (xx). The account to be given in the three volumes does not claim to be exhaustive, indeed, he writes, it is not to be "considered in any sense remotely exhaustive" (xx). Rather it offers three theological narratives relating the *triplex munus* of Christ to the three marks of the church from the Nicene-Constantinopolitan Creed. The narratives concern, therefore, the priestly catholicity of the church (Vol. 1); the prophetic apostolicity of the church (Vol. 2); and the kingly holiness of the church (Vol. 3).

In addition to this Christological (or Christocentric?) perspective there is a pneumatological dimension:

> [T]he event of the act of the Holy Spirit in the life of the church is considered accordingly in relation to the Spirit who is the Lord, the giver of life (Vol. 1); who spoke through the prophets (Vol. 2); and who with the Father and the Son is worshipped and glorified (Vol. 3). The argument is that *through the economy of the Holy Spirit in God's work of salvation* we are, as the church, enabled to participate in (Vol. 1), encounter (Vol. 2), and be transformed into (Vol. 3) the body of Jesus Christ (xxi, italics original)

These "irreducible narratives . . . are worked through systematically as three possible ways to describe the church in its relation to God the Father in Christ through the gracious event of the act of the Holy Spirit" (xxi). This appears to suggest that the Christological or Christocentric approach does not militate against, but rather serves, a fully Trinitarian context for ecclesiology. And to refer to the church as an "event of the act of the Holy Spirit" is to reject merely abstract doctrine in order to see that ecclesiology is about "positioning our lives together in such a way that we might participate in *something* of God *happening*."[1] The trilogy is therefore to be read "vertically and horizontally," that is, not only following the train of thought through each volume but also the connections across the corresponding chapters of the three volumes.

Having prepared us for what to expect in "How to Read this Book," Greggs then turns to methodology in his Preface. He begins from the weakness of ecclesiology in Protestantism where individual faith and the individual's personal relationship with God appears to have priority. The Protestant "propensity to individualism" is accentuated in today's society

---

1. Quoting Severson, "The Church: The Event of the Kingdom of God," 29–36, 32.

where "me, my Bible, and Jesus" seem to be all that is needed and whole denominations are in free fall. There is a radical need for Christians to rethink the church, not only what the church *does* but what the church *is*. In considering dogmatic topography, he considers that it is tempting to consider the church in relation to theological anthropology or in the order of *knowing*. But Greggs argues that it must be considered within the order of *being*. Ecclesiology is a derivative of economic pneumatology, which is a derivative of the doctrine of appropriations within the doctrine of the economic Trinity, which in turn is a derivative of the doctrine of the immanent Trinity. It is therefore "a long way downstream from more foundational areas of dogmatic inquiry" (xxxi). What Greggs is offering is a thick *theological* description of the church, "irregular" in the sense that it treats ecclesiology as an individual area rather than within a full dogmatics (xxxv).

Whereas ecclesiology is a derivative doctrine in the order of being, it is a foundational doctrine in the order of knowing (xxxviii). "The church is the place where the revelation of grace and salvation is received, and the Word is heard through an event of the act of the Spirit" (xxxviii). Resisting the crude attempt to think of this as an account of the church "from above", he rejects the Kantian divorce, emphasizing that the church is "a free activity of God *in space-time*." Creation is the theatre of divine action.

The methodological ambition therefore is, first, an ecclesiology giving priority to classical Christian doctrines; secondly, one which critiques the church's proclamation about itself; and thirdly, one which asks how far the church's proclamation about itself is attested in Scripture (xl-xli). *Sola scriptura* is not simply a doctrine about the individual's authority to interpret the Scriptures, but an account of the church under the authority of the Word of God. Although the church only appears explicitly towards the end of the Creed of Constantinople under the third article, it is also, Greggs notes, the subject "we" in, "We believe," and so a foundational doctrine in the order of knowing (xliii).

Drawing on scriptural and credal insights, the argument is to be given of three irreducible divine-human relations in the church, each explored in one of the three volumes: *participation, encounter, and transformation.* Greggs writes:

> The church *participates* in the wounded and resurrected body of Christ by an event of the act of the Holy Spirit; the church *encounters* the risen and ascended Christ by an event of the act of the Holy Spirit; and the church is *transformed* into the exalted and

triumphant body of Christ by an event of the act of the Holy Spirit
(xliv, italics added).

Ecclesiology must relate to specific concrete forms of the church, and
Greggs traces "variegated and overlapping ecclesiastical traditions" beginning from his own Methodist tradition (xlvi). Backwards in time we may
trace the continuity from Anglicanism as one of the Magisterial traditions
of the Reformation and also from the influence of the Moravians and so
back to the radical Reformation, and thus through both back to the Catholic
church before the Reformation and thus back before the split between East
and West. Forwards from Methodism, we come to the Holiness traditions
including the Salvation Army, worldwide Pentecostalism, and independent
evangelical churches. The ecclesiology presented will be particularly critical
of any view of the church which thinks that there is some kind of causative
action of the church which determines *ex opere operato* the presence, grace
and act of God.

Since the church is created *ex nihilo* by the Holy Spirit, it is "*an object
of faith and not of sight*" and in opposition particularly to the Roman Catholic view that the church invisible subsists within the church visible, Greggs
takes the view that the church visible (in its *simul iustus et peccator* form)
exists within the hidden or invisible church. He endorses Barth's view that
the church does not exist either in gathered individuals or in bishops or
synods or hierarchy. It is not the visible order and structure which is the
cause or location of the church's existence, but "the invisible operation of
God in Christ and the Spirit known by faith" (li).

The priority of the "invisible" church is pursued farther through com-
menting that in the first two chapters of the book of Acts, it was not the
decisions about polity (i.e., the visible church) in Chapter One, but the
coming of the Spirit in Chapter Two which marks the beginning of the
church. Greggs writes:

> The church begins at Pentecost with the coming of the Holy Spirit:
> at Pentecost the church is created out of nothing by an event of the
> act of the Holy Spirit (lii).

That sentence seems to me to raise the whole question of the relation
of the church to Israel, the *qahal* of God in the Old Testament. Positively
however, it asserts the dependence of the church on the Spirit. There is no
church which is not visible, taking a culturally influenced structural form,

but being a "true" church cannot be determined by secondary, cultural and, at worst, nontheological issues. That is to ape the church in Acts 1.

The Structure of the Three Volumes

The Preface thus makes clear Gregg's overall approach in this "irregular" exercise in Christian Dogmatics.[2] He gives us two very helpful aids to grasping the overall structure and line of argument throughout the projected three volumes. He not only blesses the reader with "Abbreviated Chapter Theses" for Volume One, but before that, he gives a most helpful "Chart of Prospective Chapter Topics" across the three volumes. All dogmatic theologians, who by definition rejoice to see the wood and not just the individual trees, will be delighted by these aids to understanding! Here the architectonic structure of the three volumes is laid bare for our contemplation.

It will help us to grasp the overall structure of the three-volume work to note that in each volume, the first chapter is on the Holy Spirit—"The Giver of Life" in Volume One, "Who Spoke by the Prophets" in Volume Two, and "Worshipped and Glorified" in Volume Three. The second chapter in each volume is Christological, devoted specifically to the *triplex munus*: the High Priesthood of Christ in Volume One, "Christ as Prophet" in Volume Two, and "Christ the King" in Volume Three. After a chapter on pneumatology and a chapter on Christology, the remaining twelve chapters in each volume are on the church. The third chapter in each volume takes up the trilogy of participation, encounter, and transformation. Across the fourth chapters, the life of the church is considered as priestly, prophetic and kingly. The fifth chapter in each volume is on baptism, the sixth on Holy Communion. The seventh takes from the creed the three themes of the Communion of Saints, the forgiveness of sins, and the life everlasting. The eighth chapter in each volume is concerned with different aspects of prayer, the ninth chapter in each volume respectively with thanksgiving and praise, preaching, and service. The tenth chapters bring us to the necessary consideration of polity—the congregation in Volume One, "Order and Oversight" in Volume Two, and "Pastoral Activity and Vocation" in Volume Three. Chapter eleven in this first volume is on "Sanctification," in Volume Two on "Speaking the Truth" and in Volume Three we look forward to a culturally relevant discussion of "Transforming Power Relations."

2. On "regular" and "irregular" dogmatics, see Barth, *Church Dogmatics*, I/1, 275ff.

The twelfth chapter across the volumes takes up the triad of Love, Faith and Hope. The thirteenth chapters sum up the theme indicated in the volume title, thus linking priesthood with catholicity (Volume One), the prophetic office of the church with its apostolicity (Volume Two), and the kingly office with holiness (Volume Three). The final chapter in each volume takes up the fourth note of the church as "One."

This quick account of the structure of the entire three volumes bears out David Fergusson's assessment that this is "a theologically rich ecclesiology." There is much to look forward to here! It is evident that the questions about polity and ministry are not ignored but they are placed in a stronger dogmatic context than has often been the case. The same may be said of sacramental theology. And it is clearly to be welcomed that preaching and prayer and sanctification and pastoral ministry and so many other topics are not considered in isolation or merely from an individualistic or anthropological or practical perspective, but are incorporated within ecclesiology, the doctrine of the church. Altogether, the connections indicated between the structure of the *triplex munus* and the phrases of the creed, along with such structures as the Pauline triad of faith, love and hope will rejoice the heart of dogmaticians. While we can never be quite sure that our architectonic structures are not contrived and just too clever, by and large, they do help us to see connections and insights which might not otherwise be clear to us. We must congratulate Tom Greggs for a creative structure across the three volumes promising to give us many new insights. It is notable however in each volume, the first chapter is on pneumatology, the second on Christology and the remaining twelve chapters on the ecclesiology arising, but that the Father and indeed the Trinity do not enter into the structure of the three-volume work. It is true (as we shall see) that they are mentioned from time to time in passing, but there is no Trinitarian structure to the three-volume work.

Is this a problem? Twenty-three years ago, when Miroslav Volf published *After Our Likeness: The Church as the Image of the Trinity*,[3] he aligned himself with John Zizioulas in advocating a Trinitarian ecclesiology over against Joseph Ratzinger's Christocentric ecclesiology.[4] That Zizioulas derived an Eastern Orthodox polity from the doctrine of the

---

3. Volf, *After Our Likeness*.

4. Volf draws mainly on Zizioulas, *Being as Communion*, and on numerous publications by Joseph von Ratzinger, but most often on *Theologische Prinzipienlehre* and *Zur Gemeinschaft gerufen: Kirche heute verstehen*.

Trinity while Volf derived a "gathered church" polity seemed to indicate some kind of special pleading from both, perhaps undermining the strategy of moving directly from the doctrine of the Trinity to the doctrine of the church. On the other hand, Vladimir Lossky claimed that the Eastern Fathers repeat continually that the church is an image of the Holy Trinity,[5] while T.F. Torrance developed an ecclesiology which was both Trinitarian and Christocentric, as the New Zealand theologian, Kate Tyler, has recently shown.[6] Is it a problem that while the Father is occasionally mentioned in the text of Gregg's first volume, neither the Father specifically nor the Trinity appears in the structure or plan of the three volumes? Is this another case of "the forgotten Father?"[7] Given the analysis that ecclesiology is a derivative of economic pneumatology, which is a derivative of the doctrine of appropriations within the doctrine of the economic Trinity, which in turn is a derivative of the doctrine of the immanent Trinity, this appears to be a problem. But it may be that this is a consequence of undertaking an exercise in "irregular" dogmatics, and certainly Greggs makes it clear that the three-volume work is not to be "considered in any sense remotely exhaustive" (xx). Perhaps we are asking too much. It may be of course that the basis for ecclesiology within the doctrine of the Trinity will become clearer in later volumes.

For the rest of this review, we shall focus on the one published volume, and while I cannot give an account of the content in the same detail, we can

---

5. Lossky, *The Mystical Theology of the Eastern Church*, 176.

6. Tyler, *The Ecclesiology of Thomas F. Torrance*. According to Tyler, *koinōnia* is the central motif of Torrance's Trinitarian ecclesiology (79), although he also works with *mystērion* in relation to the Son and *prothesis* in relation to the Father. The purpose (*prothesis*) of the Father is achieved in the *mystērion* of the Son, that is the union of deity and humanity in his Person, so that humankind may be included in the *koinōnia* of the Spirit, which is the *koinōnia* of the Holy Trinity, a *koinōnia* of loving *perichōrēsis*, opened to us by the Son's incarnation, death, and resurrection. Torrance also rejects the view that Pentecost marks the beginning of the Church, writing in what Tyler calls a "Diachronic Ecclesiology" (Tyler, 49–71) of "the anticipatory existence of Israel as the Church in the Old Testament," "The Church in the time between," and "the Church as the new creation," In his chapter on "The One Church" in *The Trinitarian Faith*, 252–301, Torrance's account of *The Evangelical Theology of the Ancient Catholic Church*, he begins with the "basic convictions" in the patristic doctrine of the Church, namely "St Paul's teaching about the *Church as the Body of Christ* together with *baptism in the name of the Father, the Son and the Holy Spirit*" (253) indicating that the doctrine of the Church is both Christocentric and Trinitarian.

7. See Smail, *The Forgotten Father*.

follow the overall line of thought and note some particular points which may provoke us to thought and spark some questions for our consideration.

Pneumatology and Ecclesiology
(Chapter One)

The church is a "Creature of the Spirit, an act of divine grace" (2). Greggs differentiates his position from the position of Schleiermacher that the church is "the common spirit" of the fellowship. At every point "*the church is an event created by an act of the Spirit of God.*" And yet, on the other hand: "The church comes into being as a church through the epicletic call for the Spirit in the gathered community" (4, see also 7). Is this a paradox or an outright contradiction, or is there some confusion here between the local gathered church and the church universal as the body of Christ?

Attention is given to the recurring phrase "an event of the act of the Holy Spirit." It is not that the act of the Spirit *is* the event of the church. The church is an event in space-time which is "caused" by the Spirit, not an event causing the Spirit to come. (That, of course, raises again the question of how we understand the *epiclesis*). Acts 2 rather than Acts 1 is the crucial passage. "The Spirit is the agent who brings the church into being" (13) and we must accordingly speak of the lordship of the Spirit over the church (14).

As the *vinculum amoris* (in Augustine's term), the Spirit is self-effacing, pointing to the Father and the Son, but to be a creature is to have life from the Spirit, the Giver of Life. It follows that the Spirit is (in Barth's terms) "the freedom of God to be present to the creature and the condition for the possibility of the human being open to revelation." Salvation happens "*to and for creation in its created medium of space-time*" (26). The relevance of this is twofold. First, the Spirit works in the human creature to turn the heart outwards from its lapsarian condition as *cor incurvatum in se* towards God (26). This theme of "the heart turned in on itself" becomes a recurring theme throughout the volume. Secondly, this is relevant to the question of mediation, that is to say, whether there is unmediated work of the Spirit in the life of the believer (as in gnosticizing versions of Protestantism) or whether revelation always comes through creaturely (cultural?) forms. No created form can mediate the presence and work of the Spirit *ex opere operato*, but we must also be wary of the notion that some creaturely forms are particularly fitting (28–30).

The Spirit's continuing work on the horizontal plain is "to move the believer within the movement of God", delivering her from the inturned heart to be

> incorporated into the eternal loving of the Son by the Father and the Father by the Son's and the movement of God's gracious and unmerited love of creation (31). Salvation is thus deliverance from that individualism which is sinful because it is the prioritization of self (34). The vertical and horizontal dimensions of love are seen in the two great commandments (39). The Spirit frees the believer from the *cor incurvatum in se* for participation in God's loving ways, participating indeed in the divine life which is the eternal life of the love of the Father and the Son within the bond of the Spirit (42). The church therefore cannot be focused on certain 'types' or classes for it is not a society of like-minded friends. The turning of the heart out from self is why there is a corporate dimension to salvation (45–46)

This is a highly significant chapter drawing on the Augustinian understanding of sin as the *cor incurvatum in se*, developed most radically perhaps by Luther, and underlying John Wesley's concept of sanctification as being filled with the Spirit of "perfect love."[8] We shall come back to that later. There is also here just a glimpse of the Trinitarian context of ecclesiology.

The Priesthood of Christ and His Church
(Chapters Two through Four)

The next three chapters, 2 to 4, are concerned with the priesthood of Christ and his church and all three chapters share a sub-heading, "The Essential Hierarchy of the church." The first chapter, Chapter Two, is focused on the Priesthood of Christ himself and begins with "The Rule of the Only Priest: The Lordship of Christ over the church." Christ is the only priest, and the church does not replace him since he is the head of the body, ascended so that his [physical] body is in heaven, and seated at the right hand of the Father to intercede for those who are in him. Greggs deliberately sets aside therefore the questions of polity and authority which usually attach themselves to discussion of priesthood in the church. These will be dealt

---

8. See Noble, *Holy Trinity: Holy People*, 114–23, drawing on McFadyen, *Bound to Sin.* and Jenson, *The Gravity of Sin.*

with a long way downstream. He begins instead with the New Testament material on the priesthood of Christ, confined largely to the Epistle to the Hebrews. Greggs quotes Barth and Torrance to the effect that the Mediator *is* the mediation (59), "which takes place uniquely in Christ's person and is fulfilled in the giving of Christ's blood in self-sacrifice on the cross. In his sacrifice, he bears our iniquity and takes the damnation deserved by humanity upon himself" (70–73). Intercession, oblation, and blessing are considered and the holiness of Christ as a setting apart not *from* the world but *for* the world (76–77).

The second of the three chapters on priesthood is the second on "The Essential Hierarchy of the Church" and is entitled "Participative Ontology and the Church's Internal Priesthood." Being "in Christ," "the church actively participates in Christ and in this participation is its existence as a priesthood" (83). Christ is the "corporate person" of the community of faith, but the church as the body of Christ "is not a replication of the incarnate person of Christ or even a continuity of it" (86). Rather, "to be formed into Christ's body means to share in the same Spirit who rested fully on Christ" (92). Crucially, this does not mean a change in our ontology: we become not less but more human as we share in the humanity of Christ. It is "very different from the lapsed humanity which expresses itself in the *cor incurvatum in se*" (98).

How then can the church be spoken of as a priesthood? The church's priesthood is not "a replacement, continuation, or supersession" of the priesthood of the temple, but participates in Christ's *unique* priesthood. The imagery of a royal priesthood in I Peter 2:9 or Revelation 1:5–6, 10 and 20:6 is not individual or multiple, but corporate. This means that priesthood is not held individually as if we were each our own priests. Pietistic tendencies to individualization must be rejected. Rather, we participate in the priesthood of the church only *as we are related to other human beings around us whom God loves* (107). "Thus, relationship with God exists within an infrastructure of mutually giving the ministry of God to others and receiving the ministry of God from others" (109). This is "the internal priesthood of the church" (112).

This leads on to the Chapter Four, the third on "The Essential Hierarchy of the Church." This is entitled, "The Priestly Ontology and the Church's Life for the World". Here the thesis is developed that traditional accounts of the hierarchy of the church are inward looking, and, given that there is only one priest (Christ), "the conceptualization of this essential hierarchy requires re-examining and reordering" (113). The corporate nature of the church's priesthood is a means by which we can speak of the church's relation to the world, of which the church is a part. (114). The corporate body must take the form of Christ, the one who lives for others, and the saying attributed to William Temple is endorsed: "The church is the only society which exists for the benefit of those who are not its members." Not only does Greggs reject the early evolution of priesthood and episcopacy in the church's early centuries and the notion of Cyprian that without the bishop there is no church, but he appears even to distance himself from the "ordaining" of "elders" in Presbyterian rites (120). The Reformation rejected clerical essentialism, but ended up speaking repeatedly about polity instead of the church's true priesthood in service to the world. Luther and even Zwingli equivocated. The ecumenical movement perpetuates this failure. The focus on polity, Greggs argues, is invariably inward-looking (124).

I am reminded of William Storrar, drawing on Torrance's point that "if the priestly agency of Christ is obscured, then inevitably a substitute priesthood arises," to suggest that in Scottish life and literature "the minister in the pulpit, so much part of the Scottish religious experience and folklore, becomes the mediating figure between us and God. In other words, the Scottish Christ."[9] Greggs appears to be close here to the views which that biblical scholar and Aberdeen graduate, F. F. Bruce, shared in the tradition of the Christian Brethren.

Most worrying of all for Greggs in making the church inward-looking is the division into the elect and the reprobate. Augustine is blamed here for this "double predestination" (125ff.). It may not be technically correct that Augustine taught double predestination, but Gregg's point is that if there are these two categories of the elect and the reprobate, the saved and the damned (which there are for both Calvinists and Arminians), then somehow the reprobate are seen to exist for the sake of the elect, the world for the sake of the church. The church's focus, it is alleged, shifted in the catholic centuries from the salvation of the world to the salvation of individuals who are saved through baptism and eucharist administered by a true priest, known to be such since he was ordained by a true bishop in the apostolic succession. Even free churches are said to fall into this logic of self-salvation, some of them pursuing "church growth" not for the sake of

9. Storrar, *Scottish Identity*, 89, drawing upon the depiction of the Scottish minister in Lewis Grassic Gibbon's *Scots Quair* trilogy, Fiona MacColla's novel about the Highland Clearances, *And the Cock Crew*, and Robin Jenkin's novel about the Disruption of 1843, *The Awakening of George Darroch*.

the world but for the sake of the survival and flourishing of a congregation or a denomination—a corporate form, Greggs suggests, of the *cor incurvatum in se* (128).

In contrast to all of this, the priestly church exists for the world. Greggs explains that the purpose of the chapter is "to move the emphasis of discussion of ecclesiology away from unending disputes about polity and order" (139). All such discussion must be subsequent to such an understanding of the priesthood of the church as participating in Christ's priestly ministry to the world. Whatever we say about offices and ministries, "*these ministries exist to serve the corporate priesthood's priestly service to the world*" (140, italics original)

As a brief reflection, we might note how close this is to current discussion in missiology as to whether mission is a function of the church or the church a function of the *missio dei*. Perhaps this is a discussion which will feature in Volume Two in the context of the prophetic apostolicity of the church.[10]

These three chapters on priesthood go a long way to clarify what Greggs means by a "Protestant" ecclesiology. In contrast to the "catholic" ecclesiology which focuses on the threefold orders of bishop, priest, and deacon, he challenges us to be true to the Protestant rejection of that whole patristic development which has no basis in the New Testament. He is embracing here, we must note, the Protestantism embodied most clearly in the Radical Reformation and in the Anabaptist and Independent traditions of the "Believers church" or "gathered church." It seems as if those traditions most clearly represent the Protestantism he advocates. The Lutheran or even the magisterial Reformed traditions, never mind the Anglican tradition, would have to be viewed by implication as compromising a truly Protestant ecclesiology. But the argument is not presented at the level of a debate about polity. It is an argument at a deeper theological level, a theological doctrine of the church.

Baptism and Holy Communion (Chapters Five and Six)

The next two chapters take this thesis on ecclesiology into the area of sacramental theology, although, as we will see, Greggs rejects that terminology.

10. See for example, Schwanz and Coleson, *Missio Dei*, taking its approach from the work of Lesslie Newbigin.

Right at the beginning of Chapter Five, which is on baptism, he questions the category or genus of "sacrament," dismissing that as an ambiguous and unbiblical term. He traces the rise of "sacrament" as a genus from Hippolytus and Tertullian, but there is no such category in Scripture. He advocates regarding baptism and Holy Communion simply as dominically ordered "practices" in order to avoid the "magical" or "mystical" view. He writes:

> Certainly. it should not be doubted that something particular happens in baptism and something particular in Holy Communion, but these particulars are not the same particular: these actions do not belong uniquely to the same genus (158)

I am not sure that Greggs make it clear exactly what happens. But still more problematical for him is the definition of the sacraments as "means of grace." Greggs rejects Wesley's use of the definition of a sacrament in the *Book of Common Prayer*: "an outward sign of an inward grace, and a *means* by which we receive the same."[11] He notes what he regards as the unhelpful historical link between the administration of sacraments and a clerical priesthood.

Baptism Greggs regards as *a human* act in response to *the Spirit's* act. It is a sign "to the individual being baptized, to the community of baptism, and to the world for which the church exists as a provisional proleptic representation of the kingdom" (166). Divine and human agencies are asymmetrical so that individuals are caught up in the movement of the Spirit. Thus. the human act of baptism is within the divine act. To present oneself for baptism is a sign that the baptism of the Spirit has already occurred (168). Baptism is "entry into the corporate priesthood", or better, "a sharing in Christ's priestly life and ministry" (176). It is a movement from being a person whose primary identity is as an individual, to one whose primary identity is now in Christ (178).

This new identity challenges the "quotidian givenness of the world" in three ways. First, it is a new identity involving reconciliation not only with God but horizontally with the human other. As entry into the church catholic it can only take place once: there can be no provisional baptism or rebaptism. Secondly, it is "worked out in defiance of the fallen relations of power, hierarchy, and privilege," the "dynamics of the *cor incurvatum in*

---

11. I am sympathetic to this rejection of the Augustinian notion of grace as some kind of entity or force or medicine, an impersonal concept which appears to go back to Plotinus's notion of the impersonal force emanating from "the One" down through the Neoplatonist pantheistic cosmos. See Burns, "Grace," 391–98.

se." A church of "boring, monotonous homogeneity" replicates the power dynamics of societies based on class, gender, race, ability and so forth (187–88). Thirdly, the community of the baptized is that of the new humanity, Christ's true humanity "turned outwards from the *cor incurvatum in se*" (189). That means, fourthly, that this community is called always to reach beyond its bounds.[12]

The chapter on the Holy Communion explicitly adopts a Zwinglian position in contrast not only to transubstantiation and consubstantiation, but differentiating it from that of Calvin. Holy Communion is symbolic, not a sacrifice, and "This is my body," is to be understood figuratively. It is only in the context of the congregation, being together *as the body of Christ* that there is Holy Communion, that it has meaning for the individual: "The real presence of Christ is the presence of his body in the community of the church" (203). It does not replicate or repeat or effect salvation in any way (212), but the Spirit is at work in the believer enabling her to see what the bread and wine symbolize and to receive them, feeding on them in her heart in faith. Again, we see the double agency, the human act within the act of the Spirit. As we participate, we are bound to one another in space-time and the hearts of the believers are turned outwards from the *cor incurvatum in se*. Greggs quotes Donald Baillie that it is not individual ministers who celebrate the sacraments, but the whole church.[13]

There is much here which we would recognize as a common Protestant position. But if there is much that Protestants hold in common here over against catholic positions, Greggs seems to make a point of dismissing "the more Calvinist elements" in Donald Baillie's doctrine of the sacraments, but he does not specify what these are.[14] It is worth noting that

12. A brief section on the baptism of infants takes the position that while the baptism of believers is the theological norm, the baptism of infants is a sign particularly of the prevenient grace of God and is *permissible* but not necessary. A final section meditates on the suitability and worldliness of water.

13. On the last point, I was reminded of an incident some decades ago, sitting at morning coffee in the Rainy Hall in New College with Prof. Alex Cheyne when someone announced college communion and named the "celebrant." Looking characteristically over his spectacles, Prof. Cheyne remarked quietly to me: "I trust we shall *all* be celebrating!"

14. Baillie, *The Theology of the Sacraments*. Baillie quotes the Westminster Confession: "Worthy receivers, outwardly partaking of the visible elements in this sacrament, do then also inwardly by faith, really and indeed, yet not carnally and corporally, but spiritually, receive and feed upon Christ crucified, and all the benefits of his death: the body and blood of Christ being then not corporally or carnally in, with, or under the

Calvin's doctrine became the position of the Church of England at the Reformation, and so the view of John Wesley.[15] That is the doctrine of the "real presence of Christ," not physically contained in the elements, but his "spiritual presence," that is, his presence in the power of the Holy Spirit. Geoffrey Bromiley suggested a more developmental view here: that Calvin was developing a doctrine of the real presence of Christ, not physically, but in the power of the Holy Spirit, which was not clearly present in Zwingli's early reaction against the notion of the physical presence of the body of Christ in the Roman mass, but which Zwingli was developing before his untimely death.[16]

To think of the work of the Spirit as occurring only subjectively in the heart of the believer would surely be the Protestant individualism which Greggs wants to avoid. Surely. we need to speak of the Spirit present and active not merely in the individual and not only in the physical elements, but also in the whole action, the gathering of the community of the church around the table, the words and the actions of the breaking of the bread, the pouring out of the wine—all of which must precede the

bread and wine; yet as really, but spiritually, present to the faith of believers in that ordinance, as the elements themselves are to their outward senses" (Chapter XXIX, vii). Baillie asks: "Is that a subjective or an objective presence? Of course it is objective. To say that it is merely subjective would mean that we *imagine* Christ to be there though He is not really there. To say 'subjective' would be to deny that very objectivity and prevenience of the divine of which it is the very function of the sacraments to remind us" (97).

15. Cf. Parris, *John Wesley's Doctrine of the Sacraments*, 89: "This view, of a real but spiritual presence, is much closer to Calvin, as mediated through the Anglican Reformers, particularly Hooker, than to either that of Luther or Zwingli." See also Borgen, *John Wesley on the Sacraments,* who like Parris refutes the claim of Franz Hildebrandt that Wesley held a Lutheran view. See also Maddox, *Responsible Grace: John Wesley's Practical Theology,* 202–205; Collins, *The Theology of John Wesley,* 259–262. Charles Wesley expresses it dramatically: "Ah, tell us no more/ The spirit and power/ of Jesus, our God,/ Is not to be found in this life-giving blood! 'Tis God we believe,/ who cannot deceive,/ The witness of God/ Is present, and speaks in the mystical Blood. Receiving the bread,/ On Jesus we feed:/ It doth not appear, His manner of working—but/ Jesus is here!"

16. See Bromiley's Introduction to Zwingli's treatise, "On the Lord's Supper" in *Zwingli and Bullinger,* 183: "For Zwingli does not dispute that Christ is truly present in the Supper. What he disputes is that he is substantially present, present in the substance of his flesh and blood, present after his human nature. . . After the Ascension he was still present, but spiritually. That thought of the spiritual presence of Christ is not emphasized, indeed it is almost taken for granted, for it was not a point at issue." The issue was Christological: was Christ present in his human nature as well as in his divine nature? "Even if Zwingli was wrong, it is still true that he had no wish to deny the presence of Christ altogether, and the reality of the spiritual presence of Christ involves something far more than a bare memorialism."

individual participation. We do not create the presence of the risen Christ subjectively by participating in the power of the Spirit. Rather the Spirit is already objectively present, and by his presence and power, acknowledged in the *epiclesis*, the risen Christ is objectively present in the power of his Holy Spirit as we symbolically represent his death in the fracture and the outpouring. How can the risen Christ be absent? Was the early Zwinglian position not over-reacting so much to catholic views that it neglected the real presence of the risen LORD in the midst of his church, a view which Calvin more fully developed?[17]

The Communion of Saints, Intercessory Prayer, and Thanksgiving and Praise (Chapters Seven, Eight and Nine)

Time and space forbid a full treatment of the next three chapters, Chapter Seven on "The Communion of Saints," Chapter Eight on "Intercessory Prayer," and Chapter Nine on "Thanksgiving and Praise." In Chapter Seven, the church is provisional and temporal whereas the communion of saints is "everlasting and universal" (251). This seems to imply that we are not to speak of the church triumphant, the bride of Christ at the Last Day. This might also be the place to note again that Greggs treats the Day of Pentecost as the initiation of the church: there is no consideration (at least in this volume) of the church's relation to Israel as the *qahal* of God, the olive tree into which we gentiles are grafted.

---

17. See Alastair Heron's discussion of this in *Table and Tradition*. According to Heron, while Calvin disagrees with Luther on the ubiquity of Christ's humanity and on any notion of consubstantiation, he agrees with Luther (and indeed with the medieval Catholic theology) on the objective presence of Christ at the Supper. "Genuine participation in the body and blood of Christ through the signs, which are certainly to be *distinguished* but not *separated* from the reality joined to them, constitutes the heart of the matter; and it is very apparent here how far Calvin is from Zwingli. He also firmly rejects Zwingli's earlier reduction of a sacrament to an expression of faith: this, as he had already stated in the 1536 *Institute*, is to make what is a genuine but secondary element in a sacrament the only one, to overlook that a sacrament is primarily God's sign of his promise, given precisely to awaken and strengthen faith. Along the same line lies his insistence that the Eucharist is a *mystery*, and his implicit subordination of *explanation* to *apprehension, recognition, acceptance* of the mystery of communion with Christ. There is also a special weight in his insistence that the Eucharist is "spiritual" because it is *the Spirit of God* who brings about the union between Christ and us" (Heron, 126). Like Bromiley, Heron sees the recognition of the role of the Spirit as "a deepening of Zwingli's argument."

In Chapter Eight, the church participates in the priestly ministry of Christ praying to "Our Father" when it engages in intercessory prayer. In Chapter Nine, thanksgiving and praise are considered as "participating graciously in grace." A question arises here as to how Chapter Nine in the projected Volume Three, which is on worship, will differ from this chapter on praise. But another larger question occurs here. Whereas intercessory prayer is seen as participating in the priestly intercession of Christ, no role seems to be given here to our High Priest leading us in our praise. Rather this is seen within the horizon, present throughout the book, of human action as occurring within the context of the grace of God. I detect here a Wesleyan doctrine of prevenient grace (with which of course I am fully in agreement). But the question arises: where in this chapter is the book's overall Christological principle of the priesthood of Christ? The priesthood is intimately connected with his humanity: as priest he not only represents God to us, but us to God. And if he is truly our human priest, does he not then lead us not only in our intercessions but also in our praise? Since the Trinitarian doctrine of worship as participating by the Spirit in the Son's communion with the Father was developed so fully by the Torrance brothers (particularly James Torrance at Aberdeen), this seems to call out for attention.[18]

The Congregation, Sanctification and Love (Chapters Ten, Eleven and Twelve)

Chapter ten turns our attention to "the primary form of polity for the church," namely the gathered community or congregation, too often ignored in ecclesiologies which focus on the clergy and orders of ministry and so "a vastly underdeveloped topic" in ecclesiology (333).[19] For Paul, the church exists in the coming together or congregating of the believers. "In the congregation," Greggs writes, "the most intimate and intensive moments of thanksgiving and intercession, initiation and sustaining, confession and forgiveness take place" (339). The believer is freed from preoccupation with

18. See J. B. Torrance, *Worship, Community and the Triune God of Grace*; Navarro, *Trinitarian Doxology*. Greggs refers to J. B. Torrance's book on p. 391.

19. This move was made by the Roman Catholic Church at Vatican II in the document *Lumen Gentium* in which the old institutional and hierarchical ecclesiology was replaced with the notion of the "people of God," a pilgrim people on their way to the heavenly city.

individual salvation and self, turned outwards and delivered from the *cor incurvatum in se* in the form of saving one's own soul. But this deliverance extends to the congregation in that whereas most communities exist for the sake of the individual or the collective self, the church is not a homogeneous religious club. Greggs is not advocating Congregationalism, a polity which can result in "clotted individualism" (Forsyth). He uses the relationship between the congregations in Jerusalem and Antioch in the book of Acts as a model for how congregations might relate within "connections" (a very Methodist word) or denominations. Gregg's focus on the congregation is surely wise and appropriate. Those of us who move in theological colleges and conferences and presbytery or synodical meetings so easily forget that the only experience of the church known to most Christians is the experience of being part of a local congregation. Greggs has surely done us a great service in directing our thinking to the dynamics within the congregation as a fundamental part of ecclesiology.

Somewhat surprisingly in a work on ecclesiology, the next two chapters are entitled "Sanctification" and "Love," two topics which in our Protestant way we have generally considered individualistically. Considering sanctification in the corporate dimension of the church is strongly to be welcomed, and Greggs finds a fundamental agreement in Luther, Wesley, and Barth on the absolute priority of divine grace, on the postlapsarian condition of humanity, and on the life of sanctification as a life of continuous repentance (371–376). It is undoubtedly valuable to get away from the often individualistic, subjectivist thinking on Christian sanctification and set it in the corporate context of the church. At the same time, if this is deliverance from the *cor incurvatum in se*—clearly a problem of the heart, the inner motivation, then this cannot be an "either-or," but it must be "both-and."

Further, is there not more to say about the sanctification of the church corporately? Do we not also need to consider here the corporate sin of the church? Are there not those who have suffered from horrendous congregational splits, from unfair dismissal, from pharisaic pride, or from racial or class prejudice, from church politics, from financial mismanagement, or from delayed justice in church courts? If we are going to think about corporate sanctification, it would be good to consider how the corporate church is *simul iustus et peccator*. Finally, the Chapter on sanctification continues a major theme of the book by turning us outside-in to consider sanctification as not for our own sake within the church, but for the world.

That leads on neatly to Chapter Twelve on "Love," marked as "one of three culminating chapters to the whole book." Clearly for someone in the Wesleyan tradition—and indeed anyone who understands the whole Augustinian tradition—this is intimately and intricately connected to the theme of sanctification. Where for some traditions, sanctification may be discussed in the very sensible practicalities of self-discipline,[20] Wesley was the heir of the Augustinian model that the only antidote to the *concupiscentia* or self-centredness of the *cor incurvatum in se* was *caritas,* God's love . . . poured into our hearts through the Holy Spirit which has been given to us (Rom 5:5, Augustine's favourite text). Wesley's theology has been called "a theology of love" and as such was deeply influenced by the Augustinian tradition.[21] Greggs proceeds here by considering 1 John (Wesley's favorite epistle) and its theme of perfection in love. He puts this in Trinitarian context, writing: "Love is the very being and activity of God's life *in se* as the Father loves the Son and the Son loves the Father in the bond of love, who is the Holy Spirit" (409).

Priestly Catholicity in the One Church
(Chapters Thirteen and Fourteen)

Chapter thirteen, the final major chapter, is entitled "Priestly Catholicity" and here the theme of this volume is summarized. The claim is that catholicity and priesthood . . . have a resonance with each other. For fifteen hundred years catholicity has been indexed to priesthood, understood as the priesthood of the so-called clergy, linked to altars and sacrifices and monepiscopal hierarchical structure. Here in this book, priesthood has been explored in a more overtly and determinately Protestant way, pushing Magisterial Protestant theology beyond its own bounds. The essential priesthood of the church has been understood not inwardly but as an expression of the outward movements of grace. The catholicity of the church is grounded in the perfect high priesthood of Christ. This is not necessarily to reject the threefold order of bishop, presbyter, and deacon, which may have practical value, but to reject it as grounds for catholicity. By virtue of the oneness of Christ, there can only be one church, but participating in the priesthood of Christ must mean that the church exists for the world. Greggs

20. As in Ryle, *Holiness*; and Packer, *A Passion for Holiness*.

21. See Wynkoop, *A Theology of Love*; Noble, "East and West in the Theology of John Wesley," 359–72; Noble, *Holy Trinity, Holy People*, chaps. 3, 4 and 5.

calls therefore for an active, loving and dynamic catholicity. He takes Wesley's great sermon, "Catholic Spirit" as his basis here.[22] As the twentieth-century ecumenical movement had its roots in the evangelical movement, this sermon may indeed be regarded as a great manifesto for the united catholicity of the church. It is not latitudinarian: doctrine matters and truth matters. But catholicity is not about uniformity but about the Christian life. Wesley takes his text from II Kings 10, the words of Jehu to Jehonadab: "Is thine heart right as my heart is with thy heart? If it be, give me thine hand." "Give me thine hand" implies a catholicity which consists in love between Christians of different traditions, praying for other traditions, and directing good works toward other traditions.

This leads to the final chapter, a coda on the fourth mark of the church, the church as one, which will be the theme of the final chapters in all three volumes. The Trinitarian context is briefly noted in the thesis statement, and catholicity is seen as a proleptic anticipation of the eschatological unity which will be ours in Christ. This will reflect the loving unity of the Holy Trinity to which all present polities move. We are reminded that priestly catholicity is only one of the three irreducible narratives and that even these three are not an exhaustive account of the doctrine of the church, but a partial attempt from one (Protestant) perspective which the author trusts will be given a loving response from other traditions. Ultimately the oneness of the church rests on the "complex" simplicity of the oneness of God (458).

Conclusion and Questions Arising

As a final response I echo the commendations of David Fergusson, Susan Durber, Gregory Jones, David Ford, Iain Torrance, and Rachel Muers. Arising from the stimulating richness of this volume, our conversation could address some questions which we may profitably discuss:

- how this ecclesiology. rich in its resources in pneumatology and Christology, could be placed structurally in the context of the full doctrine of the Trinity

- how the doctrine of the church, initiated by the coming of the Spirit at Pentecost, is related to priestly Israel as the assembly of God under the old covenant

22. Outler, "Catholic Spirit," 79–95.

- whether the two dominical sacraments recognized by the Reformers do not have a particular shape and form reflecting the heart of the Christian gospel in the cross and the resurrection and therefore constitute a particular genus

- whether we should not prefer Calvin's development of the Zwinglian position on the LORD's Supper in order to assert more clearly the "real presence" of the risen LORD in the power of the Holy Spirit (as endorsed by the Anglican tradition and Wesley)

- whether there could be further development of the role of Christ as our human high priest leading us not only in our intercessions but in our praise and worship

- whether we need to develop more fully what it means for the church to be corporately holy by recognizing its structural sin as *simul iustus et peccator,* and its ongoing need for the sanctifying work of the Holy Spirit to deliver us from the corporate *cor incurvatum in se* and to fill us with the perfect love of God

- whether the dimension of mission might be developed, reflecting on current writing in missiology.

But the very raising of these questions indicates what a rich and fertile presentation of the priestly catholicity of the church is presented in this volume. The main thrust of the argument, that priestly catholicity is not a matter of polity or structures or of the three traditional orders of bishop, priest, and deacon, or of the church controlling entry to the sacraments and to salvation, but is a matter of the church's priestly existence in Christ to serve the world, is surely a rich and relevant characterization of the heart of a "Protestant" ecclesiology.

Response to Professor Tom Noble

Dogmatic Ecclesiology Volume 1, *The Priestly Catholicity of the Church*

Tom Greggs

Introduction

IT IS A PARTICULAR honor to have had two chapters dedicated to my overly long book on ecclesiology in this volume of essays arising from the Edinburgh Dogmatics Conference. Professor Noble's chapter on my book, which is more gracious than I deserve, is a perfect example of the best of what one can hope for from a reviewer. I am deeply grateful to him for such a careful, thoughtful, and thought-provoking paper. It is always a particular joy and privilege to learn something more about one's own thinking and commitments from the reflection upon one's work by another, and this has certainly been the case in reading these reflections on my book. It is also a particular delight to be able to dialogue with a fellow Wesleyan who has such respect for the Reformation and for Calvin. There are far too few of us who realize that, after Karl Barth and T. F. Torrance, many of the old arguments between Arminians and Calvinists are—if not redundant—very much relativized. Professor Noble's voice has been so helpful, and one of the positives of writing a multi-volume work is that one can learn, react to and be informed by the wisdom and reflections of others. And it is particularly heartening to know that some of the questions which are offered pre-empt some of the issues which I hope to address in the volumes which will follow.

I want in this chapter to do three things. First, I want to offer some thoughts and reflections on some of the questions that Professor Noble raised. Second, and within these reflections, I will offer some brief (somewhat eschatological)! comments on where the next two volumes of my ecclesiology are likely to go in relation to some of these themes. Third, I have appended to this paper the provisional outline of the three volumes to give an indication of the direction my thinking is following. I have had to be more selective in my response than I would have hoped, and have orientated the comments I am offering on the fundamental issues of the trinity and the sacraments. Because I believe—as I have tried to show in the volume—in the significance of the inter-relation of doctrines to the form of doctrinal speech we offer, my conversations in this chapter have at times had to zoom out a lot first before zooming in. I hope this is not a negative from the point of view of this volume on ecclesiology, but the simple effect of my own commitment to the very "downstream" nature of ecclesiology as a doctrinal locus. In some sense, at least Professor Noble's questions and probes on trinity, are inviting comment on the schema I offer.

I wish I had time to offer broader comments on the whole range of themes raised in his chapter about my book. What I have learned from the insightful response by Professor Noble is a considerable amount about some of my own operative theological commitments which are not always as overt as I should make them. The question of the relationship of the *ekklesia* to the assembly of God in the Hebrew Bible is both something which I will, for example, look at more in the next volume of the book, *and* it displays my real concerns to guard against unbridled supersessionism in theology (concerns which are evident in other ways throughout *Dogmatic Ecclesiology Volume 1*). Similarly, my Methodist origins might well display more indebtedness to certain forms of "Radical" Reform's ecclesial conceptualization than I might be happy to admit: there is a lot of pleading at the start of the book about the being "Magisterial" in no small part to remind my own compatriots of the importance of the Reformers! It might be helpful for me to engage more critically with the sense in which I use the term "Magisterial":

The sense is not in the more Lutheran sense of a lasting, "universal" confessional tradition, nor in the more Reformed sense of a provisional and temporally and geographically situated confession. Instead, the language [of Magisterial] is used to demarcate against federated, or congregational, or radical, or independent evangelical accounts which are more narrowly construed and do not necessarily afford as much authority to the theological traditions of the past. 'Magisterial Protestant' is not used, therefore, in reference to any one person or several identified people who serve to be the *magistri* delimiting (whether in a Lutheran or Reformed way) the theology of the church by its confessional standards. Rather, it is used in the sense that those we call the Magisterial Reformers themselves left a deposit of texts and teachings which serve as the *magister*. Even in their abilities not to agree, these texts are indicative of a way of thinking about the faith, doctrine and the church which demonstrate a resonance and clear family resemblance . . . Of course, this understanding in itself believes a more Pietistic (rather than legal or confessional) and Methodist appropriation of that tradition, but it also opens up the possibilities of engaging across Protestant confessional divides. At times (as with, for example, discussions of holy communion or the priesthood of Christ), dogmatic decisions are made as to which of these texts and traditions are most helpful, but it is hoped this is done [in the book] with a degree of generosity and open-handedness.[1]

While these might be interesting points of discussion, in this chapter itself, I am limiting myself to two principal areas I think are particular "touch points" of ecclesiological discussion. Moreover, they themselves arise out of something I have also learned from Professor Noble: my commitment (since my doctorate) to attempt as far as possible not to be polemical and not to be overtly negative about those with whom I engage, or avenues I do not pursue. Some of this comes from my sense of the task of theology which the coda at the end of my book discusses.[2] My desire largely to state what I believe positively, I realize, leaves very open the questions of why I have not taken the paths I have avoided. It is two of these paths I wish to explore in relation to the issues raised in the review of my book.

1. This is a slightly rewritten version of a footnote Greggs, *The Priestly Catholicity of the Church*, xlvii n.46.

2. Greggs, *Dogmatic Ecclesiology*, vol. 1, 451–60; cf. Greggs, "On the Nature, Task and Method of Theology."

Trinity, Father, and Worship

I am very grateful for Professor Noble's series of probes on the "invisible Father," the trinity and the priestly mediation of praise. Indeed, I am very much reminded of a conversation I had with my late teacher, mentor, colleague, and friend, John Webster, just ten days before he died. John told me (sadly in light of what was to happen to him) in his inimitable Yorkshire manner that it would be "my funeral" if I started with the volume I did—rather than the third volume which considers more fully (as you will see from the outline) the Spirit within the immanent trinity. The chapter on the Spirit in the first volume which Professor Noble has reviewed considers the Spirit who is the LORD and Life Giver—the divinity of the Spirit and the Spirit as the one who brings life to the creaturely, works in creaturely media, and who creates the church. But it will be the third volume which will address the Holy Spirit "who with the Father and Son is to be worshiped and glorified." This volume will require a more detailed engagement with the immanent life of the trinity. This trinitarian discussion is something I believe is best fitted for the end of the trilogy. I will try to explain briefly why I believe this.

There is clearly a dogmatic decision in topography and order to my ecclesiology, and this is of some importance to the way I've conceived the project. While, as I hope the coda at the end explains, I sit lightly to a reductionist approach of systematics and dogmatics which says it "must only be done thus," and while I believe that the different orderings of different doctrines will offer a distinctly different texture or form of the particular dogmatic res being discussed,[3] *Dogmatic Ecclesiology* is focused on the church's ontology and divine operation *in the economy of salvation*. In one sense I am starting *in via*, in the middle in my discussion of the life of the church. In part, this is because I am not sure I believe that we can so easily separate the order of knowing and the order of being straightforwardly. There are multiple reasons for this. First and most profoundly, for me, the Scriptures themselves do not do this: there is no real discussion of God's life *in se* aside from the economy of God, aside from God's gracious relationship to creation. Even in speaking of the absolute ontological distinction of Creator and creature, there is a presupposed relationality: *Creator* is a *relational* term as well as a means of protecting the absolute qualitative

---

3. On this theme see Methodist theology, see my "The Nature, Task and Method of Theology."

distinction between God and humanity. Even in the theophanies in the Bible, there are those who receive the vision, and even then, they do not tend to see much. Second, in *speaking* of God *in se*, we are still dependent on the *we* who speak: we cannot speak of the life of God or of divine aseity without realizing that even to speak in such terms presupposes the gracious reconciliation and revelation of God. God, we might say, in God's eternal life is now never without God's creature: there is no way of conceiving the eternality and constancy of the divine life without recognizing the eternal determination of God towards all that is not God in the gracious economy of creation, reconciliation, and redemption.[4] Part of the *properly theological* commitment of this book is the *eternal* significance of the Spirit's economic life for the way we think about the divine life and the economy; and, in that sense, the need always to realize that even as we think in the order of being the priority of the self-sufficient plenitude of God's life, that order of being is still shaped by (and cannot abstractly escape from) the revealedness of the divine life, known within the church by the Spirit's grace, and received by us as creatures.

As I attempt to argue throughout my book, we might say this in the following terms. Materially, in the order of being, ecclesiology (the doctrine of the church) is a derivative doctrine of economic pneumatology (the doctrine of the events of the Holy Spirit) which is itself a derivative doctrine of the doctrine of appropriations (the doctrine of attribution of specific works to individual persons of the Trinity) *and* the doctrine of ontological pneumatology (the doctrine of the person of the Holy Spirit). The doctrine of appropriations is a derivative doctrine of the doctrine of the economic Trinity. The doctrine of the economic Trinity and the doctrine of ontological pneumatology are derivative doctrines of the doctrine of the immanent Trinity and the principle *omnia opera trinitatis ad extra indivisa sunt*. The doctrine of the immanent Trinity establishes that all of God's ways with the world are ways of sheer, superabundant and free grace. But to reflect on the church, on the Spirit, on the revealedness of God, to my mind requires a need to consider the eternal determination of God to be God *in this way* in the event of the act of the Spirit in the life of the church. I think I am with Barth in saying, we cannot, therefore, ever consider who God is *in abstracto* apart from and outside the acts and works of God: "God is God

---

4. This is a theme I have addressed at length in my earlier book, *Barth, Origen, and Universal Salvation: Restoring Particularity*. I also have a forthcoming collection of essays addressing many of these themes to be published later this year by T. & T. Clark.

in the very fact, and in such a way, that He does stand in this relation, in a definite relationship with the other."[5] To go behind this free but definite decision is to venture into abstraction from the living life of faith—a matter which is particularly significant it seems to me in dogmatic reflection on the church. We can only speak from the works of God, knowing from this divine relating to creation the attitude God has in God's act in grace and which God has revealed to the creature. It is necessary, therefore, to deal with the Christian God in the *relationship* God establishes—"a relationship outside of which God no longer wills to be and no longer is God, and within which alone He can be truly honored and worshipped as God."[6] Building on the work of my great colleague at Aberdeen, Paul Nimmo, and his helpful claim that we cannot abstract the person of the Spirit from the Spirit's work within the church and that we are wise to think of the Spirit as eternally *inecclesiandus*,[7] this relationship of the Spirit to the life of the church is, because the Spirit is constant and faithful, "an actuality which can neither be suspended nor dissolved."[8] There is no way for us to go behind that. The church rests as an event on the act of the Holy Spirit, but the Spirit—who is Holy—is faithful to the Spirit's self and to the constancy of the Spirit's act. In other words, the "being" of the church as an event is held not in its own institutions but in the reality that the One whose act brings it into being is the eternal God who is faithful and unchanging in the person of the Holy Spirit. This is not only significant for the church, but also for our conceptualization of God. And this itself has implications for the way we think about the trinity. Despite our unhelpful propensities to do so, we must be alert to our incapacity to act as if there were two trinities (one immanent and the other economic) or as if it were not as a result of the economy of the trinity's life we can even begin to hesitatingly speak of the life of God's immanence—only because God does not only live *in se* can we hesitatingly reflect on the significance of divine aseity.

Of course, there is the danger of falling prey to what I consider some of the errors of Schleiermacher's theology in such a dogmatic topography. Karl Barth himself suggested that if he were to start all over again that he

5. Barth, *Church Dogmatics*, II/2, 6.

6. Barth, *Church Dogmatics*, II/2, 7.

7. See Nimmo, "Barth and the Election-Trinity Debate," in *Trinity and Election in Contemporary Theology.*

8. Barth, *Church Dogmatics*, II/2, 7. Barth uses this phrase about the covenant of God with humanity in Jesus Christ. The logics of it are, however, being applied here in relation to the Spirit and the church.

would have written from the dominant perspective of the Holy Spirit, but stated that it was perhaps too close to the time of Schleiermacher to do this. I am certainly concerned that there might be any sublation of the human and the divine spirit which I think might well be the case for liberal theologies which followed from Schleiermacher. However, and while this is not vogue in the neo-scholastic context of much contemporary systematic theology, I do think there is wisdom in Schleiermacher's approach of culminating in the doctrine of the trinity, rather than seeing the doctrine of the divine life *in se* as the foundation; and I think this particularly because the point for Schleiermacher is that having read *The Christian Faith* forwards to the culmination in the doctrine of the trinity, it is necessary then to read the book backwards from the doctrine of the trinity.[9] This commitment to not being able to separate the order of knowing and the order of being straightforwardly is one which I think is particularly important in terms of any modern account of the triune life of God. But any more on this would be another (very long and complex) paper.

However, Professor Noble's paper also poses the question about the trinitarian form more narrowly in terms of social trinitarianism. In one sense, my answer to this is quite straightforward: as a Western theologian, indebted to the Reformation and the Augustinianism behind it, I am not sure I am best resourced by social trinitarianism. In a more critical tone, I am actually somewhat troubled by modes of thinking that consider too strong an analogy (indeed, to the extent that sometimes it passes almost beyond analogy towards something more akin to univocacy) between God and things in creation—too strong an analogy between divine persons and creaturely persons, too strong an analogy between divine relations and human relations. Indeed, in this way, I find myself—having originally been a patrologist before turning to the "dark arts" of systematics—ironically very heavily influenced by the Cappadocians, heroes supposedly of social trinitarians everywhere. I simply do not see the Cappadocians doing what the social trinitarians argue they are doing—quite the opposite. I agree with the argument of Zizoulas that the Cappadocians brought about a revolution in the way in which ontology was considered, but they did this always with regard to the considering the dis-similarity of the divine essence and creaturely essence, of the acts of God and the essence of God, of speech about

---

9. A very good account of this is offered by Shelli Poe in *Essential Trinitarianism: Schleiermacher as Trinitarian Theologian.*

what we might induce from the economy not deduce from the essence. To give just one example from Basil:

> The activities are various, and the essence simple; but we say that we know God from his activities, but do not undertake to approach near to his essence. His activities ('energies') come down to us, but his essence remains beyond our reach. ['Αλλ' αἱ μὲν ἐνέργειαι ποικίλαι, ἡ δὲ οὐσία ἁπλῆ. Ἡμεῖς δὲ ἐκ μὲν τῶν ἐνεργειῶν γνωρίζειν λέγομεν τὸν Θεὸν ἡμῶν, τῇ δὲ οὐσίᾳ αὐτῇ προσεγγίζειν οὐχ ὑπισχνούμεθα. Αἱ μὲν γὰρ ἐνέργειαι αὐτοῦ πρὸς ἡμᾶς καταβαίνουσιν, ἡ δὲ οὐσία αὐτοῦ μένει ἀπρόσιτος (PG 32, 869 A-B)].

Or else, building on Origen, St Gregory reminds us that when we are *speaking* as creatures of the divine life, we are speaking of the *likeness* of the "gold" and not the "gold itself."[10] These fathers after all were the chief opponents of the Eunomians!

All of this is an historical way of saying (more dogmatically) that I am nervous that the uniqueness of God's own life is undermined in accounts which use creaturely relations to project our ideas of relationality onto God and then project those relations back onto creation. Whoever God is, God clearly is not a committee! And in a church which loves committees, I would want to do all I can to prevent justification of that form. But more significantly, such approaches not only often provide projections of bad relations onto God to create bad trinitarianism and bad social forms (see the eternal subordination and headship debates in the USA), but also engage in a form of unhelpful "cross and switch trick" projectionism. Karen Kilby puts this nicely:

> Now of course any language that is used about God is drawn from human experience in some way or other, and so it is arguable that in talk about God it is always a matter of saying that God is just like such-and-such that we know, only unimaginably more so. What is particularly distinctive about the social theorist's strategy, however, is that what is at its heart a suggestion to overcome a difficulty is presented as a key source of inspiration and insight. So the social theorist does not just say, perhaps the divine perichoresis, which we can understand as being akin to our best relationships, only better, makes the three Persons into one God; she goes on to say, should we not model our relationships on this wonderful thing, the divine perichoresis?

10. Cant. (GNO VI85,10–87,17; trans. Norris 95).

In short, then, I am suggesting we have here something like a three-stage process. First, a concept, perichoresis, is used to name what is not understood, to name whatever it is that makes the three Persons one. Secondly, the concept is filled out rather suggestively with notions borrowed from our own experience of relationships and relatedness. And then, finally, it is presented as an exciting resource Christian theology has to offer the wider world in its reflections upon relationships and relatedness.[11]

As someone who wishes to emphasize the uniqueness of the divine life, I am minded always to prioritize the internal processional relations (and the corresponding missions, and vice versa) in relation to the divine persons: persons are predicated in their relation. God is the One God in three relations: unbegotten, begotten and spiration. Although I would disagree with *some* of her presentation of Augustine and have questions about several aspects of her approach, Kate Sonderegger in her wonderful second volume of her *Systematic Theology* helpfully states this:

there is no separate Res, no distinct Object or Enumerable Nature that *is* Divine Person. A Divine Person is not a "Thing," so to say, that could be defined or characterized or studies—or counted even—apart from the Life that It perfects. Rather we see the Divine Fire *as a Whole*, a Perfection, and as an Infinite Life we do not know It exhaustively or completely. We know, rather, that It is Completed, an Absolute. Note the passive construction here. We cannot specify the Reality of this Perfection or articulate the "entire membership" of the Infinite Life; we do not know the Personal Processes "from the inside," as it were, from Its own Principles, as Thomas would style this. This is the Greater Unlikeness. We know and confess and adore Its Being Completed, the Persons' Consummation and Sabbath Rest. From the creaturely view we behold the Whole Life in Its Integrity, Its Termini, and we receive the New Name, ever Ancient, of Father, Son, and Spirit, all Holy, Thrice Holy.[12]

It is for these reasons, therefore, that I have derived my ecclesiology from economic pneumatology rather than the doctrine of the immanent trinity, and more specifically rather than a social trinitarian model.

In terms, furthermore, of where the Father is: He is there as the mysterious origin of these external, economic relations which are consistent

11. Kilby, "Perichoresis and Projection," 441–42.

12. Sonderegger, *Systematic Theology*, vol. 2, 554.

and constant with the missions. The Father is there in all trinitarian relations since *omnia opera trinitatis indivisa sunt*. The Father, we might say, is always not an independent person, but eternally the Father of Jesus Christ who with the Son sends the Holy Spirit: the Father is there in the Father's eternal relationality—naming the eternal relationship of unbegotteness in the divine life. But I am glad to have been pushed to articulate this more. There is real help in Professor Noble's challenge about praise and worship and priestly mediation on this front; and I am grateful. I think discussion of these matters is there in the sections on oblation and thanksgiving,[13] and some of the material on glory and on the reflections on Ephesians. But I can see how if this were a stand/alone volume, it would look very imbalanced. I hope that by the time we get to the third volume and deal with the glorification of the Spirit with the Son and Father and with worship, there might be a chance to rebalance things.

Enough on the trinity (so to speak)! that is a whole other book, but since I believe that ecclesiology is a downstream doctrine, I guess I should be more explicit about what I think is upstream, and what I hope I will come to more by the time I complete the third volume. And so now to more directly ecclesiological questions.

Sacraments: Genus, Real Presence, Means of Grace

Professor Noble raises a range of questions around what I prefer to think of as the "brave" rather than "radical" discussion of what is usually understood as sacramentology. There are a series of questions raised helpfully around the approach to sacraments in the volume: first in relation to my rejection of a genus, and second in relation to my preference in the volume for a Zwinglian—albeit I hope "high" Zwinglian—approach to Holy Communion. There is a lot to discuss here: whether Calvin's presence is quite as pervasive within our traditions as we often presume; whether Zwingli says what we often presume him to say; whether there is unity around the idea of two dominical sacraments within the Magisterial Protestant tradition. Each of these areas deserves a chapter in its own right, and I hope I will be forgiven for being brief around these complex matters.

With regard to the question of the genus, in some sense I am not terribly invested in this issue—which might be a surprise given it is a daring statement within the book. I am not terribly invested except that I do not

13. Greggs, *Dogmatic Ecclesiology*, vol. 1, chap. 9.

see the genus in any meaningful way in Scripture. What I guess I want to do is to say, therefore, that I do not think the genus *adds* anything, and may well detract from things we would want to say, and cause more problems for us than it solves. Looking at the particularity of both holy communion and baptism is, I feel, more theologically informative for all kind of reasons than long discussions about the genus. Furthermore, in a volume so determined not to be focused on *particular* forms of polity, I am nervous that often the demarcation of the genus is related to questions of presidency. I do not find those questions of order odious per se: order is an essential mark of the church since the gospel orders itself (something I will discuss in volumes 2 and 3); but arguments about particular order (which often slip in an oleaginous manner into discussion about distinctive priesthood of certain groups within the church) are ones I wish not to enter into.

But I have other questions about the genus as well. I wonder how well we are served by Luther's back and forth about two or three sacraments, and whether penance should be included. And I must say I find Calvin's discussion of the genus a bit of special bargaining. Fearful as I am of saying this in such a hallowed context of chapters by Reformed colleagues, the argument of Calvin seems to me to go: we can use the word "*sacramentum*" since it simply renders the word "*musterion*" into Latin, and the word "*musterion*" is all over Scripture—with multiple examples offered. So, says Calvin, we can call the LORD's Supper and baptism "sacraments" because there are so many texts in the New Testament which use "*musterion*." The problem is that Calvin never shows one instance of baptism or the LORD's Supper (as I can see) being called "*musterion*" in Scripture.[14] It is logically akin to saying, the word "apple" is used in scripture, so it is fine to call these two activities "apples," if I were to engage in a *reductio ad absurdum* argument. The only link which I can really see being made is in terms of circumcision as a *seal.* And one of my concerns has been to decouple baptism and circumcision.

But there are two other issues which are related and more significant, perhaps, than the genus question: first the question of "real" spiritual presence, and second whether baptism and holy communion are (within a genus) *particular* as a means of grace, and what we might mean by means of grace.

In terms of the real presence of Christ by the Spirit, I am really delighted to see Professor Noble framing the question in part in terms of the

---

14. Calvin, *Institutes of the Christian Religion*, IV.14.2.

resurrection. It is the theme of the resurrection in relation to holy communion and baptism which I wish to explore particularly in the second volume on which I am working at the moment—on prophetic apostolicity and the *encounter with the risen Christ who speaks prophetically in His resurrected life*. Volume 1 was concerned to try to think about corporate priesthood, and the demarcation of divine and human action seemed very important at this point—ensuring we do not confuse the priesthood of Christ and church with some notion of priestly efficacy in ecclesial practice. The once for all, completed aspect of all that Christ *has done* (read: "memorialism") seemed most important to emphasize here. However, in the next volume which will address much more overtly the church as *creatura verbi*, the *living encounter* through the Spirit with the resurrected and ascended Christ will be emphasized more as an expression in the present of the living Word whose presence is known by the Spirit. In one sense, there is an irony to the *Last* Supper: it is not the last meal Jesus shares with His disciples, but is, instead, succeeded by the meals He shares with His followers *at which he teaches* in His resurrection. It is, therefore, *under* a consideration of the living gospel and the living Word of God which I want to consider the real and living presence of Christ, so as not to separate communion from the Word or the gospel, and so as to retain what I think is the primary trope for all the Reformers of holy communion and baptism as the *visible Word*. This emphasis on the visible Word is the shared Augustinian heritage the Reformers have: in the communion, the gospel is present as *verbum visibile*.[15] We should remember that even for Calvin (who is at one end of the Reformed spectrum):

> We can therefore say, that in it the Lord displays to us all the treasures of his spiritual grace, inasmuch as he associates us in all the blessings and riches of our Lord Jesus. Let us recollect, then, that the Supper is given us as a mirror in which we may contemplate Jesus Christ crucified in order to deliver us from condemnation, and raised again in order to procure for us righteousness and eternal life. It is indeed true that *this same grace is offered us by the gospel*, yet as in the Supper we have more, ample certainty, and fuller enjoyment of it, with good cause do we recognize this fruit as coming from it.[16]

15. Augustine, *Tract 80 on Jn* 15:3.

16. John Calvin, *Short Treatise on the Support of Our Lord* (1541); emphasis added.

Calvin also writes, despite everything he is about to say about Holy Communion, in *The Institutes*:

> Now, from the definition I have set forth we understand that a sacrament is never without a preceding promise but is always joined *as a sort of appendix*, with the purpose of *confirming and sealing* the promise itself, and of *making it more evident to us* and *in a sense* ratifying it. By this means God provides first for our ignorance and dullness, then for our weakness.[17]

It is clear that sacraments (so called) are not separate or distinct from the gospel. They contain the "same grace [which] is offered us by the gospel" and are such as "a sort of appendix." Indeed, there is actually in *The Institutes* very limited discussion of Zwingli or Bucer, limited to discussion of the analogy of the soldier's oath and to a rather vague sentence with the idea that some of the positive contribution on the sacraments had been overlooked by Bucer and Zwingli.

I am tempted in light of some of the responses I've had to the book which have picked up on my Zwinglianism to wish that I'd have used Bullinger as my principal interlocutor here—not because I believe Bullinger makes the points I want to make any better than Zwingli, but because Bullinger is a much less contentious figure who has been much less misrepresented in most of the literature. Zwingli is in fact very clear that there is a real presence at the LORD's Table. In the Confession addressed to Francis I (one of the later things he wrote), he writes that Christ is not just present (per se) but present at the LORD's Table: "Christum credimus vere esse in coena immo non esse Domini coenam nisi Christus adsit." Zwingli's concern is just that we are not literally, physically eating the body of Christ; but he is happy to affirm the presence of Christ is there spiritually and that Christ is even consumed: "Adserimus igitur non sic carnaliter et crasse manducari corpus Christi in coena, ut isti perhibent, sed verum Christi corpus credimus in coena sacramentaliter et spiritualiter edi, a religiosa, fideli et sancta mente." Anderson Scott states in light of this: "We have here the assertion of the real presence of Christ in the Supper, and of that presence as essential to its validity; further, the assertion that the body of Christ is eaten in the Supper 'sacramentally and spiritually.'"[18] The same points about real presence are made in the articles on which Luther and Zwingli agreed (reflecting the same kinds of themes which can be found in Calvin).

17. Calvin, *Institutes*, IV.14.3.
18. Scott, "Zwingli's Doctrine of the Lord's Supper," 168.

The issue was whether the true body and blood were present *"coporaliter"* in the bread and wine.

Zwingli believed that he was following a deeply Augustinian approach to the communion. But more profoundly for him, it was Scripture that was the source of the argument he made. His key text was John 6:63: "It is the spirit that gives life; the flesh is useless." Peter Stephens (a predecessor of mine at Aberdeen who was also a Methodist) notes that this is "the key text for Zwingli . . . a wall of bronze which nothing can shake, let alone shatter . . . an unbreakable adamant which stands unshattered when attacked and shatters all weapons used against it."[19] The Spirit is the one who is dynamically at work, therefore, in the life of the church in the communion. Through this work of the Spirit, Zwingli is able to state: "by the signs themselves, the bread and wine, Christ himself is as it were set before our eyes, so that not merely with the ear, but with eye and palate we see and taste that Christ whom the soul bears within itself and in whom it rejoices."[20] Because of this, Stephens and Bromiley in their accounts can both argue that Zwingli never denied that Christ's body is truly, sacramentally, and mysteriously present in the supper. There is a "spiritual" and "sacramental" eating of Jesus Christ in the eucharist.

For me, in my own attempts to think with Zwingli, it is in the faithful "doing" of this act ("Do this in remembrance of me": Luke 22:19 and 1 Cor 11:14) by the community (not in the elements themselves) that Christ is commemorated, with the elements as symbols which metronymously serve the purpose of the commemoration. In commemorating this act of salvation completed once and for all in Christ within Christ's body, the church by the Holy Spirit remembers its own present existence as the body of Christ in which it actively participates as the Spirit frees it to share in Christ's humanity and priestly life. It is worth noting, indeed, that "commemoration" does not deny real presence. Commemoration is a biblical concept which actually involves *making present* in a manner which accords to the metronymous nature of the breaking of bread and sharing of wine: events are recalled—in the changing contexts of the here and now—before and in the eternal, constant and faithful presence of God, such that the effects of the events are operative and present now. For example, when Israel celebrates the Passover (to which the Last Supper is clearly related), there is a commemoration (*zikkaron*) of the liberation from Egyptian slavery, and

19. Stephens, *The Theology of Huldrych Zwingli*, 232.
20. Zwingli, *An Exposition of the Faith*, 248.

the Passover Haggadah contains the instruction:[21] "In every age everyone is bound to regard himself as if he himself had come out of Egypt."[22] In sharing symbolically in the bread and wine which metronymously commemorate the body and blood of Christ, through the Holy Spirit the body of Christ is actively present in the community of faith in its given historical and geographical present. But the key issue is the issue of divine sovereignty: even in these acts, God is sovereign and free, and our capacity to speak faithfully of the act's constancy stems from the constant faithfulness of the divine life not the actions of the human. This is a point which Bromiley and Bouvier consider key to both Zwingli and Bullinger. The practices are not themselves in their performance "*means* of grace."

My personal reason for following the approach I do in the book is to develop systematically my actualistic and event-orientated language as well as my nervousness of drawing "straight lines" from human action to God's action. Certainly, there will be a development and more positive unpacking in the following books on real presence (volume two) and the heavenly banquet (volume 3). But I remain concerned to retain this actualism and the primacy of divine sovereignty of God in relation to *all* the actions and activities of the church. I am very indebted here (again) to my colleague Paul Nimmo and a paper he gave at the Edinburgh Dogmatics Conference some years ago, which makes plain what is at stake in different Reformed approaches to the LORD's Supper. He makes plain, indeed, that Calvin should not always be considered the "go to" figure. Despite much of the literature, as Nimmo argues: "the characterization of the Reformed tradition as a whole as one in which the Eucharist is conceived in instrumentalist terms as a means of grace may have to be revised."[23] Here, Nimmo is building on Paul Rorem's taxonomy of Reformed approaches to the communion:

---

21. Jeremias and Leenhardt convincingly show that there are close parallels between the Haggadah and the words of institution at the LORD's Supper. See Jeremias, *The Eucharistic Words of Jesus*, esp. 41–49; Leenhardt, "This is My Body, esp. 39–40.

22. See Haag, *Clergy and Laity: Did Jesus Want a Two-Tier Church?*, 81; cf. Haag, *Gedächtnis, biblisch in Lexikon für Theologie und Kirche*, 4:570–72; Haag, *Vom alten zum neuen Pascha: Geschichte und Theologie des Osterfestes*, 115–17. There is worth in the translation of *anamnesis* by Gregory Dix, *The Shape of the Liturgy*, 161: "in the Scriptures both of the Old and New Testament, *anamnesis* and the cognate verb have the sense of 're-calling' or 're-presenting' before God an event of the past, so that it becomes *here and now operative by its effects*." See also the neat summary by Anthony C Thiselton in *Systematic Theology*, 332.

23. Nimmo, "The Eucharist in Post-Reformation Scotland," 479.

Does a given Reformed statement of faith consider the Lord's Supper as a testimony, an analogy, a parallel, even a simultaneous parallel to the internal workings of God's grace in granting communion with Christ? If so, the actual ancestor may be Heinrich Bullinger, Zwingli's successor in Zurich. Or does it explicitly identify the Supper as the very instrument or means through which God offers and confers the grace of full communion with Christ's body? The lineage would then go back to John Calvin, despite the opposition he faced among his Reformed brethren on this very point.[24]

The key distinction which exists within the Reformed tradition is nicely summarized in this way by Bryan Spinks: "Whereas Calvin (following Martin Bucer) could speak of sacraments as being instruments (*instrumenta*) and of exhibiting (*exhibent*) the grace they signify, Bullinger declined to use such language, allowing only that sacraments might be implements (*organa*), but his preferred terms were sign and signify."[25]

The issue of instrumentalism is that which I am trying to avoid, and why I am nervous of the category and language of sacraments as particular "means of grace" and of Calvin's approach. For Calvin, a sacrament is "a testimony of divine grace toward us, confirmed by an outward sign."[26] So far, I am agreed. But he also argues that the two sacraments are in a way which is particular to them "means and instruments of [God's] secret grace."[27] This is where I draw the line in my own theology.

But why, as Wesleyan, am I pointing all this out? The concern I have as a Methodist is two-fold. First, Wesley, as a pre-Tractarian High-Anglican, was Cranmerian. Methodist liturgy is such. All too often, Cranmer has been presented as a Calvinist on the grounds of his insistence (which Wesley follows) on the "real presence." But, as I've tried to show, that is not what is at stake between Calvin and Zwingli. The issue is the *instrumentalism* at play. While he has been critiqued (for political reasons more than historical or theological, it seems to me), Dom Gregory Dix clearly recognized this in his characterization of Cranmer and his liturgy.[28] The key distinction is the instrumentalism of Calvin's account. Wesley's (pre-Tractarian) high Anglicanism could very happily rest with Zwingli. Zwingli would have been

24. Rorem, "Calvin and Bullinger on the Lord's Supper," 384.

25. Spinks, *Do This in Remembrance of Me*, 278.

26. Calvin, *Institutes*, IV.14.1.

27. Calvin, "Exposition of the Heads of Agreement," 227.

28. Dix, *The Shape of the Liturgy*.

happy with Wesley's statement: "we learn that the design of this sacrament is, in the continual remembrance of the death of Christ, by eating bread and drinking wine, which are the outward signs of the inward grace, the body and blood of Christ."[29] Now, it is true that Wesley does use the language of means of grace: there is a whole sermon on this. But the question for me is not what does "means of grace" mean generally, but how is he using the term. It is, indeed, interesting to note that most English translations of Zwingli and Bullinger translate the term *organa* as "means" (the term in English which usually denotes "*instrumenta*"), and yet this is the key point of difference between Zwingli and Bullinger, on the one side, and Calvin on the other. This, therefore, is my second issue. For all that Wesley talks of "means," this is not in the usual instrumentalist manner in which most accounts of "means" operate. For Wesley, not only is there no objective, independent operation of God in the sacrament, but there is also no limitation of these means to the usual two dominical sacraments. Wesley lists a run of means of grace and not just the usual two. Furthermore, his discussion of the LORD's Supper *follows* Scripture and points in the very language of means to *remembrance*. This is much closer to the idea in Zwingli of the *implements* (*organa*) of grace than Calvin's *instrumenta*. And, most strangely—although Wesley discusses baptism at length at other points[30]—Wesley does not list baptism among the primary of these means. He instead states: "The chief of these means are prayer, whether in secret or with the great congregation; searching the Scriptures (which implies reading, hearing, and meditating thereon) and receiving the Lord's Supper, eating bread and drinking wine *in remembrance of him*; and these we believe to be ordained by God as ordinary channels of conveying his grace to the souls of men."[31]

What his discussion indicates is the care we need when we separate off "sacraments" into a separate genus from other marks and practices of the life of the church, or of affording them an (objective, perhaps)? instrumentalist status which is higher than all else. It is this point which brings us full circle into why I am concerned about the genus.

---

29. John Wesley, "The Duty of Constant Communion," Notably, Wesley's text for this sermon is: "do this in remembrance of me." There is very little mention of any language of means in this sermon—if any, in fact.

30. Wesley wrote on infant and adult baptism, and on the role of godparents, and famously altered the baptism liturgy in the *Book of Common Prayer* for his *Sunday Service* (1784).

31. Wesley, "The Means of Grace," 381.

Conclusion

I hope that in these reflections what I have shown minimally is how very seriously I have taken such an important review of the first volume of my *Dogmatic Ecclesiology*. These forays into detail might not only give a sense of the ways in which I think of the doctrine of the church as downstream from more foundational commitments, overtly why I have chosen not to take some of the paths available to me. Along the way, I have also hoped to give glimpses of where the next two volumes might go, and I am alert to all I can learn from reviews and the reflections of others along the way. I will certainly be taking into account the questions and points posed by Professor Noble, and already I can see the need for my account of the prophetic work of the church as involving speaking against structural and corporate sin within the church, and of both the affirmations and the concerns I have with aspects of the *missio dei* understanding of mission when I come to speak more of the trinity in volume 3; these are both points at which I will be glad to reference Professor Noble's insightful comments.

APPENDIX: Chart of Prospective Chapter Topics

	Volume 1: *Participating in Priestly Catholicity*	Volume 2: *Encountering Prophetic Apostolicity*	Volume 3: *Transforming into Kingly Holiness*
	Prolegomena		
Chapter 1	The Spirit: The Giver of Life	The Spirit: Spoke through the Prophets & The Apostles	The Spirit: Worshiped and Glorified
Chapter 2	The High Priesthood of Christ	Christ as Prophet	Christ the King
Chapter 3	Participative Ontology internal to the Church	Ontology of Encounter internal to the Church	Transformative Ontology internal to the Church
Chapter 4	The Priestly Life of the Church	The Prophetic Life of the Church	The Kingly Life of the Church
Chapter 5	Baptism: Entry into the Priesthood of the Church	Baptism: Encountering New Life in the Presence of Death	Baptism: Becoming a Child of God
Chapter 6	Holy Communion and Participation	Holy Communion and Encounter	Holy Communion and Transformation
Chapter 7	Communion of Saints	Forgiveness of Sins	Life Everlasting
Chapter 8	Intercessory Prayer	Penitential Prayer	Prayer of Worship & Adoration
Chapter 9	Thanksgiving & Praise	Preaching	Service
Chapter 10	Congregation	Order & Oversight	Pastoral Activity & Vocation
Chapter 11	Sanctification	Speaking the Truth	Transforming Power Relations
Chapter 12	Love	Faith	Hope
Chapter 13	Priestly Catholicity	Prophetic Apostolicity	Kingly Holiness
Chapter 14	Coda: The Church as One	Coda: The Church as One in Context	Coda: The Church as One in Penultimacy

Bibliography

Abbott, Walter, ed. *The Documents of Vatican II*. London: Chapman, 1967.

Aisthorpe, Steve. *The Invisible Church*. Edinburgh: St Andrew Press, 2016.

Ames, William. *The Marrow of Theology*. Translated by John Dykstra Eusden. Grand Rapids: Baker, 1968.

———. *The Marrow of Theology*. Translated by John Eusden. 1968. Reprint, Grand Rapids: Baker, 1997.

Arcadi, James M., and James T. Turner, Jr. eds. *T&T Clark Handbook of Analytic Theology*. T&T Clark Handbooks. London: T. & T. Clark, 2021.

Ascough, Richard S. *Paul's Macedonian Associations: The Social Context of Philippians and 1 Thessalonians*. WUNT 2/161. Tübingen: Mohr Siebeck, 2003.

Augsburg Confession VII.

Baillie, D. M. *The Theology of the Sacraments*. London: Faber & Faber, 1957.

Baillie, John. *Baptism and Conversion*. London: Oxford University Press, 1964.

Barth, Karl. *Church Dogmatics*. 14 vols. Edinburgh: T. & T. Clark, 1936–77.

———. *Church Dogmatics, II/2: The Doctrine of God, Part 2*. Edinburgh: T. & T. Clark, 1957.

———. *Church Dogmatics, IV/2: The Doctrine of Reconciliation, Part 2*. Edinburgh: T. & T. Clark, 1958.

———. *Church Dogmatics, IV/3: The Doctrine of Reconciliation, Part 3*. Edinburgh: T. & T. Clark, 1962.

———. *Church Dogmatics, IV/3.1*. Edinburgh: T. & T. Clark, 1962.

Basil the Great. *On the Holy Spirit*. Yonkers, NY: St Vladimir's Seminary Press, 2011.

Bavinck, Herman. *Reformed Dogmatics*. Vol. 1: *Prolegomena*. Grand Rapids: Baker, 2003.

———. *Reformed Dogmatics*. Vol. 3: *Sin and Salvation in Christ*. Grand Rapids: Baker, 2006.

Beasley-Murray, George R. *Baptism in the New Testament*. Exeter: Paternoster, 1972.

Beilby, James K., and Paul Rhodes Eddy, eds. *Justification: Five Views*. Spectrum Multiview Books. Downers Grove, IL: InterVarsity, 2011.

Berkhof, Hendrikus. *Christian Faith:An Introduction to the Study of the Faith*. Grand Rapids: Eerdmans, 1979.

———. *The Doctrine of the Holy Spirit*. Richmond, VA: John Knox, 1964.

Bévenot, Maurice. *De Unitate Ecclesiae, 6 in Cyprian, The Lapsed; the Unity of the Catholic Church*. London: Longmans, Green, 1957.

Black, David Alan, ed. *Perspectives on the Ending of Mark: Four Views*. Nashville: B&H, 2008.

Bolt, John. *Reformed Dogmatics: Holy Spirit, Church and New Creation.* Vol. 4. Grand Rapids: Baker, 2008.

Borgen, Ole E. *John Wesley on the Sacraments.* Grand Rapids: Asbury, 1972.

Bosch, David J. *Transforming Mission: Paradigm Shifts in Theology of Mission.* Maryknoll, NY: Orbis, 1991.

Bray, G. L. *The Church.* Grand Rapids: Baker, 2016.

Bromiley, Geoffrey W. *Zwingli and Bullinger.* London: Westminster, 1953.

Brunner, Emil. *The Christian Doctrine of the Church, Faith and the Consummation: Dogmatics,* Vol. 3. London: Lutterworth, 1962.

——. *The Misunderstanding of the Church.* Translated by Harold Knight. London: Lutterworth, 1952.

Burns, J. Patout. *Augustine through the Ages: An Encyclopedia.* Edited by Allan D. Fitzgerald. Grand Rapids: Eerdmans, 1999.

——. "Grace." In *Augustine through the Ages: An Encyclopedia,* edited by Allan D. Fitzgerald. Grand Rapids: Eerdmans, 1999.

Burtchaell, James Tunstead. *From Synagogue to Church: Public Services and Offices in the Earliest Christian Communities.* Cambridge: Cambridge University Press, 1992.

Calvin, John. "Exposition of the Heads of Agreement". in *Tracts and Letters.* Vol. 2. Edinburgh: Banner of Truth, 2009.

——. *Institutes of the Christian Religion.* Grand Rapids: Eerdmans, 1972.

——. *Institutes of the Christian Religion.* Edited by John T. McNeill. Translated by Ford Lewis Battles. Library of Christian Classics 20–21. London: Westminster, 1960.

——. *New Testament Commentaries.* Edinburgh: Saint Andrew Press, 1964.

——. *Short Treatise on the Support of Our Lord.* 1541

Castaldo, Chris. *Holy Ground: Walking with Jesus as a Former Catholic.* Grand Rapids: Zondervan, 2009.

A Catechism of Catholic Doctrine Approved by the Archbishops and Bishops of Ireland. Dublin: Gill, [1951].

Chow, Alexander. "Calvinist Public Theology in Urban China Today." *International Journal of Public Theology* 8 (2014) 158–75.

Clarke, Andrew D. "'Be Imitators of Me': Paul's Model of Leadership." *Tyndale Bulletin* 49 (1998) 329–60.

——. "Lexicography and New Testament Categories of Church Discipline." *Tyndale Bulletin* 64 (2013) 129–51.

——. *A Pauline Theology of Church Leadership. Library of New Testament Studies.* London: T. & T. Clark, 2008.

——. *Serve the Community of the Church: Christians as Leaders and Ministers.* Grand Rapids: Eerdmans, 2000.

Cockayne, Joshua. "Analytic Ecclesiology: The Social Ontology of the Church." *Journal of Analytic Theology* 7 (2019) 100–123. chrome-extension:// efaidnbmnnnibpcajpcglclefindmkaj/https://research-repository.st-andrews.ac.uk/ bitstream/handle/10023/18443/Cockayne_2019_JAT_AnalyticEcclesiology_VoR. pdf?sequence=1&isAllowed=y.

Collins, K. J. *The Theology of John Wesley* Nashville: Abingdon, 2007.

Crisp, Oliver. *Analyzing Doctrine: Toward A Systematic Theology.* Waco: Baylor University Press, 2019.

——. *Deviant Calvinism: Broadening Reformed Theology.* Minneapolis: Fortress, 2014.

————. *Divinity and Humanity: The Incarnation Reconsidered*. Cambridge: Cambridge University Press, 2007.

————. *Regeneration Reconsidered, Freedom, Redemption and Communion: Studies in Christian Doctrine*. London: T. & T. Clark, 2021.

————. *Retrieving Doctrine: Essays in Reformed Theology*. Downers Grove, IL: InterVarsity, 2011.

————. *The Word Enfleshed: Exploring the Person and Work of Christ*. Grand Rapids: Baker, 2016.

Cyprian, Saint. *The Lapsed: The Unity of the Catholic Church*. Translated by Maurice Bévenot. London: Longmans, Green, 1957.

Davie, Grace. *Religion in Britain: A Persistent Paradox*. Oxford: Wiley Blackwell, 2015.

Dix, Gregory. *The Shape of the Liturgy*. Westminster: Dacre, 1947.

Dulles, Avery. *Models of the Church*. Expanded ed. 1987. Reprint, New York: Image, 2014.

Edwards, Jonathan. *Concerning the End for which God Created the World in Ethical Writings,*. Edited by Paul Ramsey. The Works of Jonathan Edwards 8. New Haven: Yale University Press, 1989.

————. *Religious Affections*. Edited by John E. Smith. The Works of Jonathan Edwards 3. New Haven: Yale University Press, 1959.

————. *Writings on the Trinity, Grace and Faith*. Edited by Sang Hyun Lee. The Works of Jonathan Edwards 21. New Haven: Yale University Press, 2002.

Evans, William B. *Imputation and Impartation: Union with Christ in American Reformed Theology. Studies in Christian History and Thought*. Milton Keynes, UK: Paternoster, 2008.

Fergusson, David, and Mark W. Elliott. *History of Scottish Theology*. Vol. 1. Oxford: Oxford University Press, 2019.

Finney, Mark T. *Honour and Conflict in the Ancient World: 1 Corinthians in Its Greco-Roman Social Setting*. LNTS 460. London: T. & T. Clark, 2011.

Flett, John. *The Witness of God: The Trinity, Missio Dei, Karl Barth and the Nature of Christian Community*. Grand Rapids: Eerdmans, 2010.

Forsyth, Alexander C. *Mission by the People: Re-discovering the Dynamic Missiology of Tom Allan and his Scottish Contemporaries*. Eugene, OR: Pickwick Publications, 2017.

Fransen, Peter. "Sacraments: Signs of Faith." *Worship* 37 (1962) 31–50.

French, Peter. *Corporate Ethics*. New York: Harcourt Brace, 1995.

————. "The Corporation as a Moral Person." *American Philosophical Quarterly* 16 (1979) 207–15.

Glare, P. G. W. *Oxford Latin Dictionary*. 2nd ed. Oxford: Oxford University Press, 2012.

Green, Michael. *Baptism: Its Purpose, Practice and Power*. London: Hodder & Stoughton, 1987.

————. *Man Alive*. London: InterVarsity, 1967.

Greggs, Tom. *Barth, Origen, and Universal Salvation: Restoring Particularity*. Oxford: Oxford University Press, 2009.

————. *Dogmatic Ecclesiology Vol. 1: The Priestly Catholicity of the Church*. Grand Rapids: Baker, 2019.

————. "The Nature, Task and Method of Theology: A Very Methodist View." *International Journal of Systematic Theology* 20 (2018) 309–34.

Guder, Darrell L. "Reformed Theology, Mission and Ecumenism." In *The Cambridge Companion to Reformed Theology*, edited by Paul T. Nimmo and David A. S. Fergusson,

319–34. Cambridge Companions to Religion. Cambridge: Cambridge University Press, 2016.

Haag, Herbert. *Clergy and Laity: Did Jesus Want a Two-Tier Church?* Tumbridge Wells, UK: Burns & Oats, 1997.

———. "Gedächtnis, biblisch." In *Lexikon für Theologie und Kirche*, edited by Josef Höfer und Karl Rahner, 4:570–72. 11 vols. 2nd ed. Freiburg: Herder, 1957–67.

———. *Vom alten zum neuen Pascha: Geschichte und Theologie des Osterfestes.* Stuttgart: KBW, 1971.

Haney, Mitchell R. "Corporate Loss of Innocence for the Sake of Accountability." *Journal of Social Philosophy* 35 (2004) 391–412.

Harland, Philip A. *Associations, Synagogues, and Congregations: Claiming a Place in Ancient Mediterranean Society.* Minneapolis: Fortress, 2003.

———. "'The Most Sacred Society (*thiasos*) of the Pythagoreans': Philosophers Forming Associations." *Journal of Ancient History* 7 (2019) 207–32.

Hellerman, Joseph H. *The Ancient Church as Family.* Minneapolis: Fortress, 2001.

Heppe, Heinrich. *Reformed Dogmatics.* Edited by Ernst Bizer. Translated by G. T. Thomson. London: Collins, 1950.

Heron, Alasdair. *The Holy Spirit.* London: Marshall, Morgan & Scott, 1983.

———. *Table and Tradition: Towards an Ecumenical Understanding of the Eucharist.* Edinburgh: Handsel, 1983.

Hobbes, Thomas. *Leviathan,* edited by Michael Oakeshott. Oxford: Blackwell, n.d. [1651].

Holland, Tom. *Dominion: The Making of the Western Mind.* London: Little, Brown, 2019.

International Theological Commission. *The Reciprocity between Faith and Sacraments in the Sacramental Economy.* Vatican City: Libreria Editrice Vaticana, 2021.

Jenson, Matt. *The Gravity of Sin: Augustine, Luther and Barth on homo incurvatus in se.* London: T. & T. Clark, 2006.

Jeremias, Joachim. *The Eucharistic Words of Jesus.* Translated by Arnold Ehrhardt. London: SCM, 1966.

Judge, Edwin A. "The Conflict of Educational Aims in New Testament Thought." *Journal of Christian Education* 9 (1966) 32–45. Reprinted in *The First Christians in the Roman World: Augustan and New Testament Studies,* 693–708.

———. "Cultural Conformity and Innovation in Paul: Some Clues from Contemporary Documents." *Tyndale Bulletin* 36 (1984) 3–24.

———. "The Early Christians as a Scholastic Community." *Journal of Religious History* 1 (1960) 4–15. Reprinted in *The First Christians in the Roman World: Augustan and New Testament Studies,* 526–52.

———. "The Early Christians as a Scholastic Community: Part II." *Journal of Religious History* 1 (1961) 125–37. Reprinted in *The First Christians in the Roman World: Augustan and New Testament Studies,* 526–52.

———. *The First Christians in the Roman World: Augustan and New Testament Studies.* Edited by James R. Harrison. WUNT 229. Tübingen: Mohr Siebeck, 2008.

———. "Higher Education in the Pauline Churches." In *Learning and Teaching Theology: Some Ways Ahead,* edited by Leslie James Ball and James R. Harrison, 23–31. Sydney: Morning Star, 2014.

———. "On This Rock I Will Build My *Ekklesia*: Counter-Cultic Springs of Multiculturalism." In *The First Christians in the Roman World: Augustan and New Testament Studies,* edited by James R. Harrison, 619–68. WUNT 229. Tübingen: Mohr Siebeck, 2008.

———. "The Social Identity of the First Christians: A Question of Method in Religious History." *Journal of Religious History* 11 (1980) 201–17.

Justin Martyr. *First Apology 61 Ante-Nicene Fathers*. Grand Rapids, Michigan: Eerdmans, many dates.

Kilby, Karen. "Perichoresis and Projection: Problems with Social Doctrines of the Trinity." *Blackfriars*, 81.956 (2000) 432–45.

Kittle, Simon. "Grace and Free Will: Quiescence and Control." *Journal of Analytic Theology* 3 (2015) 89–108.

Kloppenborg, John S. *Christ's Associations: Connecting and Belonging in the Ancient City*. New Haven: Yale University Press, 2020.

———. *Voluntary Associations in the Graeco-Roman World*. London: Routledge, 1996.

Koffeman, Leo J. "'Ecclesia reformata semper reformanda' Church Renewal from a Reformed Perspective." *HTS Teologiese Studies/Theological Studies* 71.3 (2015) 1–5.

Laffin, Michael Richard. *The Promise of Martin Luther's Political Theology: Freeing Luther from Modern Political Narrative*. London: Bloomsbury, 2016.

Lane, Anthony N. S. "Becoming a Christian: Initiation in the New Testament and in British Evangelicalism." In *The Interface of Science, Theology, and Religion: Essays in Honor of Alister E. McGrath*, edited by Dennis Ngien, 11–27. Eugene, OR: Pickwick Publications, 2019.

———. "Did the Apostolic Church Baptise Babies? A Seismological Approach." *Tyndale Bulletin* 55.1 (2004) 109–30.

———. *Regensburg Article 5 on Justification: Inconsistent Patchwork or Substance of True Doctrine?* Oxford: Oxford University Press, 2019.

———. *Sin and Grace: Evangelical Soteriology in Historical Perspective*. London: Apollos, 2020.

Last, Richard. *The Pauline Church and The Corinthian Ekklesia: Greco-Roman Associations in Comparative Context*. SNTSMS 164. Cambridge: Cambridge University Press, 2015.

Leenhardt, F. J. "This is My Body." In *Essays on the Lord's Supper*, edited by Oscar Cullman and F. J. Leenhart, 24–86. Translated by J. G. Davies. London: Lutterworth, 1958.

Lehmann, Helmut T., gen ed. *Luther's Works*. Vol. 53, *Liturgy and Hymns*. Edited by Ulrich S. Leupold. Philadelphia: Fortress, 1965.

Leith, John H. ed. *Creeds of the Churches*. 3rd ed. Louisville: John Knox, 1982.

Levin, Janet. "Functionalism." In *Stanford Encyclopedia of Philosophy*. https://plato. stanford.edu/entries/functionalism/.

Lewis, Charlton T., and Charles Short, eds. *A Latin Dictionary*. Rev. ed. Oxford: Clarendon, 1879.

Lindbeck, George. "The Church." In *Keeping the Faith: Essays to Mark the Centenary of Lux Mundi*. Philadelphia: Fortress, 1988.

List, Christian, and Philip Pettit. *Group Agency: The Possibility, Design, and Status of Corporate Agents*. Oxford: Oxford University Press, 2011.

Lossky, Vladimir,. *The Mystical Theology of the Eastern Church*. Cambridge: James Clarke, 1957.

McDonnell, Killian. *John Calvin, the Church, and the Eucharist*. Princeton: Princeton University Press, 1967.

McFadyen, Alastair. *Bound to Sin: Abuse, Holocaust and the Christian Doctrine of Sin*. Cambridge: Cambridge University Press, 2000.

McGrath, Alister E. *Iustitia Dei: A History of the Christian Doctrine of Justification*. 4th ed. Cambridge: Cambridge University Press, 2020.

———. *A Life of John Calvin: A Study in the Shaping of Western Culture*. Oxford: Blackwell, 1990.

MacCulloch, Diarmaid. *A History of Christianity*. Harmondsworth, UK: Penguin, 2009.

Maddox, R. L. *Responsible Grace: John Wesley's Practical Theology*. Nashville: Kingswood, 1994.

Minear, Paul S. *Images of the Church in the New Testament*. 1960. Reprint, Louisville: Westminster John Knox, 2004.

Muller, Richard. *Calvin and the Reformed Tradition: On the Work of Christ and the Order of Salvation*. Grand Rapids: Baker, 2012.

Murray, Paul. *Receptive Ecumenism and the Call to Catholic Learning: Exploring a Way for Contemporary Ecumenism*. Oxford: Oxford University Press, 2008.

Navarro, Kevin J. *Trinitarian Doxology: T. F. and J. B. Torrance's Theology of Worship as Participation by the Spirit in the Son's Communion with the Father*. Eugene, OR: Pickwick Publications, 2020.

Nevin, John Williamson. *The Mystical Presence: A Vindication of the Reformed or Calvinistic Doctrine of the Holy Eucharist*. Philadelphia: Lippincott, 1846.

Newbigin, Lesslie. *A Word in Season: Perspectives on Christian World Mission*. Grand Rapids: Eerdmans, 1994.

Nietzsche, Friedrich. *Thus Spoke Zarathustra*. Cambridge: Cambridge University Press, 2005.

Nimmo, Paul T. "The Eucharist in Post-Reformation Scotland: A Theological Tale of Harmony and Diversity." *Scottish Journal of Theology* 71 (2018) 460–80.

———. *Trinity and Election in Contemporary Theology*. Edited by Michael T. Dempsey. Grand Rapids: Eerdmans, 2011.

Nimmo, Paul T., and David A. S. Fergusson, eds. *The Cambridge Companion to Reformed Theology*. Cambridge Companions to Religion. Cambridge: Cambridge University Press, 2016.

Noble, T. A. "East and West in the Theology of John Wesley." [2003 Tercentenary Conference, "John Wesley, Life, Legacy and Legend"]. *Bulletin of the John Rylands University Library of Manchester* 85 (2003) 359–72.

———. *Holy Trinity: Holy People: The Theology of Christian Perfecting*. Eugene, OR: Cascade Books.

Numbers, Ronald L. *Galileo Goes to Jail and Other Myths about Science and Religion*. Cambridge: Harvard University Press, 2010.

Origen of Alexandria. *Homilies on Numbers*. Ancient Christian Texts. Downers Grove, IL: InterVarsity, 2009.

Outler, Albert C., ed. *The Works of John Wesley*. Vol. 2. Nashville: Abingdon, 1985.

Oxford English Dictionary Online. Oxford: Oxford University Press, 2000.

Packer, J. I. *A Passion for Holiness*. Cambridge: Crossway, 1992.

Pannenberg, Wolfhart. *Systematic Theology*. Vol. 3. Translated by Geoffrey W. Bromiley. Grand Rapids: Eerdmans, 1998.

Parris, John R. *John Wesley's Doctrine of the Sacraments*. London: Epworth, 1963.

Perkins, William. *A Golden Chain or Description of Theology*. Edinburgh: Robert Walde-Graue, 1592.

Peterlin, Davorin. *Paul's Letter to the Philippians in the Light of Disunity in the Church*. Novum Testamentum Supplements 79. Leiden: Brill, 1995.

BIBLIOGRAPHY

Poe, Shelli. *Essential Trinitarianism: Schleiermacher as Trinitarian Theologian*. London: T. & T. Clark, 2017.

Putnam, Robert D., and David E. Campbell. *American Grace: How Religion Unites and Divides Us*. New York: Simon & Schuster, 2010.

Quick, Oliver Chase. *The Christian Sacraments*. London: Nisbet, 1955.

Rahner, Karl. *The Church and the Sacraments*. Tunbridge Wells, UK: Burns & Oates, 1974.

Benedict XVI, Pope. *Introduction to Christianity*. San Francisco: Ignatius, 2004.

———. *Theologische Prinzipienlehre*. Munich: Wewel, 1982.

———. *Zur Gemeinschaft gerufen: Kirche heute verstehen*. Freiberg: Herder, 1991.

Robertson, Charles K. *Conflict in Corinth: Redefining the System. Studies in Biblical Literature*. Oxford: Lang, 2001.

Rorem, Paul. "Calvin and Bullinger on the Lord's Supper." *Lutheran Quarterly* 2 (1988) 357–89.

Ryle, J. C. *Holiness: Its Nature, Hindrances, Difficulties, and Roots: Being a Series of Papers on the Subject*. 2nd ed. London: Hunt, 1879.

Schaff, Philip. *The Creeds of Christendom, volume III: The Evangelical Protestant Creeds with Translations*. New York: Harper, 1877.

Schwanz, Keith, and Joseph Coleson, eds. *Missio Dei: A Wesleyan Understanding*. Kansas City, MO: Beacon Hill, 2011.

Scott, C. Anderson. "Zwingli's Doctrine of the Lord's Supper." *Expositor* 3 (1901) 161–71. https://biblicalstudies.org.uk/pdf/expositor/series6/03-161.pdf.

Sergienko, Gennadi A. *"Our politeuma is in Heaven!": Paul's Polemical Engagement with the "Enemies of the Cross of Christ" in Philippians 3:18-20*. Carlisle: Langham Monographs, 2013.

Severson, Eric. "The Church: The Event of the Kingdom of God." In *Essential Church: A Wesleyan Ecclesiology*, edited by Diane Leclerc and Mark A. Maddix, 29–36. Kansas City Missouri: Beacon Hill, 2014.

Smail, Tom. *The Forgotten Father*. Exeter: Paternoster, 1980.

Smith, Claire S. *Pauline Communities as "Scholastic Communities:" A Study of the Vocabulary of "Teaching" in 1 Corinthians, 1 and 2 Timothy and Titus*. WUNT. Tübingen: Mohr Siebeck, 2009.

Smith, T. ed. *Letters of Samuel Rutherford*. Edinburgh: Oliphant, Anderson, & Ferrier, 1881.

Snoddy, Richard. *The Soteriology of James Ussher: The Act and Object of Saving Faith*. Oxford: Oxford University Press, 2014.

Sonderegger, Katherine. *Systematic Theology* Vol. 2. Minneapolis: Fortress, 2021.

Spinks, Bryan D. *Do This in Remembrance of Me: The Eucharist from the Early Church to the Present Day*. London: SCM, 2013.

Spurlock, R. Scott. "Boundaries of Scottish Reformed Orthodoxy 1560–1700." In *History of Scottish Theology*, edited by David Fergusson and Mark W. Elliott, . Oxford: Oxford University Press, 2019.

Stephens, W. P. *The Theology of Huldrych Zwingli*. Oxford: Oxford University Press, 1986.

Stockitt Robin., and John S. Dawson. *Leaving Church: What Can We Learn from Those Who Are Done with Church?* Cambridge, UK: Grove, 2020.

Storrar, William. *Scottish Identity: A Christian Vision*. Edinburgh: Handsel, 1990.

Stout, Jeffrey. *Blessed Are the Organized: Grassroots Democracy in America*. Princeton: Princeton University Press, 2010.

Strong, A. H. *Systematic Theology*. 1886. Reprint, London: Pickering & Inglis, 1906.

Stump, Eleonore. *Aquinas*. Arguments of the Philosophers. New York: Routledge 2003.

Thiselton, Anthony C. *Systematic Theology*. London: SPCK, 2015.

Torrance, James B. *Worship, Community and the Triune God of Grace*. Carlisle, UK: Paternoster, 1996.

Torrance, Thomas F. *The Trinitarian* Faith. Edinburgh: T. & T. Clark, 1988.

Tyler, Kate. *The Ecclesiology of Thomas F. Torrance*. Lanham, MD: Lexington/Fortress Academic, 2019.

Varro, Marcus Terentius. *On the Latin Language*.

Volf, Miroslav. *After Our Likeness: The Church as the Image of the Trinity*. Grand Rapids: Eerdmans, 1998.

Wainwright, Geoffrey, ed. *Keeping the Faith: Essays to Mark the Centenary of Lux Mundi*. Philadelphia: Fortress, 1988.

Wallace, R. S. *Calvin's Doctrine of the Christian Life*. Edinburgh: Oliver & Boyd, 1959.

Walls, Andrew. *The Cross-Cultural Process in Christian History*. Edinburgh: T. & T. Clark, 2002.

Wesley, John. "The Duty of Constant Communion." In *The Works of John Wesley*. Edited by Albert C. Outler. 35 vols. Nashville: Abingdon, 1984.

————. "The Means of Grace." In *The Works of John Wesley*. Edited by Albert C. Outler. 35 vols. Nashville: Abingdon, 1984.

————. Sermon 19, "Catholic Spirit." In *The Works of John Wesley* 2. Edited by Albert C. Outler. Nashville: Abingdon, 1985.

Whale, J. S. *The Protestant Tradition: An Essay in Interpretation*. Cambridge: Cambridge University Press, 1955.

Williams, Demetrius K. *Enemies of the Cross of Christ: The Terminology of the Cross and Conflict in Philippians*. JSNTSup 223. London: Sheffield, 2002.

Williams, Rowan. *Why Study the Past? The Quest for the Historical Church*. London: Darton, Longman & Todd, 2005.

Wood, Susan K. "Baptism." In *Oxford Handbook of Ecumenical Studies*, edited by Geoffrey Wainwright and Paul McPartlan. Oxford: Oxford University Press, 2021.

Wright, David F., ed. *Baptism: Three Views*. Downers Grove, IL: InterVarsity, 2009.

————. *Infant Baptism in Historical Perspective*. Milton Keynes, UK: Paternoster, 2007.

————. *What Has Infant Baptism Done to Baptism? An Enquiry at the End of Christendom*. Carlisle, UK: Paternoster, 2005.

Wynkoop, Mildred Bangs. *A Theology of Love: The Dynamic of Wesleyanism*. Kansas City, MO: Beacon Hill, 1972.

Yarnold, Edward. "The Sacraments of Christian Initiation." In *Commentary on the Catechism of the Catholic Church*, edited by Michael J. Walsh, 242–58. London: Chapman, 1994.

Zink, Jesse. "Five Marks of Mission: History, Theology, Critique." *Journal of Anglican Studies* 15 (2017) 144–66.

Zizioulas, John. *Being as Communion: Studies in Personhood and the Church*. Crestwood, NY: St Vladimir's Seminary Press, 1985.

Zwingli, Huldrych. *An Exposition of the Faith*. Edited by Geoffrey W. Bromiley. Library of Christian Classics 24. Philadelphia: Westminster, 1953.

Name and Subject Index